D0401690

Geologic Time Scale

For chronological order from past to present, read from the bottom up.

GEOLOGIC TIME (in millions of years)				DEVELOPMENT OF PLANTS AND ANIMALS
EON	ERA	PERIOD	EPOCH	
Phanerozoic	Cenozoic	Quaternary	Holocene — 0.008	Humans develop
			Pleistocene — 1.8 —	Ice Ages
		Tertiary	Pliocene — 5.3 —	"Age of Mammals"
			Miocene — 23.8 —	
			Oligocene — 33.7 —	
			Eocene — 55.5 —	
			Paleocene — 65.0 —	
	Mesozoic	Cretaceous — 145	"Age of Reptiles"	Extinctions of dinosaurs and many other species
		Jurassic — 213		First flowering plants
		Triassic — 248		First birds
				Dinosaurs dominant
	Paleozoic	Permian — 286	"Age of Amphibians"	Extinctions of trilobites and many other marine animals
		Pennsylvanian — 325		First reptiles
		Mississippian — 360		Coal swamps
				Amphibians abundant
		Devonian — 410	"Age of Fishes"	First insect fossils
		Silurian — 440		Fishes dominant
				First land plants
		Ordovician — 505	"Age of Invertebrates"	First fishes
		Cambrian — 544		Trilobites dominant
				First organisms with shells
Proterozoic — 2500		Precambrian (makes up about 86% of the geologic time scale)		First multi-celled organisms
Archean — 3800				First one-celled organisms
Hadean — 4500				Age of oldest rocks

Hiking THE
SOUTHWEST'S GEOLOGY
FOUR CORNERS REGION

RALPH LEE HOPKINS

THE MOUNTAINEERS BOOKS

To my wife Lindy.
And to all of the Colorado Plateau's geologists past and present,
in whose footsteps I have followed.

 Published by
The Mountaineers Books
1001 SW Klickitat Way, Suite 201
Seattle, WA 98134

© 2002 by Ralph Lee Hopkins

All rights reserved

First edition, 2002

No part of this book may be reproduced in any form, or by any electronic, mechanical, or other means, without permission in writing from the publisher.

Published simultaneously in Great Britain by Cordee, 3a DeMontfort Street, Leicester, England, LE1 7HD

Manufactured in China

Acquiring Editor: Cassandra Conyers
Project Editor: Christine Ummel Hosler
Copyeditor: Erin Moore
Series Cover and Book Design: The Mountaineers Books
Cartographer: Moore Creative Designs
All photographs © 2002 by Ralph Lee Hopkins

Cover photograph: Sculpted layers of Navajo Sandstone, Paria Canyon–Vermilion Cliff Wilderness, Arizona
Frontispiece: The artistry of erosion, Balanced Rock, Arches National Park, Utah

Library of Congress Cataloging-in-Publication Data

Hopkins, Ralph Lee.
  Hiking the Southwest's geology : Four Corners Region / Ralph Lee
Hopkins.— 1st ed.
     p. cm.
Includes bibliographical references (p.   ) and index.
  ISBN 0-89886-856-4 (pbk.)
  1. Hiking—Four Corners Region—Guidebooks. 2. Geology—Four Corners
Region—Guidebooks. 3. Four Corners Region—Guidebooks. I. Title.
  GV199.42.F68 H66 2002
  917.92'5904—dc21
                              2002008328

♲ Printed on recycled paper

Contents

Preface: How to Use this Book 9

Acknowledgments 11

Introduction 13
    What Is the Colorado Plateau? 13
    The Colorado Plateau through Time 14
    Foundations: Rocks of the Colorado Plateau 16
    Global Forces: Plate Tectonics and the Colorado Plateau 31
    Preparing to Hike the Geology 39

PART 1. ARIZONA'S PLATEAU HIKES 43
CHAPTER 1. THE MOGOLLON RIM 44
    Hike 1. Fossil Springs: The Ancestral Mogollon Rim 48
    Hike 2. North Wilson Trail in Oak Creek Canyon: A Tale of Two
             Canyons 52

CHAPTER 2. THE SAN FRANCISCO VOLCANIC FIELD 57
    Hike 3. Inner Basin: San Francisco Mountain's Glaciated Caldera 60
    Hike 4. Bonito Lava Flow: Arizona's Youngest Lava Flow at Sunset
             Crater 64
    Hike 5. Grand Falls: Lava Meets the Little Colorado River 67
    Hike 6. Red Mountain: Anatomy of a Cinder Cone 71

CHAPTER 3. THE GRAND CANYON 74
    Hike 7. Horseshoe Mesa: Hike through Time below the South Rim 79
    Hike 8. Cape Final: North Rim View of the Grand Canyon
             Supergroup 85
    Hike 9. Powell Plateau: North Rim's Island in the Sky 88
    Hike 10. Toroweap Point: Western Grand Canyon's Lava Cascades 92

CHAPTER 4. THE PAINTED DESERT 96
    Hike 11. Blue Mesa: Stone Trees in Petrified Forest National Park 98
    Hike 12. Canyon De Chelly: Ancient Wind-Blown Dunes and the
             Paleozoic–Mesozoic Unconformity 101
    Hike 13. Coal Mine Canyon: Ghosts and Painted Spires 105
    Hike 14. Monument Valley: Red Rock Buttes and Mesas 109
    Hike 15. Coyote Buttes: Exhumed Desert Sand Dunes 112

PART 2. UTAH'S PLATEAU HIKES 117
CHAPTER 5. THE SLICKROCK COUNTRY 118

Hike 16. Honaker Trail: Entrenched Meanders of the San Juan
          River 123
Hike 17. Twin Towers: Stone Ruins in Hovenweep National
          Monument 128
Hike 18. Natural Bridges: The Bridges of White Canyon 131
Hike 19. Fisher Towers: Red Rock Towers of Conglomerate 137

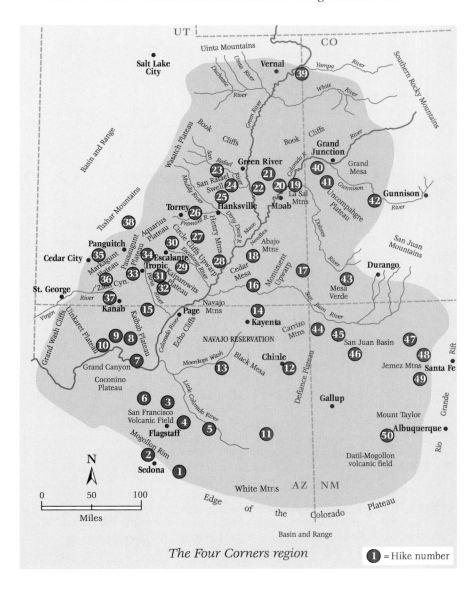

The Four Corners region

1 = Hike number

Hike 20. Delicate Arch: Sandstone Icon in Arches National Park 140
Hike 21. Devils Garden: Standing Stones in Arches National Park 145
Hike 22. Upheaval Dome: Salt Dome or Meteorite Impact Crater? 150
Hike 23. Little Grand Canyon: Heart of the San Rafael Swell 154
Hike 24. San Rafael Reef: World of Standing Stone 157
Hike 25. Goblin Valley: Hoodoo Playground 160
Hike 26. Rim Overlook: Sandstone Cliffs of Capitol Reef 162
Hike 27. Strike Valley Overlook: Tilted Rocks along Waterpocket Fold 165
Hike 28. Mount Hillers: Laccoliths of the Henry Mountains 168
Hike 29. Dry Fork Coyote Gulch: Sandstone Slot Canyons 171
Hike 30. Lower Calf Creek Falls: Desert Oasis between Sandstone Cliffs 174
Hike 31. Kodachrome Basin: Mysterious Sandstone Pipes 176
Hike 32. The Cockscomb: Slot Canyons along the East Kaibab Monocline 180

CHAPTER 6. THE HIGH PLATEAUS 183
Hike 33. Bryce Canyon: Fairyland of Hoodoos 186
Hike 34. Table Cliffs Plateau: Atop the Grand Staircase 191
Hike 35. Cedar Breaks: The Colorado Plateau's Faulted Western Rim 193
Hike 36. Zion Canyon: The Subway along the Left Fork of North Creek 196
Hike 37. Coral Pink Sand Dunes: Recycled Jurassic Sand 200
Hike 38. Bullion Canyon: Waterfalls and a Glaciated Hanging Valley 204

PART 3. COLORADO'S PLATEAU HIKES 207
CHAPTER 7. THE WESTERN SLOPE 208
Hike 39. Harpers Corner: Bird's-Eye View of Faults and Folds 211
Hike 40. Monument Canyon: Sandstone Monuments and the Great Unconformity 214
Hike 41. Unaweep Canyon: Ancient River Channel and the Great Unconformity 217
Hike 42. North Vista Trail: Black Canyon of the Gunnison 222
Hike 43. Mesa Verde: Sandstones of the Cretaceous Seaway 225

PART 4. NEW MEXICO'S PLATEAU HIKES 229
CHAPTER 8. THE SOUTHEASTERN PLATEAU 230
Hike 44. Ship Rock: Rocks from the Deep 234
Hike 45. Bisti Badlands: Fantasy in Stone 237
Hike 46. Chaco Canyon: Ancient Voices and Ancient Shorelines 239
Hike 47. Ghost Ranch: New Mexico's Red Rock Country 242
Hike 48. Frijoles Canyon: Waterfalls and Volcanoes at Bandelier 246
Hike 49. Tent Rocks: Volcanic Landscape in the Jemez Mountains 250
Hike 50. El Malpais: Lava Tubes of the Bandera Flow 254

Glossary 258

Appendices 267
    A. Recommended Reading 267
    B. Key References 269
    C. Geologic Maps 274
    D. Addresses and Contact Information 277

Index 280

Spring wildflowers and the Three Sisters

Preface: How to Use this Book

Hiking the Southwest's Geology is an invitation to explore the magical landscapes of the Four Corners region where Arizona, Utah, Colorado, and New Mexico meet. Also known as the Colorado Plateau, this is an area of "in-your-face" geology where colorful rock layers lie naked under the cobalt blue southwestern sky. Here the artistry of erosion has sculpted the earth into an infinite variety of forms. With every step, the canyon walls and red rock mesas challenge you to ponder their origins. Take time to stop and listen. Use your imagination. Just think, not that long ago (geologically speaking that is!) there was no Grand Canyon.

This book is intended to get you started thinking about geology and how today's landscapes came to be. No previous knowledge of geology is required. Both the general introduction and the chapter introductions provide basic information and background for each hike. Beginners especially should read these introductions before heading out on selected hikes. Hikes are given a difficulty rating of easy, moderate, or strenuous based largely on total distance and elevation change.

Important geologic terms and concepts are defined in the glossary at the back of the book. By referring often to the geologic time scale and to Table 1, Highlights of the Colorado Plateau's Geologic Time Scale, you will become familiar with the different eras and periods of geologic time. If you are interested in more in-depth overviews, see Appendix A, Recommended Reading. Appendix B lists key references for each hike and Appendix C lists geologic maps keyed to hikes by chapter sections, should you want to pursue anything in greater detail than presented in the text. Addresses and contact information end the listing in Appendix C.

This book suggests a few places to begin your explorations of the Southwest's geology, although there are a lifetime of possibilities. The hikes described here include some of the Southwest's most popular trails, as well as routes that are more remote and off the beaten track. Most are easily completed as day hikes, but a few are better suited to overnight backpacking trips. Be sure to inquire about local conditions and regulations when planning your trip. Keep in mind that all trails within wilderness areas, national parks, and national monuments are off-limits to bicycles and other forms of mechanized travel. Dogs are also prohibited in many areas. Please respect private property and remember that archeological sites are protected by law.

   Hiking the Southwest's Geology is offered with the hope that as you come to understand more about the land you visit you will do more to protect it. Please do your part to minimize impact so that those who follow in your footsteps will find little or no trace of your visit.

Delicate Arch—symbol of Utah's slickrock country, Arches National Park, Utah

Acknowledgments

This book fulfills my dream of writing about my geologic "home" and the land where I discovered rocks and geologic time as a young boy on my first trip west. This book would not have been attempted or completed without the encouragement, support, and love from my wife, Lindy Hopkins.

I would also like to thank everyone who offered encouragement, suggested geology hikes, and took time to accompany me in the field. A warm thank you to Stefan and Jay Lundgren for your hospitality in Sedona and our time together photographing, to Bill and Carolyn Hilton for suggesting hikes and distracting me with desert wildflowers, and to Wayne Ranney for your thoughts on hikes and red rocks. Special thanks to Ron Blakey and Gene Stevenson for your knowledge of the Colorado Plateau and time and help with the manuscript. Thanks also to the great staff at The Mountaineers Books, and to Erin Moore for her help in improving the final manuscript. And finally, thank you to my colleagues at Lindblad Expeditions for your support in allowing flexibility in my travels and the time to finish this book.

Geology is a science where we build on the work of others. The maps and diagrams in this book have been modified from a variety of authors whose books and publications have contributed so much to our understanding of the Colorado Plateau. Specifically, I would like to thank Ron Blakey (for his many published papers on paleogeography), Don Baars (*The Colorado Plateau* and *Navajo Country*), Robert Fillmore (*The Geology of the Parks, Monuments, and Wildlands of Southern Utah*), Frank DeCourten (*Shadows of Time*), Wendell Duffield (*Volcanoes of Northern Arizona*), Wayne Ranney (*Geology of Sedona's Red Rocks*), and the Utah Geological Association (*Geology of Utah's Parks and Monuments*). The maps donated by Trails Illustrated were also greatly appreciated.

The author takes full responsibility for any errors or omissions of geologic facts, dates, and other information. I welcome suggestions for improving the next edition.

Introduction

The Southwest is a geologic wonderland. It is a landscape of deep canyons, layercake cliffs, and red rock mesas in the Four Corners region where Arizona, Utah, Colorado, and New Mexico meet. This is slickrock country—the very heart of the American Southwest—where an infinite variety of breathtaking landforms are sculpted in stone. Here, geology is everywhere on display.

The Four Corners region lies within the *Colorado Plateau,* a geographically distinct province carved by the Colorado River and its tributaries from a spectrum of flat-lying layers subtly shaded by past geologic events. The Southwest's arid climate leaves the land largely free of vegetation, allowing the artistry of weathering, erosion, and time to accentuate each and every layer. It is a landscape of the imagination with a kaleidoscope of landforms, quite unlike any other place on earth. Found here are the Grand Staircase, Petrified Forest, and Monument Valley, and also the largest collection of natural arches, bridges, and standing stones. It comes as no surprise that the Colorado Plateau contains the highest concentration of national parks and monuments anywhere in the world, including Grand Canyon National Park, where in a single view you can look back in time through nearly 2 billion years of Earth history.

This book invites you to explore the Four Corners region of the American Southwest from the perspective of how the Colorado Plateau's scenic landscapes formed. Each hike is a journey through time that winds through a chapter in the story of the Colorado Plateau's formation. Within the canyons, cliffs, and mesas lie tales of ancient environments and past geologic events, and also clues about the geologic forces that continue to shape the land today.

WHAT IS THE COLORADO PLATEAU?

John Wesley Powell, the pioneering geologist who in 1869 led the first river expedition through the Grand Canyon, originally named the Southwest's canyon country the "Colorado Plateaus." At that time, he defined the "Plateaus" as the area drained by the Colorado River and its tributaries. Today, this region is known simply as the Colorado Plateau.

The view from Horseshoe Mesa, Grandview Trail, Grand Canyon National Park, Arizona

The Colorado Plateau is a sprawling landscape larger than New England and is fundamentally different than the land that surrounds it. It stretches from the western edge of the southern Rocky Mountains in Colorado and New Mexico, all the way to the eastern edge of the *Basin and Range* country of Utah and Arizona. It also reaches south from the Uinta Mountains near the Wyoming border in northern Utah to the *Mogollon Rim* of central Arizona and New Mexico.

Despite its name, the Colorado Plateau is not a single plateau but an amazingly diverse landscape of countless canyons and plateaus, buttes, and mesas—all sculpted from a thick stack of flat-lying sedimentary rock layers or *strata*. The region is punctuated by picturesque mountains, created where rising bubbles of magma warped and pushed up through sedimentary layers. It is rimmed by mountains and high plateaus capped by lava flows. And although the region is best known for its endless expanse of horizontal strata, in places the layers are broken along faults or warped and bent upright along great folds called *monoclines*.

The Colorado Plateau is also a land of contrast. It is largely a high desert landscape with elevations averaging more than 5000 feet above sea level. In its deepest canyons, such as the Grand Canyon, the land falls away below 2000 feet and can be an inferno during the summer months. But where the mountains and plateaus reach above 8000 feet, there are cool forests and alpine meadows.

The Colorado Plateau has a long and unique geologic history that has helped shape the landscape we see today. Its features lie naked at the surface for all to see, making the Colorado Plateau one of the world's best outdoor classrooms to study geology. It is geology that defines this wondrous landscape.

THE COLORADO PLATEAU THROUGH TIME

For much of its geologic history, the Colorado Plateau has remained a relatively stable platform while wildly fluctuating influences have swept its surface. The land was repeatedly flooded by seas, crossed by raging rivers, submerged beneath lakes, and parched by wind-blown dunes of vanished deserts. All of these actions contributed to the layer after layer of sediments which became the Plateau's distinctly colorful geologic "layercake." This layercake is best exposed in the Grand Canyon and along the Grand Staircase.

Geologic upheaval has surrounded the Colorado Plateau throughout its history. To the east, while the Rocky Mountains were thrust skyward not once, but several times, the Plateau underwent only comparatively minor uplifting. To the south and west, while the Basin and Range Province has stretched into mountains and valleys around Phoenix and in western Utah, it has encroached on only portions of the Plateau's southern and western borders.

TABLE 1

Highlights of the Colorado Plateau's Geologic Time Scale

Major events that shaped the landscape.
For chronological order from past to present, read from the bottom up.

MILLIONS OF YEARS	GEOLOGIC TIME	GEOLOGIC EVENTS
1.8–present	Pleistocene to Holocene	Ice Age glaciers cap the Aquarius Plateau, La Sal Mountains, and San Francisco Peaks; boulders of Fremont River Terraces; volcanic activity; San Francisco Mountain Volcanic Field and Sunset Crater; lava dams in the Grand Canyon.
25–present	Oligocene to Holocene	Uplift of the Colorado Plateau; enlivened rivers carve Colorado River basin; creation of the Grand Canyon and Oak Creek Canyon during last 5 million years.
30–present	Oligocene to Holocene	Rio Grande Rifting: block faulting down-drops New Mexico's Rio Grande Valley; Basin and Range extension: normal faults slice High Plateaus and Mogollon Rim.
30–19	Oligocene to Pliocene	Major volcanic activity: Tushar Mountain calderas, High Plateaus basalts; intrusions form laccolith mountain ranges (Henry, Abajo, and La Sal Mountains).
45–35	Eocene	Lakes submerge large parts of Utah and Western Colorado: Claron Formation of Bryce Canyon and Cedar Breaks.
65–45	Cretaceous to Eocene	Laramide orogeny: warps Colorado Plateau rocks into local uplifts (Monument, Circle Cliffs, San Rafael Swell) and monoclines (Comb Ridge, Waterpocket Fold, Cockscomb).
145–65	Cretaceous	Cretaceous seaway floods the region: Mancos Shale and sandstones of the Mesa Verde Group (Mesa Verde and Chaco Canyon).
245–145	Triassic to Jurassic	Winds pile sand into Wingate, Navajo, and Entrada dune fields; dinosaurs leave footprints and bones in the Morrison Formation river channels; Shinarump Conglomerate forms in river channels draining the Mogollon Highlands.
325–245	Pennsylvanian to Permian	Desert wind-blown dunes: Coconino, De Chelly Sandstone, and Sedona's red rocks; marine limestones; Ancestral Rocky Mountains: basement uplifts and Umcompahgre Highlands; streams deposit Cutler Formation; thick salt in Paradox Basin.
544–325	Cambrian to Mississippian	Colorado Plateau intermittently below sea level; marine sedimentary rocks blanket region with sandstone, limestone, and shale. Rocks of Ordovician, Silurian, and much of the Devonian are missing. What happened during this time is one of the great mysteries of the Colorado Plateau.
800–544	Precambrian	Erosion bevels surface that becomes the basement for the Colorado Plateau's geologic layercake.
1,700–800	Precambrian	Continental accretion assembles North America; metamorphic basement rocks (Vishnu Schist); rifting creates local basins for sediments of Grand Canyon Supergroup.

15

Volcanoes and lava flows also surround the Colorado Plateau. In Utah, lava flows and ash layers blanket the high plateaus along the Plateau's western margin. To the east, the San Juan Mountains in Colorado erupted the lava and ash that cover much of the area around present-day Durango. In New Mexico, the explosive Jemez Mountains caldera and the lava flows of Malpais National Monument line the Plateau's southeastern edge. Across the border in Arizona, the volcanic White Mountains crowned the Plateau's southern edge along the Mogollon Rim. Farther west, near Flagstaff, the San Francisco Volcanic Field spread ash and lava across a wide area that also boasts the region's most recent volcano, Sunset Crater, which erupted less than 1000 years ago.

The Colorado Plateau has survived as an island of relative calm. Taken together, the Plateau's sedimentary layers still stack like the layers of a birthday cake, one on top of the other, with the oldest rocks on the bottom where they began. Although some layers have been eroded away or were deposited only in localized areas, the sequence of geologic events can still largely be read from bottom to top.

Despite its wrinkled edges, the layered rocks of the Colorado Plateau were bent, folded, and broken only locally during the uplifts of the Ancestral Rocky Mountains about 300 million years ago, and again about 65 million years ago during the Laramide orogeny. More recently, this entire landscape was raised as the modern-day Rocky Mountains pushed higher during the past 25 million years. And about 10 million years ago, the rate of uplift accelerated, energizing the region's rivers, which swept down from their newly heightened headwaters in the Rockies, cutting deeply into the sedimentary pile. This action was further enhanced during the past 2 million years by floodwaters from melting Ice Age glaciers.

And although the exact history and course of the rivers remains uncertain, the Colorado River and its tributaries sliced through the Colorado Plateau on a course toward their eventual outlet in the Gulf of California. Some geologists interpret canyon downcutting as a testimony to uplift. Others believe it was the shortcut, provided by the opening of the Gulf of California between about 5 to 10 million years ago, which initiated the action. The debate continues. There is agreement, however, that somewhere along the way the Grand Canyon was carved and that, geologically speaking, it is a very recent feature of the landscape.

FOUNDATIONS: ROCKS OF THE COLORADO PLATEAU

Interpreting the landscape begins with rocks. Each rock carries its own story, and geologists have translated these stories into a language that everyone can understand. By knowing only a little bit about rocks, and also a few of their names, you can pick up one on the trail and expand it

TABLE 2

Common Rock-Forming Minerals

MINERAL NAME	COLOR	APPEARANCE
Feldspar	White, gray, or pink	Distinct crystal surfaces
Quartz	White, colorless to transparent	Glassy, irregular, and chunky
Mica	Gray, black, dark brown	Flat, flaky crystals
Hornblende	Dark green to black	Elongate crystals
Augite	Dark green to black	Elongate, rectangular crystals
Olivine	Pale green	Glassy, small, round
Calcite	White, gray, tan	Sugary crystals

into an entire landscape that once existed or a major event that once occurred. To understand how the Colorado Plateau is assembled, let's first look at the rocks—the building blocks of the region.

Rocks are natural combinations of minerals and form the most basic components of the landscape. The composition and arrangement of minerals in each rock reveal information about how it formed and where it came from. At the Grand Canyon, the Colorado River has sliced through the Colorado Plateau's rock pile, exposing nearly 2 billion years of geologic history. This is the best place to consider the three basic rocks types: sedimentary, igneous, and metamorphic. While the three basic rock types are exposed in other areas of the Colorado Plateau, the Grand Canyon provides the region's largest, and deepest, cross-section of rocks.

SEDIMENTARY ROCKS

Imagine gazing into the Grand Canyon from any of its precipitous overlooks. Horizontal stripes of multicolored rocks extend as far as the eye can see. Each horizontal band represents a different layer of sedimentary rock.

Sedimentary rocks are composed of fragments or grains of older rocks—mud, sand, and gravel—or the skeletal remains of organisms such as shells and coral. These sediments were transported and deposited in layers by the actions of water and wind in ancient oceans, lagoons, rivers, and desert sand dunes. Thus each layer records past environments that existed millions of years ago. As each layer of sediment became buried by newer material, its grains were compacted and bound together by cement, most commonly by the minerals quartz or calcite, forming the rock layers now visible on the Colorado Plateau.

17

Sandstone is a common sedimentary rock on the Colorado Plateau.

The walls of the Grand Canyon display the four most common sedimentary rock types on the Colorado Plateau. They are limestone, sandstone, shale, and conglomerate.

Several layers of *limestone* are found within the Grand Canyon. The top layer on both rims is composed of light-gray limestone within the Kaibab Formation. Limestone is formed by accumulation of the remains of organisms as fossils or fossil fragments in warm, shallow oceans and lakes. These fossils are composed primarily of the mineral calcite, which organisms manufacture into shells and skeletons from the calcium carbonate found in their water environment. When the organisms die, their shells and skeletons are swept by tides and currents and ultimately deposited on the ancient sea or lake floor. The Kaibab limestone was formed during the Permian, about 250 million years ago, when the Plateau was submerged under a warm, shallow sea.

Sandstone, the next sedimentary rock type, is also well represented in the Grand Canyon. Perhaps the most prominent sandstone layer is a white stripe about one third of the way down into the Canyon. This stripe is called the Coconino Sandstone. Sandstone is formed by the accumulation of "sand size" mineral grains or rock fragments that are weathered from preexisting rocks. Since quartz is the most durable of rock-forming minerals, most sandstones are composed predominantly of quartz grains. The further from the source of sediment, the greater the quartz composition because less resistant grains weather away. Closer to the source, less durable minerals, commonly feldspar, may be mixed with the quartz.

Sandy sediment tends to accumulate along bars in rivers, on ocean beaches, in shallow water offshore, or as wind-blown dunes. The Coconino Sandstone was deposited as a wind-blown sand dune complex that stretched across much of the southern Colorado Plateau during the Permian. As another example, the towering red rock buttes of Monument Valley along the Utah/Arizona border are made of the De Chelly Sandstone, which was also deposited by winds at about the same time.

Shale is a third sedimentary rock type found on the Plateau. At the Grand Canyon, the Hermit Shale forms a red slope directly beneath the Coconino Sandstone. Accumulation of silt and clay results in rocks called *siltstone* and *mudstone.* Collectively, they are known as shale. Shales result in low-energy environments where silt and mud settle, like river floodplains, coastal tide flats and lagoons, and deeper water environments offshore. The

TABLE 3

Common Sedimentary Rocks

ROCK NAME	GRAIN SIZE	FEATURES
Shale/mudstone and *siltstone*	Clay and silt	Thin bedded, mud cracks, forms slopes
Sandstone	Sand	Mostly quartz, cross-bedded, forms ridges and cliffs
Arkose sandstone	Sand	Contains feldspar
Conglomerate	Pebbles, cobbles, boulders	Thick bedded, contains rounded rock fragments
Limestone	Crystalline	Fizzes in acid, may contain fossils, forms cliffs
Gypsum/halite	Crystalline	Soft, friable, interlocked network of crystals

Hermit Shale represents an ancient system of rivers and floodplains on the southern Colorado Plateau. Elsewhere on the Plateau, another prominent shale layer is the Mancos Shale, which formed in a marine environment when Cretaceous seas flooded across the Plateau about 100 million years ago.

Conglomerate is the fourth major sedimentary rock type found on the Colorado Plateau. Conglomerates are typically mixtures of coarse-grained sediments like pebbles, cobbles, and boulders cemented together by quartz or calcite minerals precipitated in the spaces between the particles. On the Plateau, the Shinarump Conglomerate is a widespread layer that was deposited by a gravelly stream that blanketed much of the area during the Triassic. The Shinarump is not represented in the Grand Canyon; rather, conglomerates in the canyon are primarily found along boundaries between some of the layers that formed during periods of erosion, and are also found in localized lenses associated with ancient stream channel deposits.

The stream-deposited Triassic Shinarump Conglomerate is a widespread layer on the Colorado Plateau.

STRATIGRAPHY AND GAPS IN THE RECORD

Layered rocks or *strata* dominate the Colorado Plateau. How these rock layers fit together is called *stratigraphy*. In order to describe the Colorado Plateau's stratigraphy, geologists have subdivided the layers into formations, members, and groups in which different rock layers or sequences of layers are given names. These names are typically derived from the place where the rocks are best exposed, or where they were first studied in detail.

Each *formation* has recognizable characteristics, making it distinguishable from adjacent rock sequences. For example, the Tapeats Sandstone, a formation near the bottom of the Grand Canyon, forms a consistent cliff along the Canyon's Inner Gorge that looks much different than the igneous and metamorphic basement below and the slope-forming Bright Angel Shale above.

If the formation has distinguishable layers within it, it can be subdivided into *members*. East of the Grand Canyon, in Petrified Forest National Park, the Chinle Formation is subdivided into several different members, including the Petrified Forest Member where a high concentration of petrified wood is found.

In cases where formations are similar or represent the same time period, they are lumped into larger units called *groups*. For example, a series of colorful red sandstone formations make up the Supai Group found in the upper walls of the Grand Canyon. Groups can also be lumped together into an even thicker package called a "supergroup," such as the Grand Canyon Supergroup exposed in the eastern Grand Canyon.

Although the stratigraphy of the Colorado Plateau is often referred to as "layercake geology," the relationships between formations are complicated by several factors.

First, geologists have not been consistent when naming formations, or members within formations. In some cases, the names have even changed altogether. For example, the Redwall Limestone layer of Arizona and Utah is called the Leadville Limestone in Colorado, and the Madison Limestone in Wyoming.

Second, formations are not continuous across the entire Colorado Plateau. Formations that thin laterally and ultimately disappear are said to "pinch out." The Navajo Sandstone, for example, one of the Plateau's most famous layers and best known for the towering cliffs in Zion Canyon, thins to the northeast toward the Colorado border

Tilted layers of the Grand Canyon Supergroup below the Great Unconformity, Grand Canyon National Park, Arizona

and is absent in the cliffs of Colorado National Monument.

The third complicating factor when considering stratigraphic formations is a gap in the record between formations called an *unconformity*. An unconformity is a surface that represents a break in the geologic record where a portion of the stratigraphic sequence is missing from the layercake. This gap can be caused by erosion of preexisting rocks or from a lack of deposition over a specific period of time. The result is two formations of considerably different ages stacked together. For example, in the Grand Canyon the Cambrian Tapeats Sandstone sits horizontally on top of tilted Precambrian sedimentary layers, a relationship called an *angular unconformity* because the rock layers meet at an angle. Incredibly, the gap in the rock record between the Tapeats and the underlying Precambrian rock represents a time span of about 560 million years!

AGE	FORMATION		ENVIRONMENT
	UNCONFORMITY		
CRETACEOUS	MESAVERDE	FORMS CLIFFS	Beach and sandbars
CRETACEOUS	MANCOS	GRAY SLOPES	Ocean floor
CRETACEOUS	DAKOTA	CAPS MESAS	Beach
	UNCONFORMITY		
JURASSIC	MORRISON	DINOSAUR BONES	Rivers and floodplain
	UNCONFORMITY		
JURASSIC	WANAKAH		Tidal flat
JURASSIC	ENTRADA	LARGE CROSS-BEDS	Wind-blown dunes
JURASSIC	NAVAJO		
JURASSIC	KAYENTA	RIPPLE MARKS	Rivers
JURASSIC	WINGATE	LARGE CROSS-BEDS	Wind-blown dunes
	UNCONFORMITY		
TRIASSIC	CHINLE	MULTICOLORED RED ROCKS	Rivers and floodplain
	UNCONFORMITY		
TRIASSIC	MOENKOPI (225 million)	RED ROCKS	Floodplain
	GREAT UNCONFORMITY		
PRECAMBRIAN	BASEMENT		Metamorphic and igneous

Granite (1.4 billion)   Gneiss and schist (1.7 billion)

Stratigraphy of Colorado's Uncompahgre Plateau, where more than 1 billion years are missing along the Great Unconformity

So to rephrase the "layercake geology" metaphor, the rock layers of the Colorado Plateau are like a sloppy cake made by a messy (or hungry) baker, where some of the layers pinch and swell or ultimately disappear, while other layers interfinger, one blending into another. To make matters worse, some layers were partially "eaten" (that is, eroded) before the next layer was placed on top, or perhaps the baker forgot to spread (that is, never deposited) certain layers at all. And as far as giving the same rock layer different names, this is like calling the same layer "custard" in one confection and "vanilla cream" in another.

SEDIMENTARY STRUCTURES

Occasionally, during deposition of sediments, a geologic process may leave a fingerprint, a distinctive pattern within a sedimentary layer. These features, called *sedimentary structures,* are preserved in place when other layers are deposited on top of them. For example, *ripple marks* are created when wind or currents leave their mark in sand or silt along shorelines or dune environments. *Cross-beds* are parallel, sloped layers that form by advancing crests of windblown dunes or submerged, water-transported sediments. Mud cracks are formed as sediment dries out, such as in a lakebed, tidal flat, or riverbed.

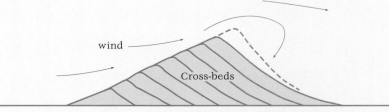

wind

Cross-beds

Cross-section of migrating sand dune

Cross-beds form as dune crests advance downwind.

Eventually, these structures may become exposed by erosion, revealing features of the ancient environment where their sediments accumulated. For example, cross-bed patterns in the Colorado Plateau's Navajo, Coconino, and De Chelly Sandstones record the passage of huge Sahara-like sand dunes, indicating that when the sand was deposited, desert conditions once existed across the Four Corners region.

Ripple marks in sandstone, Moenkopi Formation, Capitol Reef National Park, Utah

WHY ARE THE ROCKS RED?

The Colorado Plateau is also known as "red rock" country. As sunset approaches the colors of the rock layers become increasingly more intense. But why are the rocks red?

The unusually colorful hues in the Colorado Plateau's rocks are the result of small amounts of oxide minerals trapped in the rock. *Oxides* are formed when metals like iron and manganese combine with oxygen. In general, iron oxides tend to stain the rock varying shades of red and yellow, while manganese oxides add pastels like purple and lavender. Similar to rust, red iron oxide minerals—most commonly hematite—coat individual grains within a rock, or are precipitated within the chemical cement (calcite or quartz) that binds the rock together. Like magic, it only takes tiny amounts of hematite within the rock, typically less that three to five percent, to color the rocks red. So when someone asks you, why are the rocks red? You can answer with confidence: it's because of the iron-bearing mineral hematite. Like rust, hematite has turned the rocks red!

The beautiful streaks that adorn the canyon country sandstone walls are known as *desert varnish*. Desert varnish forms when windblown clay and soil particles cling to moist surfaces dripping down the canyon walls. Over time, aided by microbial action, the clay particles attract minute amounts of iron and manganese that build up to form the patina or "varnish" that paints the canyon walls.

Rock glow in Utah's slickrock country

IGNEOUS ROCKS

Although sedimentary rocks dominate the Colorado Plateau, igneous and metamorphic rocks are also important aspects of the geologic story. They include the oldest rocks in the region and their appearances contribute layers other than horizontal. Examples of these rock types are found at the very bottom of the Grand Canyon beneath the lowest sedimentary layer. Here lie the ancient contorted rocks of the Inner Gorge, part of the Colorado Plateau's igneous and metamorphic basement rocks.

Igneous rocks, like the pink-colored Zoroaster Granite that composes the igneous portion of the Grand Canyon basement, are borne from molten material, or *magma,* generated at great depth within the earth. Magma, which is relatively buoyant, tends to rise, forcing its way through the Earth's crust as a hot liquid. If magma is unable to reach the surface, it cools slowly to form a *pluton,* a name derived from Pluto, the Greek god of the underworld. The slow cooling allows time for crystals to grow large enough to be seen with the naked eye, which is one way that plutonic rocks can be identified. Plutonic igneous rocks are called *intrusive* igneous rocks, since they "intrude" the surrounding rocks.

The Grand Canyon's Zoroaster Granite forms light-colored bands of cooled magma that once squeezed between cracks in the dark Vishnu Schist, a metamorphic rock we will discuss below. Granite is only one in a series of intrusive rock types that owe their light color to the dominant

TABLE 4

Common Igneous Rocks

INTRUSIVE/PLUTONIC (COARSE-GRAINED)	COLOR (COMMON MINERALS)	EXTRUSIVE/VOLCANIC (FINE-GRAINED)
Granite	Light-colored, can be pink to red (quartz, feldspar, mica, minor hornblende)	Rhyolite
Granodiorite	Light gray (feldspar, quartz, hornblende, mica minor augite)	Dacite
Diorite	Medium to dark gray (feldspar, hornblende, mica, augite)	Andesite
Gabbro	Dark gray to greenish black (feldspar, augite, olivine, minor hornblende)	Basalt

Church Rock diatreme was a conduit for an explosive volcanic eruption near Kayenta, Arizona.

minerals quartz and feldspar. Granite is also peppered with dark mineral flakes such as biotite mica and needles of hornblende. There are "hybrid" granites, such as granodiorite or quartz monzonite, that look something like granite but contain slightly different blends of minerals. Geologists generally refer to granite and all of its similar gradations using the term *granitic*.

At the dark end of the intrusive rock color spectrum, igneous rocks such as *gabbro* contain darker-colored minerals rich in iron and magnesium, including hornblende, augite, and olivine. Intermediate between the light- and dark-colored extremes are medium to dark gray igneous rocks like *dacite* and *diorite*.

If magma travels all the way to the Earth's surface before it cools, it is extruded as *lava*, which flows across the landscape as hot, molten material under the influence of gravity. In the western Grand Canyon during the last million years or so, lava spilled from volcanoes on the rim and flowed over the cliffs into the Canyon forming *lava cascades*, masses of cooled lava that adhere to the steep canyon walls. Lava may be thrown from a volcano as a fountain, building a *cinder cone*, or it may also erupt more explosively in clouds of ash, lava, and glowing avalanches of debris that build tall *composite* or *stratovolcanoes*.

The products of these eruptions form *extrusive igneous rocks*, better known as *volcanic rocks*, named after Vulcan, the Greek god of fire. Since volcanic rocks cool relatively quickly, there is little time for crystals to grow very large. In fact, a hand lens is often needed to see the tiny crystals. Cooling also may take place so rapidly that crystals have no time to form, and the magma quenches into a natural glass called *obsidian*. Another possible feature in volcanic rocks is small holes, or *vesicles,* that are sometimes left behind by gas bubbles trapped in the lava as it cools.

There is a broad spectrum of extrusive igneous rock types that ranges from light to dark in color. Since both intrusive and extrusive rocks come from molten material, their mineral content is basically the same. Thus, for each variety of intrusive, or plutonic, rock, there is an equivalent extrusive, or volcanic, rock type. The key difference is their texture—plutonic rocks have larger mineral crystals because they cooled more slowly underground and volcanic rocks have smaller mineral crystals since they cooled rapidly at the Earth's surface.

Names of common extrusive igneous rocks found on the Colorado Plateau include light-colored *rhyolite* (the extrusive equivalent of granite), grayish *andesite* (intermediate in composition like the intrusive diorite), and dark-colored *basalt* (like the igneous rock gabbro). A rock composed of volcanic ash rather than lava is called *tuff* or *breccia.*

METAMORPHIC ROCKS

As mentioned above, the Grand Canyon Vishnu Schist is a *metamorphic rock,* the third and final of the rock types. Metamorphic rocks can be strikingly beautiful and complex—and hard. The name is derived from the Greek "meta," meaning "change," and "morphe," meaning "form." Metamorphic rocks are preexisting igneous or sedimentary rocks that become exposed to heat and pressure deep within the earth or along the margins of intrusions. The heat and pressure causes the rocks to change form. A variety of metamorphic rocks are represented on the Colorado Plateau, but are exposed only in a few of the deeper canyons.

The Vishnu Schist was once an assemblage of sedimentary rock deposited nearly 2 billion years ago and later altered by heat and pressure. These rocks are now an interlocking texture of mica and other minerals. This change, called *metamorphism,* caused old minerals to recrystallize into new minerals, resulting in altered shapes and sizes of the mineral crystals and development of new structures within the rock.

Under low temperature and pressure conditions, metamorphism may be minimized, so that features of the original (or *parent*) rock are still recognizable. With gentle cooking, the existing mineral grains simply enlarge and become fused. In this way, the sedimentary rock shale transforms into the metamorphic rock slate, sandstone transforms into quartzite, and limestone transforms into marble.

As temperature and pressure intensify, the alignment of the minerals becomes more pronounced, which further transforms the rock. This is what happens when slate is altered to *schist.* If conditions further intensify, the minerals in schist may segregate into light and dark layers to form the metamorphic rock called *gneiss* (pronounced "nice"). In gneiss, dark layers of platy or elongate minerals such as mica and hornblende alternate

TABLE 5

Common Metamorphic Rocks

ROCK NAME	PARENT ROCK	TEXTURE/FEATURES
Quartzite	Sandstone	Interlocking crystals, sugary appearance
Marble	Limestone/dolomite	Fine to coarse interlocking crystals
Slate	Shale/siltstone	Fine-grained, splits into thin sheets
Schist	Shale/siltstone	Visible crystals that are elongate and aligned
Gneiss	Granite, sandstone, or sandstone/shale	Banded, may be folded or contorted

with layers of light-colored quartz and feldspar. During intense heat and pressure, the mineral banding in schist and gneiss may become deformed, often bent, folded, and swirled into complex patterns like ribbons of multi-colored taffy. Massively deformed metamorphic rocks such as these, called *banded* gneiss, compose the Colorado Plateau's basement rocks, exposed in the depths of the Grand Canyon and Black Canyon, and along the walls of the canyons that flank the Uncompahgre Plateau near Grand Junction.

If the temperature and pressure conditions reach extremes, partial melting of the parent rock can occur, producing magma. The resulting rock, called *migmitite,* is a mixture of igneous and metamorphic rocks and is the most deformed and confused of all. If conditions go even further, the rocks completely melt and the resulting magma is recycled back into igneous rock. Thus, they come full circle and the cycle can begin again.

Metamorphic basement rocks exposed in Unaweep Canyon on the Uncompahgre Plateau, Colorado

GLOBAL FORCES: PLATE TECTONICS AND THE COLORADO PLATEAU

The link between plate tectonics and the geologic history of the Colorado Plateau is not an obvious one. Throughout much of its history, the Colorado Plateau has managed to remain relatively stable. Its edges have been ruffled, its surface rippled, and its face scorched from time to time by volcanoes. But the Plateau's thick stack of sedimentary layers has escaped relatively unscathed. Its very stability, in contrast to the chaos around it, still puzzles geologists.

The concept of *plate tectonics* holds that the Earth's surface or *crust* is divided into about a dozen giant slabs of rock called *plates*. Some plates bear granitic continents, like the North American Plate, where the Colorado Plateau is located. Other plates carry islands and basaltic ocean floor, such as the Pacific Plate, which is largely submerged beneath the Pacific Ocean. Plate tectonics describes how these plates move around the globe over time, an idea first called continental drift. The moving plates carry the continents, shifting them around on the surface of the earth.

The radioactive-heat engine in the Earth's interior drives the constant wandering of plates. The plates, which are rigid sections of rock, ride around on top of a hot, dense material in the upper part of the Earth's *mantle*. Relative to the size of the earth, the patchwork of moving plates that covers the Earth is very thin, like crackers on top of a huge cauldron of pea soup. The Earth's mantle can be compared to the boiling soup, where convection cells rise to the surface, begin to cool, and then sink down to where they are reheated and rise again. Convection cells in the mantle may drive the motion of the plates on the Earth's surface, although the exact mechanism remains unknown.

Much of the geologic action at the Earth's surface, like earthquakes, volcanic eruptions, and mountain building, takes place at the boundaries between plates. Plates interact in three basic ways: they *converge* or collide, they pull apart (a process called *rifting*), or they bump and grind past each another, like along the San Andreas Fault in California.

Although perhaps not as dramatically as in surrounding regions, plate tectonic processes have had a profound effect on the Colorado Plateau. Today, the Colorado Plateau lies far inland from the major boundaries between plates where all the action is. But this has not always been the case.

Geologists now recognize that the continental margin of western North America is a mosaic of fragments, or *microplates,* added to the continent during phases of its assembly. This process, called *continental accretion,* in its early phases helped build the basement foundation for the Colorado Plateau. Nearly 2 billion years ago during the Precambrian, microplates began rafting onto an ancient continent whose southern margin was where Wyoming is today. Although exact details remain uncertain, the coast consisted of a chain of offshore volcanic islands associated with *subduction* zones, where one plate is forced beneath the other. This action created conditions of great heat and pressure, generating complex arrangements of metamorphic and igneous rocks. Subduction is one way the earth recycles its crust—though the crackers sink into the pea soup, heading to the bottom of the pot, the material does rise again.

This was the Colorado Plateau's beginning. As accretion continued, the volcanic and sedimentary rocks along this ancient continent were in-

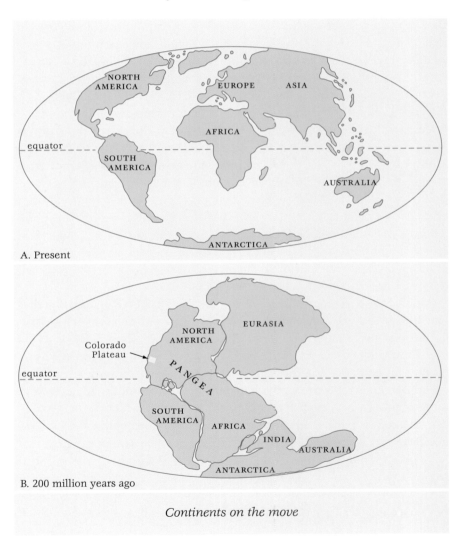

Continents on the move

tensely metamorphosed into schist and gneiss. These rocks became part of North America's Precambrian basement rock, and include the Grand Canyon's 1.7-billion-year-old Vishnu Schist and the basement rocks exposed along the Uncompahgre Plateau and in the Black Canyon. These contorted metamorphic rocks were also laced by granitic intrusions, including the Grand Canyon's Zoroaster Granite, before being exposed to a long period of erosion. It was the eons of erosion that followed these ancient plate tectonic events that created the basement platform for the Colorado Plateau's thick stack of sedimentary rocks. The foundation had been laid.

Continued plate tectonic actions through time have jostled the Colorado Plateau's basement foundation. Major events include the rise of the Ancestral Rocky Mountains about 300 million years ago, which caused uplift and erosion along the Uncompahgre and Defiance Plateaus, and the widespread uplift and warping of the sedimentary stack about 65 million years ago during the Laramide orogeny. Later, about 30 million years ago, a change in plate tectonic interactions caused renewed uplift of the Colorado Plateau. At this same time, the land surrounding the plateau began to pull apart as the Basin and Range and Rio Grande Rift caused major faulting along the Plateau's margins. And the action continues today. The Colorado Plateau continues to rise, and faults still nibble at the edges.

THE LARAMIDE OROGENY

Nowhere else are the rippling affects of the Laramide orogeny on the Colorado Plateau's geologic layercake better displayed than at the Grand Canyon. The prominent tilt of the Canyon's otherwise horizontal rock layers are easily seen on each limb of the Kaibab Uplift, and the faults that underlie each limb are exposed in the basement rocks deep in the Grand Canyon's inner canyons. The Kaibab Uplift is what geologists call "a classic Laramide structure."

The *Laramide orogeny* climaxed between about 65 and 50 million years ago, at the same time that the Rocky Mountains were first thrust skyward in what is now Colorado. During this time, movement along deep-seated faults in the basement rocks upset the Plateau's thick stack of sedimentary layers. Many of these faults followed preexisting zones of weakness that date back to faulting during Precambrian time.

Like a rug draped over a step, the Grand Canyon's overlying sedimentary rocks are warped, forming broad uplifts marked by steep

Tilted layers along Waterpocket Fold, a monocline formed during the Laramide orogeny, Capitol Reef National Park, Utah

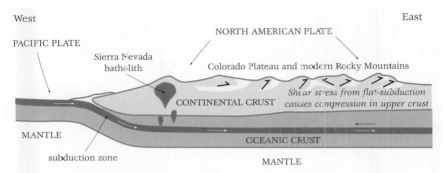

The plate tectonic setting during the Laramide orogeny

monoclines. These monoclines are large-scale, step-like folds whose strata are inclined in the same direction.

The origins of the Laramide orogeny, though probably triggered by continental accretion and subduction on the continent's west coast and beneath the North American plate, remain a mystery. Uplift and mountain-building so far inland from the plate boundary is a geologic anomaly, although a possible modern analog may exist in western South America where the Andes Mountain chain is currently rising.

Geologists speculate that about 65 million years ago the pace of Atlantic sea-floor spreading may have quickened, accelerating the rate of subduction of the Pacific sea floor beneath North America. This may have flattened the angle of subduction, causing the Pacific Plate to impinge on the region's basement rocks. The basement squeezed like an accordion, sending some rocks skyward to become mountains (as in Colorado).

In contrast, on the Colorado Plateau uplift was less severe and only warped the overlying layers into more gentle structures bounded by monoclines. In addition to the Grand Canyon's Kaibab Uplift, prominent Laramide structures include the Monument and Defiance Uplifts (where Monument Valley and Canyon De Chelly are located today), New Mexico's Zuni Uplift, Colorado's Uncompahgre Uplift, and Utah's Circle Cliffs Uplift and San Rafael Swell.

The artistry of erosion has sculpted the tilted limbs of these structures into spectacular landforms. Many of these uplifts extend for more than 100 miles across the naked earth of the Colorado Plateau. And from what we observe at the Grand Canyon, each of these great monoclines are underlain by step-like faults in the Colorado Plateau's basement.

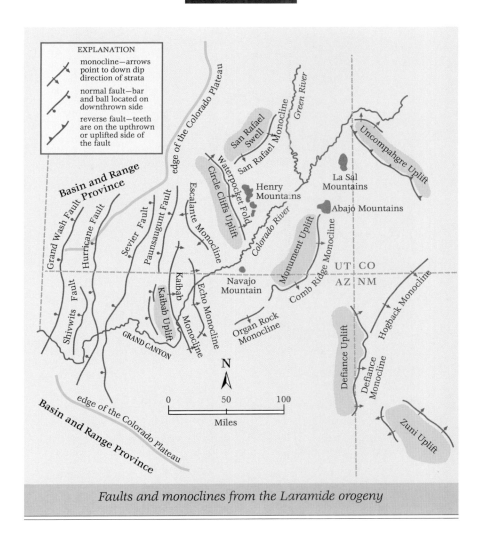

EXPLANATION

monocline—arrows point to down dip direction of strata

normal fault—bar and ball located on downthrown side

reverse fault—teeth are on the upthrown or uplifted side of the fault

Faults and monoclines from the Laramide orogeny

GEOLOGIC STRUCTURES—FAULTS, FOLDS, AND FRACTURES

Through time, geologic upheavals caused major disruptions in the rocks of surrounding regions, but the Colorado Plateau was affected to a much lesser degree. As the Rocky Mountains surged upward about 65 million years ago during the Laramide orogeny, the Plateau region was corrugated by minor uplifts that warped or domed the rock layers. Even during all of the tumult, the layers were rarely shaken enough to break.

Several things can happen when stress is applied to rigid layers of rock. First, the layers can bend, creating a *fold*. The simplest type of fold is a *monocline*, where the rock layers change from horizontal to steeply inclined to horizontal again, like a rug draped across a step. Monoclines

36

A. Monoclines reflect faulting at depth

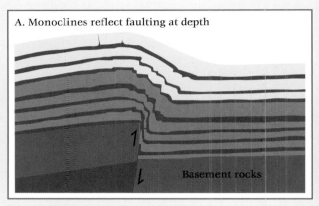

Basement rocks

B. Normal faults are a result of extension

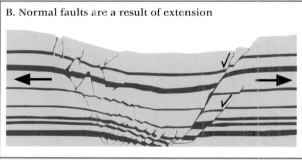

C. Thrust faults are the result of compression

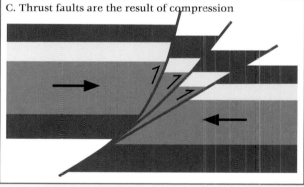

D. Laccoliths dome the sedimentary layers

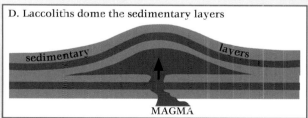

sedimentary layers

MAGMA

Common geologic structures of the Colorado Plateau

37

Fault zone along the East Kaibab monocline, Kaibab Plateau, Arizona

are very common on the Colorado Plateau where sedimentary layers are draped across breaks (or *faults*, described below) in the underlying Precambrian basement. Rocks can also bend upward into an arch or dome creating an *anticline*. In the case where rocks are warped downward, forming a basin, a *syncline* is created.

Often as rocks are folded, they break to form *fractures* (also called *joints*). Fractures are important in the formation of different landforms because broken rock provides zones of weakness that can be attacked by weathering and erosion. The formation of cliffs, arches, monuments, and other landform features is typically influenced by the orientation of fractures.

Finally, rocks may break and slide against one another, creating a *fault*. Faults are considered *normal* if one side simply drops down relative to the other. *Reverse faults* result when one side is pushed up relative to the other. A *thrust fault* occurs when the rocks slide over the top of one another, rather than just up and down. And a final type of fault, called *strike-slip*, occurs

38

when rocks slide horizontally past one another. The San Andreas Fault is the best known example of a strike-slip fault.

All of these geologic structures can occur on any scale—from small outcrops to major features extending for dozens of miles. They are important indications of the history of movements that the rocks have undergone through time.

PREPARING TO HIKE THE GEOLOGY

Hiking the geology does not require any expensive or fancy equipment. Simply using this book and adding a few special items to your backpack will prepare you to "geologize" in the field.

WHAT TO BRING

Since the Colorado Plateau has widely ranging elevations, the temperature and weather conditions can change drastically. As you prepare, ask yourself: What do I need to survive the worst conditions I might possibly encounter?

Hiking the geology at Mesa Arch, Canyonlands National Park, Utah

Start with the basics, including sturdy boots, appropriate clothing, food and water, a hat, sunscreen, raingear (both jacket and pants), and a backpack or waist pack for your gear. Also, be sure to carry the Ten Essentials: (1) flashlight with extra batteries, (2) map, (3) compass, (4) extra food, (5) extra clothing (something warm), (6) sunglasses, (7) first-aid kit, (8) pocket knife, (9) waterproof matches, and (10) candle or firestarter. In the Colorado Plateau, water should be your Eleventh Essential on all hikes.

For exploring the geology, a few other items are wise to bring: (1) a small magnifying glass or *hand lens* to examine rocks up close, (2) a waterproof notebook and pencil to record observations and questions about the landscape for later investigation (you always think you will remember, but write it down anyway!), and (3) a felt-tip, waterproof pen for marking any rock samples you might wish to collect (but remember that collecting is prohibited in many of the parks and monuments described in this book).

TOPOGRAPHIC AND GEOLOGIC MAPS

Geologists love maps. Perhaps you already have the bug. If you do, welcome to map paradise, because each hike description in this book lists the maps most useful for that specific hike. Topographic maps, or "topo maps" for short, provide basic information about elevation, the nature of the landscape (steep or flat), place names, and trail locations. When you're out on the trail, it's good practice to know your location on your topo map at all times. It's also a good idea to keep it in a zip-lock bag to protect it from getting wet.

The parallel lines on topographic maps, like rings around a bathtub, connect points of equal elevation. The lines are also spaced by elevation gain, so the closer the lines, the steeper the terrain. Standard topographic maps are provided by the U.S. Geological Survey (USGS). The format most useful and easy to read is the USGS 7.5-minute quadrangle map, because it has the largest scale; this also means that in certain cases you may need several quadrangle maps to cover a single hike. An alternative series of topographic maps is published by National Geographic Trails Illustrated Series (to order, call 1-800-962-1643). These useful, waterproof maps cover many of the popular hiking destinations in the Four Corners region. Both types of topo maps are available for sale at stores that sell outdoor gear and are on file to view at many university libraries.

Geologic maps are another type of map entirely. They are works of art (and science!). By using different colors for each rock formation or each group of formations, geologists have plotted dizzying spectrums of the rocks that form the landscape. Standardized symbols show features such as faults and folds, and each geologic map carries a legend describing the rocks and symbols. The USGS has published a number of geologic maps that cover areas of the Colorado Plateau, and each state also has its own series of maps. Geologic maps can be ordered from the USGS and state agencies, or copied from those at many university libraries. To locate the geologic maps for each hike in this book, find the numbers listed under "Geologic maps:" preceding the hike description and look up those numbers in Appendix C, Geologic Maps.

Be sure to inquire about local conditions. Flash floods are a real danger!

A NOTE ABOUT SAFETY

Safety is an important concern in all outdoor activities. No guidebook can alert you to every hazard or anticipate the limitations of every reader. Therefore, the descriptions of roads, trails, routes, and natural features in this book are not representations that a particular place or excursion will be safe for your party. When you follow any of the routes described in this book, you assume responsibility for your own safety. Under normal conditions, such excursions require the usual attention to traffic, road and trail conditions, weather, terrain, the capabilities of your party, and other factors. Keeping informed on current conditions and exercising common sense are the keys to a safe, enjoyable outing.

The Mountaineers Books

Mount Hayden is a pillar of Coconino sandstone along the Grand Canyon's North Rim.

Part 1
ARIZONA'S PLATEAU HIKES

Chapter 1
THE MOGOLLON RIM

The *Mogollon Rim* (pronounced "moge-E-yon") describes both a prominent landform and a major geologic boundary that marks the southern margin of the Colorado Plateau.

Best known for the red rock cliffs near Sedona, Arizona, the Mogollon Rim is the boundary between the Plateau country to the north and the desert mountains and valleys to the south. It is an abrupt boundary formed by a long, erosional escarpment stretching diagonally across the entire state of Arizona and well into New Mexico, a distance of nearly 300 miles.

Geologically, the Mogollon Rim marks the boundary where the generally flat-lying "layercake geology" of the Colorado Plateau falls off into a faulted and broken landscape—a transition zone with the Basin and Range in central Arizona and southern New Mexico. High, forested plateaus rimmed by a series of discontinuous cliffs define the edge of the Mogollon Rim. In places its trend has been obscured where the rim is buried under thick piles of volcanic rock, for example at the San Francisco Mountain and Mormon Lake, and in the White Mountains Volcanic Fields in Arizona and the Datil-Mogollon Volcanic Field in New Mexico. But, importantly, the volcanic rocks help date the development of the Mogollon Rim along the Colorado Plateau's southern edge.

In Arizona, the Mogollon Rim is held up by prominent, cliff-forming Permian sedimentary rocks capped by Tertiary-age basalt lava flows. The rock layers exposed below the "rim" include the colorful Schnebly Hill Formation—which forms Sedona's famed red rocks—the massive yellow cliff of the Coconino Sandstone, and the upper, hard-to-see gray ledges of the Toroweap and Kaibab Formations.

These sedimentary rocks record deposition by wind and water along the margin of a shallow sea during early Permian time, between about 275 and 250 million years ago. The cross-bedded layers in the Schnebly Hill and Coconino Sandstone represent wind-blown dunes that swept an ancient desert coastline not unlike the sandy desert found today along the Atlantic coast of Namibia. The Toroweap and Kaibab Formations represent fluctuating depositional environments, from coastal wind-swept dune sands of the Toroweap, to near-shore shallow marine conditions where sandy limestone and dolomite of the Kaibab accumulated.

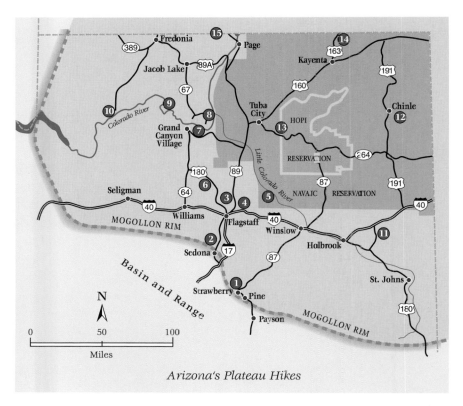

Arizona's Plateau Hikes

The geologic history of the Mogollon Rim is surprisingly complex and involves a fascinating tale of uplift, erosion, faulting, more erosion, and volcanic activity, then even more erosion.

The story begins about 65 million years ago when central Arizona was uplifted by compressional forces during the Laramide orogeny, but the mountain-building event that vaulted Colorado's Rocky Mountains skyward only gently warped the Colorado Plateau's layers into localized uplifts and monoclines. In Arizona, this tectonic event formed a huge mountain range, called the *Mogollon Highlands*. The Laramide orogeny uplifted Precambrian basement rocks and, in the process, folded the overlying stack of Paleozoic and Mesozoic sedimentary rocks into a huge dome.

The overall result of these events, which occurred over a span of at least 10 to 20 million years, was that the southern edge of the Colorado Plateau was uplifted and tilted to the north. A long, intense period of erosion followed which stripped the mountains bare of their sedimentary cover, exposing a Precambrian igneous and metamorphic core. Meanwhile, to the north, the southern edge of the Colorado Plateau was stripped of its softer, Mesozoic sedimentary rocks until only the resistant Kaibab Formation remained at the surface.

Across the broad, tilted erosional surface on top of the Kaibab Formation, northward flowing streams deposited sand and gravel containing Paleozoic and Precambrian cobbles derived from the ancient highlands to the south. These sediments, called the *rim gravels* because they are found scattered today along the Mogollon Rim, provide the most important clues that these ancient highlands ever existed.

Although geologists debate the exact age of the rim gravels, recent work indicates that they are younger than 54.6 million years, the age of a volcanic cobble found in the gravel, but older than 28 million years, the age of a lava flow found directly on top of the gravel. It is speculated that the streams that deposited the rim gravels may have drained into the great Tertiary Lakes that existed to the north in Utah, Colorado, and Wyoming during this time.

Basalt boulders on red rock below the Mogollon Rim near Sedona, Arizona

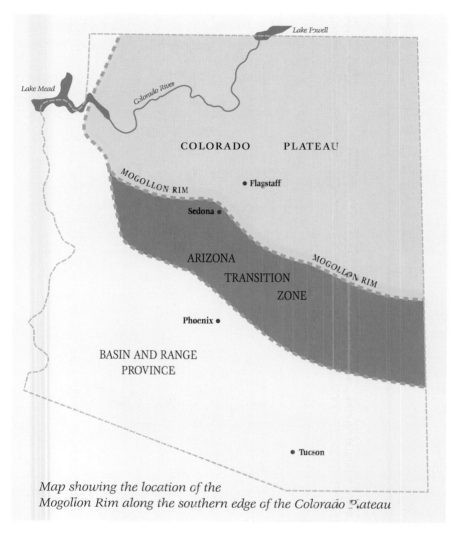

Map showing the location of the Mogollon Rim along the southern edge of the Colorado Plateau

Over time, weathering and erosion continued to etch away at the Colorado Plateau's southern edge. Eventually the northward flowing streams began to break through the erosion surface on top of the Kaibab, exposing the softer sedimentary layers below. As these layers began to retreat to the north, a cliff edge or *escarpment* developed that was similar to the cliffs along the modern-day Mogollon Rim. These ancient cliffs, which exposed the same colorful red rocks of the Schnebly Hill Formation found today around Sedona, formed an ancestral Mogollon Rim and became the retreating edge of the Colorado Plateau.

The age of the ancestral Mogollon Rim appears to vary along its length. Lava flows that entomb the ancient cliffs range in age from about 26 to 10 million years. Near Sedona, the House Mountain volcano erupted right along the ancestral Mogollon Rim and marks the position of the escarpment 15 million years ago.

Based on the position of the escarpment today, the rate of retreat for the Mogollon Rim near Sedona is calculated at about 3 feet for every 2000 years. If this current rate continues, it is speculated that the Mogollon Rim will arrive in downtown Flagstaff in about 79 million years!

Hike 1

FOSSIL SPRINGS

THE ANCESTRAL MOGOLLON RIM

View a portion of the ancestral Mogollon Rim on this hike to Fossil Springs, where life-giving water transforms a dry and rocky creekbed into a verdant oasis.

DISTANCE ■ **8 miles round trip**

ELEVATION ■ **5640 to 4320 feet**

DIFFICULTY ■ **Moderate**

TOPOGRAPHIC MAP ■ **USGS Strawberry, AZ**

GEOLOGIC MAP ■ **1**

KEY REFERENCES ■ **1, 2**

PRECAUTIONS ■ **Avoid this hike during the mid-day heat of summer. Please do all you can to limit your impact at the springs.**

FOR INFORMATION ■ **Payson Ranger District**

About the Landscape: Fossil Creek is one of the major canyons dissecting the Mogollon Rim and offers a window into the complex geologic history of the plateau's southern margin. Here, a major change in the thickness of volcanic rocks that cap the southern edge of the Colorado Plateau suggests that an ancestral Mogollon Rim, similar to the colorful cliffs near Sedona today, once existed in this area. Erosion has revealed this ancient escarpment and exposed the colorful Paleozoic sedimentary layers hidden beneath the dark veneer of volcanic rocks that buried the Colorado Plateau's southern edge 10 million years ago.

This pleasant hike along the edge of the Mogollon Rim leads to Fossil Springs, which gushes from ledges at the top of the Redwall Limestone transforming a dry, rocky creekbed into a cascading creek with a perfect swimming hole.

Trail Guide: To reach the Fossil Springs trailhead, turn off Arizona State Route 87 in Strawberry onto Fossil Creek Road and drive west 4.9 miles to the sign for the Fossil Springs Trail (after 2.5 miles this paved road turns to gravel and becomes Forest Road 708). Turn right and drive 0.25 mile to the trailhead.

From the parking area and trail register, the hike starts out following an old road toward the rim of Fossil Creek Canyon. After about 0.25 mile, the trail makes its first big switchback and cuts down through the volcanic layers that cap the Mogollon Rim.

The first outcrops along the trail are medium gray basalt formed by molten lava that flowed across the southern edge of the Colorado Plateau. Note the large vesicles in the basalt caused by gas bubbles trapped in the lava when it cooled. Exposed farther down the trail are tan to yellow layers of tuff and breccia where angular boulders are encased within volcanic ash from explosive eruptions. The source of this volcanic material was the Hackberry Mountain volcano to the south along the Verde River. About 10 million years ago, volcanic activity completely smothered the southern margin of the Colorado Plateau, which impounded the southward-flowing Verde River and created a huge lake along the southern margin of the Colorado Plateau.

At about the 1-mile point, the trail begins to descend more steeply. After another 0.5 mile, a color change to red along the trail indicates that we

Ground water transforms Fossil Creek into a flowing river below the Mogollon Rim.

are now below the volcanic layers which cap the rim. The next trailside outcrops are red sedimentary rocks also exposed in the cliff-walled butte that rises above the trail on the skyline. For about the next 1 mile the trail levels out as it contours through the red rock layers.

Not all geologists agree about the name of these red rocks, which stretch along the Mogollon Rim just west of Sedona to the east beyond Payson. They were first described as the Supai Formation, following the use of rock layer names from the Grand Canyon. More recent work, however, has shown that these rocks belong to a sequence of layers not present at the Grand Canyon, called the Schnebly Hill Formation. Along the Mogollon Rim, the Permian Schnebly Hill overlies the Permian Hermit Shale and Pennsylvanian Naco Group.

Here in Fossil Creek Canyon, the Schnebly Hill Formation consists of a thick red rock sequence of sandstone, siltstone, and mudstone. These sedimentary rocks accumulated along an arid, sandy coastline where wind-blown sand dunes dominated the ancient landscape. At about the 2-mile point, large boulders of the Fort Apache Limestone have rolled down from the cliffs above to come to rest along the trail. Although no fossils are visible to the naked eye, this limestone represents marine deposits left behind by a warm, shallow sea that covered portions of northeastern Arizona about 275 million years ago during the Permian.

At about the 3-mile point, the trail passes a campsite on the left and begins to descend steeply again. Along this section of the trail the opposite or west wall of the canyon is in full view. Most noticeable is the impressive gray cliff in the bottom of the canyon. This is a terrace of *travertine,* a type of limestone deposited by the water that flowed from Fossil Springs (not yet in view) over the millennia. The travertine accumulated on top of red and gray layers of the Pennsylvanian Naco Group, the rock layers directly below the Schnebly Hill Formation. The position of these traver-

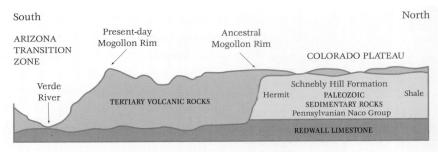

Cross-section showing ancestral Mogollon Rim buried beneath Tertiary volcanic rocks along Fossil Creek

tine layers above the canyon floor indicates that Fossil Creek was once much higher than it is today. Over time, the creek has cut down through the 200-foot-thick layer of travertine to where the present Fossil Springs now gushes forth below the base of the cliff.

Another important feature of the opposite wall of the canyon is the incredible change in thickness of the volcanic rocks. Above and to the right of the travertine cliff, red rocks of the Schnebly Hill Formation are covered by only a thin veneer of dark basalt along the rim of the canyon. In contrast, just above the travertine cliff and continuing to the left, the Schnebly Hill red rocks are absent and the volcanic rocks thicken dramatically.

This thickening in the volcanic rocks represents a buried cliff face of the ancestral Mogollon Rim. Uplift of the area during the Laramide orogeny about 65 million years ago pushed Arizona's Precambrian basement skyward, creating a highland to the south in central Arizona called the Mogollon Highlands. Erosion of the Mogollon Highlands stripped off the sedimentary layers on top of the Precambrian basement rocks, and carved a steep cliff into the retreating edge of the Colorado Plateau. This cliff was preserved beneath the volcanic rocks from the Hackberry Mountains, which buried this ancestral Mogollon Rim about 10 million years ago.

About 3.5 miles from the trailhead the trail reaches a sign at the intersection with the Mail Trail, to the right, and the Flume Trail, to the left. From this point, follow the trail to the left (downstream) about 0.5 mile to Fossil Springs. The trail crosses the dry, boulder-strewn creekbed and passes directly below the cliff of travertine. When you start to hear the sound of running water, take the first fork to the left and follow the narrow trail through the brush to the springs.

After the long, dry hike down into the canyon, arriving at Fossil Springs is like a dream come true. Fossil Springs is actually a series of springs gushing directly from the source in limestone layers of the Redwall Limestone. The Redwall Limestone is a widespread layer on the Colorado Plateau and represents an ancient tropical sea deposited about 350 million years ago during the Mississippian. If you look closely along the creekside ledges you will find brachiopod fossils scattered in the rocks. Hence the name—Fossil Springs.

In a matter of yards from where you pass the first spring, Fossil Creek is transformed into a flowing river shaded by tall, lush sycamore trees. About 100 yards downstream from the first spring you will discover the perfect swimming hole, complete with rope swing.

After you have been rejuvenated by the magical springs and fully pondered the origins of this unique canyon, return to the trailhead by the route you came.

NORTH WILSON TRAIL IN OAK CREEK CANYON

A Tale of Two Canyons

Hike along the Oak Creek Fault to Wilson Bench for a view of Sedona's famed red rocks.

DISTANCE ■ **4 miles round trip**

ELEVATION ■ **4750 to 6200 feet**

DIFFICULTY ■ **Strenuous**

TOPOGRAPHIC MAP ■ **USGS Munds Park, AZ**

GEOLOGIC MAP ■ **2**

KEY REFERENCE ■ **3**

PRECAUTIONS ■ **Avoid afternoon thunderstorms on top of Wilson Bench during the summer monsoon season. Shade can keep this trail muddy and snowbound until spring. A Red Rock Pass ($5 per day/$15 per week) is required for parking at the trailhead.**

FOR INFORMATION ■ **Red Rock Ranger District, Red Rock–Secret Mountain Wilderness**

About the Landscape: Oak Creek Canyon is one of the jewels of the southern Colorado Plateau's Mogollon Rim. The differences in the rocks on opposite sides of the canyon reveal a fascinating story about recurrent faulting events along the Oak Creek Fault, an "ancestral" Oak Creek Canyon entombed by lava, and the carving of modern-day Oak Creek Canyon.

This hike winds through a cool, forested canyon, then climbs to the top of Wilson Bench, a basalt-capped plateau on the lower flank of Wilson Mountain. The views along the trail offer an excellent opportunity to compare and contrast the rock layers that make up the walls of Oak Creek Canyon. A vista at the end of the hike provides sweeping views of the red rocks of Sedona.

Trail Guide: The trailhead for this hike is found at the Encinoso Picnic Area, located in Oak Creek Canyon about 5.2 miles north of Sedona on U.S. Highway 89A. Signs mark the trailhead at the north end of the parking area near the entrance.

The trail starts out heading north beside the highway before turning west and climbing gently up a forested slope to a fire-scarred clearing beyond a powerline. The volcanic boulders along the trail are eroded from the basalt lava flows that cap both rims of the canyon. This clearing is the perfect spot to lean against a boulder and study the differences in the rock layers exposed in each wall of Oak Creek Canyon.

Hiking the North Wilson Trail in Oak Creek Canyon

Notice that the east rim of the canyon is much lower in elevation than the west rim. The difference in elevation between rims is caused by the Oak Creek Fault, which drops the east side of the canyon down relative to the west side. The displacement or offset of rock layers along the fault varies between 700 and 1000 feet, which follows the general north-south trend of the Oak Creek Canyon. Since the fault offsets 6 to 8 million-year-old lava flows that cap the rim, the most recent movement along the fault is younger than 6 million years. But, as you will learn, there is much more to the story.

Also notice that the rock layers that make up each side of the canyon are different. The higher, west wall is composed of a colorful stack of sedimentary rocks capped by a relatively thin, dark layer of basalt. From bottom to top the layers include the red and orange Schnebly Hill Formation, the massive yellow cliff of the Coconino Sandstone, and the hard-to-see gray ledges of the Toroweap and Kaibab Formations immediately below the basalt cap.

In contrast, the lower, east wall of Oak Creek Canyon has a much thicker sequence of basalt (over 500 feet) capping the rim, and a portion of the sedimentary sequence present on the west wall below the basalt is missing. The missing rock includes all of the Kaibab and Toroweap Formations, and most of the Coconino Sandstone. This dramatic change in the stratigraphy in the canyon walls provides important clues about the recurrent history of motion along the Oak Creek Fault, and the origin of the canyon itself. The plot thickens.

Beyond the clearing the trail enters a forested canyon between two basalt-capped hills. These hills are on the down-dropped or east side of the Oak Creek Fault. At about the 0.75-mile point, the trail turns to the south and begins to climb the south hill. The trace of the Oak Creek Fault follows the sharp ravine between the trail and the base of the cliff to the west.

As the trail climbs there are several good views of the sheer cliff face of the canyon's west wall. Note the gradual change from the mostly red rocks in the Schnebly Hill Formation to the massive yellow layers of the Coconino Sandstone. As the trail switchbacks higher, several breaks in the trees offer views to the north. The Oak Creek Fault passes between the west side of the canyon, on the left, and the lower basalt-capped hill, on the right. Again, notice that the sedimentary layers present in the canyon's west wall are missing in the down-dropped hill east (right) of the fault.

This dramatic change in the rocks across the fault tells a story of multiple events and change in the sense of motion along the Oak Creek Fault.

About 65 million years ago during the Laramide orogeny, compressional forces squeezed the land together forcing it to bend, buckle, and break along what would become the Oak Creek Fault. The result of this action

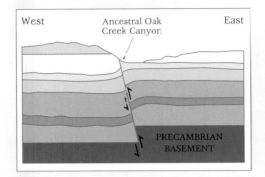

A. Erosion carves the ancestral Oak Creek Canyon along the Oak Creek Fault, which began to move during the Laramide orogeny, but with up-to-the-east movement.

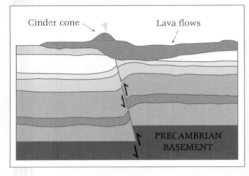

B. Lava flows fill the ancestral canyon between about 6 to 3 million years ago.

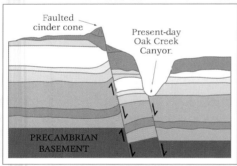

C. The Oak Creek Fault was reactivated less than 6 million years ago, but with down-to-the-east movement. For a second time, Oak Creek Canyon was carved along the fault zone.

Oak Creek Canyon: A Tale of Two Canyons

was that the east side of the fault was pushed up about 600 feet higher than the west side of the fault—exactly the opposite of the offset shown in the canyon walls today.

Over time, erosion stripped away the uplifted rocks east of the fault, removing all of the Kaibab and Toroweap Formations and a portion of the Coconino Sandstone and in the process carving an ancestral Oak Creek Canyon along the ancient trend of the Oak Creek Fault. At the time the ancestral canyon was carved, the Mogollon Rim was much farther south than where it is today. Then between about 6 and 8 million years ago, basalt flows filled the ancestral canyon, entombing it beneath the Mogollon Rim's lava cap. Today, the thickened lava east of the fault preserves a portion of the ancestral Oak Creek Canyon, while the present-day canyon has carved even deeper into the Mogollon Rim.

About 1.25 miles from the trailhead, the trail turns back to the south and begins a more gradual climb for about the next 0.25 mile, where it finally levels out on top of Wilson Bench (also called First Bench). The top of the west wall of Oak Creek Canyon, which is Wilson Mountain, is now in full view.

Along the western skyline a cinder cone of bright-red volcanic rock sits on top of the darker basalt that caps the rim. The vertical outcrop of dark basalt immediately below the cinder cone is a feeder *dike,* which acted as a conduit for molten lava gushing towards the surface when the cinder cone was erupting. This cinder cone was the source of the fifth and final lava flow that buried ancestral Oak Creek Canyon between 6 and 8 million years ago. Since the cinder cone is broken by the fault, it existed before down-to-the-east faulting. Thus, modern-day Oak Creek Canyon is younger than 6 million years old.

The last 0.5 mile of trail across Wilson Bench makes for pleasant, nearly flat walking. We are now eye-level with the east rim of Oak Creek Canyon, although a branch of the Oak Creek Fault actually drops the east rim down another 150 feet below Wilson Bench. To the west, Wilson Mountain rises on the west side of the Oak Creek Fault. Remember that Wilson Bench is on the down-dropped, east side of the fault. The San Francisco Peaks, a composite volcano located near Flagstaff, dominates the skyline to the north.

Ultimately the North Wilson Trail reaches a T-junction with the Wilson Mountain Trail. The trail to the right leads to the top of Wilson Mountain (another 2 miles). The trail to the left winds about 2 miles downhill to Midgley Bridge along U.S. Highway 89A.

If time permits, turn left and continue about 100 yards to a short spur trail on the right for a sweeping view of Sedona's famed red rocks and beyond to the Verde Valley within the Arizona Transition Zone. From this vantage point, the Oak Creek Fault makes a dogleg to the east (left) where it meets another branch of the fault that continues south. Notice that the spectacular red rocks (Schnebly Hill Formation) of Schnebly Hill and Munds Mountain are on the uplifted or western side of the fault.

Once you have enjoyed the scenery in all its geologic splendor, retrace your route back to the trailhead.

Chapter 2
THE SAN FRANCISCO VOLCANIC FIELD

For about the past 6 million years, a great number of volcanoes have con-spired as partners in crime to engulf a large portion of the southern Colo-rado Plateau's landscape. This moonscape of volcanic rock, called the *San Francisco Volcanic Field,* covers 1800 square miles across northern Arizona from Williams eastward past Flagstaff, and forms the hilly and mountain-ous terrain between the Grand Canyon and the Mogollon Rim. Here, great volumes of molten magma have welled up from below, squeezing to the surface along faults, erupting from central vents in flows of red-hot lava, or ejecting smoldering pyroclastic embers of ash and cinders. About 150,000 years ago, lava flows from a single cinder cone, Merriam Crater, diverted the course of the Little Colorado River, creating Grand Falls and changing the Colorado Plateau's landscape forever.

The San Francisco Volcanic Field is one of the world's best localities for studying volcanic landforms and was used by Apollo astronauts as a train-ing ground for landing on the moon. Most of the around 600 volcanoes within the San Francisco Volcanic Field are classified as cinder cones built by short-lived, sporadic eruptions of cinders and volcanic bombs made of basalt. Also dotting the landscape are numerous lava domes, larger and more rounded volcanoes constructed by thick, viscous flows of molten dacite or rhyolite. Flagstaff's Elden Mountain is a textbook example of a

Sunset Crater is the youngest volcano on the Colorado Plateau.

lava dome with overlapping lobes of dacite clearly visible on the mountain's south flank. Bill Williams Mountain and O'Leary Peak, near Sunset Crater, are other prominent examples of lava domes.

Geologists recognize an age progression within the San Francisco Mountain Volcanic Field along a general northeast trend. Over time, the focus of eruptions has migrated from 6-million-year-old Bill Williams Mountain, the oldest volcano in the field, to Sunset Crater Volcano, where the most recent eruption in the field occurred less than 1000 years ago. This approximately 50-mile migration translates into an average motion of about 0.5 inch per year, which is about the rate of tectonic plate movement. Like a miniature, land-based version of the Hawaiian Island chain—which are a series of volcanoes formed as the Pacific Plate moves over a hot spot welling up through the Earth's mantle—the volcanoes in the San Francisco Volcanic Field may reflect plate tectonic motion over magma upwelling beneath the North American Plate. If this model is correct, it is only a matter of time until the next eruption happens somewhere east of Sunset Crater.

San Francisco Mountain is the scenic centerpiece of the San Francisco Volcanic Field. Known by locals simply as "the peaks," San Francisco Mountain stands tall as the volcanic field's only composite or stratovolcano. The mountain's core consists of a complex arrangement of mostly andesite lava flows, tuff, breccia, and localized intrusions fed by a magma chamber that presumably still underlies the volcanic field. Its dramatic history is marked by nearly 3 million years of explosive eruptions that resulted in the mountain's original steep, classic profile.

San Francisco Mountain's snow cone profile, however, was dramatically altered by a catastrophic event that sculpted out the "Inner Basin" caldera, whose origin is still being debated by geologists. San Francisco Mountain, along with the White Mountains along the Mogollon Rim, is also the site of some of the southernmost Ice Age glaciers on the Colorado Plateau. Despite the event that took out much of the top of the original mountain, Humphreys Peak, San Francisco Mountain's tallest summit at 12,663 feet, is still the highest point in Arizona.

THE COLORADO PLATEAU'S RING OF FIRE

Although the Colorado Plateau is best known for its colorful landscapes of flat-lying sedimentary rock, great outpourings of volcanic rock help define its margins.

The fireworks along the Colorado Plateau's "Ring of Fire" began in the middle Tertiary about 35 million years ago, when boiling magma worked its way upward through faults and fractures that edge the plateau. This magma may have originated by intense friction between grinding tectonic plates deep underground, or perhaps was generated by upwelling when a slab of oceanic crust was shoved beneath the North American plate by subduction.

Whatever the underlying cause, this fiery phase was initially dominated by large-scale explosive volcanic activity. Repeated eruptions of andesite and rhyolite built tall composite volcanoes of ash, lava, and breccia, which later collapsed to form calderas. This action was centered in Colorado's San Juan Mountains, active along the eastern

Map showing the location of volcanic rocks and the major volcanic fields that define the Colorado Plateau's "Ring of Fire"

margin of the plateau between about 35 and 20 million years ago, and Utah's Tushar Mountains Volcanic Field, active along the western margin of the plateau between about 30 and 21 million years ago.

More recent volcanic activity rimming the Colorado Plateau is dominated by vast outpourings of fluid basalt lava. Major centers of less explosive basalt-dominated eruptions began about 10 million years ago in the San Francisco Mountains and Springerville Volcanic Fields along the Plateau's southern margin in Arizona, and in the Datil-Mogollon Volcanic Field across the border in New Mexico. In Utah, lava flows cap the Markagunt, Aquarius, and Sevier Plateaus along the Colorado Plateau's western margin.

The age of basalt volcanism on the Colorado Plateau shows a general decrease in a northeast direction in parts of Arizona, Utah, and New Mexico. Like the Hawaiian Island chain forming today over a hot spot beneath the moving Pacific Plate, this trend suggests that the location of volcanic activity may be related to plate tectonic motion over areas of upwelling magma beneath the Colorado Plateau.

And the action continues. Although there are no eruptions happening on the Colorado Plateau at present, Arizona's Sunset Crater erupted less than 1000 years ago. Stand by for more.

Hike 3

INNER BASIN

SAN FRANCISCO MOUNTAIN'S GLACIATED CALDERA

Hike into the throat of an extinct composite volcano.

DISTANCE ■ 6 miles round trip

ELEVATION ■ 8600 to 10,600 feet

DIFFICULTY ■ Strenuous

TOPOGRAPHIC MAP ■ USGS Humphreys Peak, AZ

GEOLOGIC MAP ■ 3

KEY REFERENCE ■ 4

PRECAUTIONS ■ Beware of violent summer thunderstorms. If possible, avoid this popular hike on weekends. To help protect Flagstaff's water supply, no camping is permitted in the Inner Basin.

FOR INFORMATION ■ Peaks Ranger District

About the Landscape: Starting at Locket Meadow, this hike leads to the scenic Inner Basin, a lush alpine valley ringed by high peaks. The Inner

Basin is a bowl-shaped valley, or *caldera,* scooped out of San Francisco Mountain. San Francisco Mountain's multiple peaks are the erosional remains of a once complete composite or stratovolcano that is unique within the San Francisco Volcanic Field. Today, four of the peaks are over 11,000 feet, and two reach above 12,000 feet—including Humphreys Peak, San Francisco Mountain's (and Arizona's) tallest summit at 12,663 feet.

Curiously, the shape of San Francisco Mountain with its scalloped Inner Basin caldera closely resembles Mount St. Helens in the Pacific Northwest's Cascade Range. Geologists speculate that San Francisco Mountain may have blown its top in an eastwardly directed eruption less than 430,000 years ago, with a display of fireworks similar to Mount St Helens's 1980 eruption. They envision that magma surging up within the volcano created a huge east flank bulge which ultimately became over-steepened and collapsed. Perhaps initiated by an earthquake, this collapse removed the confining "lid" on the volcano, triggering an eruption powered by gas and superheated water held within the magma.

Since no ash deposits have been found that can be linked to a single explosive eruption, other geologists maintain that the Inner Basin formed by a catastrophic collapse of San Francisco Mountain not necessarily related to an explosive eruption. A number of debris fans found around the mountain's base suggest that more than one collapse event may have occurred to form the Inner Basin.

The San Francisco Peaks are the eroded remains of a once-taller volcano.

Whatever process formed the Inner Basin, it seems clear that the caldera formed after 430,000 years ago, the age of the youngest lava flows on top of Humphreys Peak. That the caldera formed before 220,000 years ago is indicated by the age of Sugarloaf Mountain, a rhyolite lava dome that welled up within the mouth of the Inner Basin after the mountain had collapsed. Ice Age glaciers and stream erosion later modified the shape of the Inner Basin, steepening the headwalls of the caldera, widening the basin, and mantling the interior valley with glacial moraines. Everyone seems to agree that glaciers could not have created the Inner Basin in the first place.

Geologists estimate that prior to the mountain's collapse the summit of San Francisco Mountain rose to about 16,000 feet above sea level. Such a lofty summit would have been taller than California's Mount Whitney (14,496 feet), making San Francisco Mountain perhaps once the tallest mountain in the contiguous forty-eight states.

Trail Guide: To reach the trailhead in Locket Meadow, drive about 12 miles north from Flagstaff on U.S. Highway 89. Opposite the entrance road to Sunset Crater Volcano, turn left at the sign for "Forest Access" onto Forest Road 420. Watching for signs pointing towards "Locket Meadow," follow this dusty dirt road 0.7 mile and then turn right at the T-intersection onto Forest Road 552. After about 1.2 miles bear right and continue following FR 552 as it climbs about 3 miles to Locket Meadow. Turn right and follow the one-way campground road 0.4 mile to the day-use area and trailhead marked by the signboard (and restroom) on the right.

Note: For much of its length, the Inner Basin Trail follows a road used by the City of Flagstaff Water Department for maintenance of its water supply. The city has captured water from a series of springs fed by snow-melt within the Inner Basin, and has also drilled a number of wells. You may see an occasional official vehicle along this hike.

From the gated trailhead, the Inner Basin Trail follows the maintenance road winding uphill through the forest. Rocks and boulders of all sizes are strewn along the road and throughout the forest. Instead of being sorted by size by moving water in a river or stream, these rocks were transported by Ice Age glaciers. The ice sheets transported these boulders downslope and left them spread across the floor of the valley when the glaciers melted about 10,000 years ago.

At the 1.5-mile point the trail reaches the Watershed Cabins at Jack Smith Spring and the junction with the "Pipeline Road." The Inner Basin Trail continues straight ahead beyond the trail register, climbing more steeply now through stream-dissected ridges of glacial till. Bear left at the next junction and past the next spring and pump house.

About 2 miles from the trailhead, the trail reaches a large alpine meadow. This is San Francisco Mountain's Inner Basin, and its wide profile is typical of a glaciated valley. Here, the peaks that rim the caldera finally come into view. The Inner Basin Trail continues straight ahead, passing another spring and pump house on the right.

The last mile of this hike leaves the maintenance road behind and climbs steeply through the Inner Basin along an old road. The rocks along the road are a grab bag of volcanic rocks that make up the San Francisco Mountain volcano. When you take a moment to catch your breath, see if you can identify the light to medium gray andesite, gray dacite, and pink to maroon rhyolite. If you look closely with a hand lens you can see crystals "floating" inside some of the rocks. These include white crystals of feldspar, clear crystals of quartz, and black rectangular crystals of pyroxene. All these crystals formed within hot magma that welled up inside the volcano. Once extruded during an eruption, the magma cooled rapidly, trapping these crystals inside a fine-grained matrix.

Although it is possible to continue climbing until the Inner Basin Trail meets the Weatherford Trail, the turnaround point for this hike is a treeless ridge where there is a commanding view of the entire Inner Basin. To the east, a clear view looks beyond the eastern edge of the San Francisco Volcanic Field to the Painted Desert country.

You are standing inside the throat of an extinct volcano. San Francisco

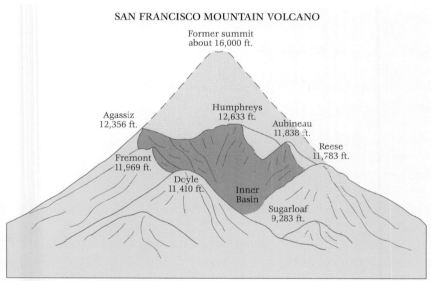

SAN FRANCISCO MOUNTAIN VOLCANO

Diagram showing the original shape and elevation of San Francisco Mountain volcano before the collapse that formed the Inner Basin

Mountain was not built by a single eruption but rather has a long history of activity dating back almost 3 million years. It was only between 430,000 and 220,000 years ago that the San Francisco Mountain volcano collapsed to form the Inner Basin.

From this vantage point within the Inner Basin, you can see the complex layering of volcanic rocks exposed beneath the tall peaks that rim the caldera. These rocks are composed of layers of lava, ash, and breccia extruded during the explosive volcanic eruptions that constructed San Francisco Mountain. The rocky ridge in the center of the Inner Basin is part of the internal plumbing system of magma once hidden inside the volcano. The hard dikes and other intrusive rocks that make up the core of the ridge are resistant to erosion and therefore remain standing high above the rest of the Inner Basin.

Once you have taken in the view, return to the trailhead by the route you came.

Hike 4

BONITO LAVA FLOW

ARIZONA'S YOUNGEST LAVA FLOW AT SUNSET CRATER

This easy walk along the edge of the Bonito lava flow reveals features of this once-molten river of magma that spilled from the base of Sunset Crater.

DISTANCE ■ 1-mile loop

ELEVATION ■ 6940 to 6980 feet

DIFFICULTY ■ Easy

TOPOGRAPHIC MAP ■ USGS Sunset Crater West, AZ

GEOLOGIC MAP ■ 4

KEY REFERENCE ■ 5, 6

PRECAUTIONS ■ Please remain on the trail to protect the fragile environment created by the loose volcanic soil.

FOR INFORMATION ■ Sunset Crater Volcano National Monument

About the Landscape: Less than 950 years ago, native peoples living in the shadow of the San Francisco Peaks may have had little warning of the fiery events to follow. If they were lucky, earthquake tremors caused by magma rising toward the surface alerted them to danger in time to escape the area. Indeed, no bodies have been uncovered in the cinders, although ponderosa pine beams from pit house dwellings inundated by the fallout were used to help date the timing of the eruption.

Although the exact date is still in question, the fireworks began around A.D. 1064 when magma rocketed skyward from a 6-mile-long fissure that cracked open in the earth on the southern Colorado Plateau. This action formed a "curtain of fire," but later the eruption concentrated at the northeast end of the fissure where it constructed an almost perfectly symmetrical cinder cone that today is called Sunset Crater. Although no one knows exactly how long the show lasted, at least several generations of families witnessed fireworks that continued intermittently, creating havoc on their crops each time hot embers rained down from the sky.

The Lava Flow Trail at Sunset Crater offers a close look at the Bonito lava flow, the youngest volcanic feature in the San Francisco Volcanic Field. When walking across this flow that formed just "yesterday," it's anyone's guess as to how long it will be before the next eruption occurs.

Trail Guide: To reach the Lava Flow trailhead, drive about 12 miles north from Flagstaff on U.S. Highway 89 to the sign for Sunset Crater Volcano and Wupatki National Monuments. Turn right and follow the paved road 2 miles to the entrance station and visitor center. From the visitor center, drive 1.5 miles to the sign for the Lava Flow Trail. Turn right and drive to the trailhead parking area.

This hike begins by following a wheelchair-accessible, paved loop for about the first 0.25 mile, then follows an unpaved trail in the shadow of Sunset Crater along the margin of the Bonito lava flow. The Bonito flow formed when lava spilled from the northwest flank of Sunset Crater, causing partial collapse of the crater itself. Sections of the crater's rim rafted out on the flow like icebergs calving off a glacier. Subsequent stages of the eruption rebuilt the cinder cone, creating the fresh and youthful Sunset Crater, a textbook example of a cinder cone.

Life returns to the 1000-year-old lava flows around Sunset Crater.

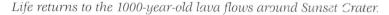

From the information kiosk, where interpretive pamphlets are available, the trail immediately crosses a bridge that spans a ravine representing *fissure* that formed as the lava was flowing and cooling, causing deep cracks at the surface.

As the trail traverses a level cinder-covered section of the lava flow, stay left at the first intersection, then right at the next intersection. The loose cinders on either side of the trail—also called *scoria*—accumulated as air-fall deposits late in the eruption of Sunset Crater. Pick up a cinder and look at it through your hand lens to see its frothy, glassy texture. These pyro-clastic fragments were gaseous blobs of molten basalt that cooled in the air before hitting the ground.

Continue following the paved trail to the Squeeze-up Overlook on the left. This ridge of lava formed when red-hot lava from inside the flow "squeezed up" through fractures in the hardened and brittle outer surface of the flow.

About 50 yards past the squeeze-up, turn left at the junction with the unpaved trail. As the unpaved trail cuts down through the edge of the Bonito flow, look at the large slabs of basalt along the trail. The dark volcanic rock is filled with tiny holes called vesicles, caused by gas bubbles trapped in the lava when it cooled. This rough, blocky lava is called *a'a lava,* a Ha-waiian term for the rough-textured type of lava that forms when the brittle outer surface of the flow breaks apart as the hotter liquid core of the flow continues to move. *Pahoehoe,* the smooth type of lava, is uncommon here.

After crossing the lava flow, the trail turns left and follows along the flow's margin. Sunset Crater towers directly ahead (east), rising 1000 feet above the trail. The "sunset" colors on the crater's rim were caused by hot gases, which altered or oxidized the cinders, turning them red.

The trail bends around to the left where it starts its gentle climb back up onto the flow. Visible on the skyline ahead (north) is O'Leary Peak, an older volcano that formed about 200,000 years ago when viscous, silica-rich rhyolite lava constructed a steep-sided lava dome. Back on top of the flow, the trail passes mounds of lava on the right that represent *spatter cones,* which are also called *hornitos* ("little ovens" in Spanish). Like min-iature volcanoes, these features form when red-hot molten lava is squeezed through openings in the cooling outer crust of the flow. The spattering of the escaping lava builds up a steep-sided heap of welded spatter.

As the unpaved trail continues toward the junction with the paved loop it passes the entrance to a lava tube on the left. Access to this 225-foot-long cave has been blocked off by the park service, although a quick peek in-side reveals cool air trapped underground.

Back on the paved trail, the towering San Francisco Peaks dominate the western skyline as you return to the trailhead.

GRAND FALLS

LAVA MEETS THE LITTLE COLORADO RIVER

Hike over lava that filled a section of the Little Colorado River canyon, changing the course of the river and creating Arizona's largest waterfall.

DISTANCE ■ 1 mile round trip

ELEVATION ■ 4620 to 4460 feet

DIFFICULTY ■ Easy

TOPOGRAPHIC MAP ■ USGS Grand Falls, AZ

GEOLOGIC MAP ■ 4

KEY REFERENCE ■ 6

PRECAUTIONS ■ The dirt road to Grand Falls is bumpy but suitable for all cars, although it may become impassable when wet. The trailhead is not marked and the trail is crude. Please use caution scrambling down to river level; several spots are difficult to negotiate. Avoid the temptation of climbing the ledges to get under the falls. It is very dangerous.

FOR INFORMATION ■ Navajo Parks and Recreation Department

About the Landscape: Grand Falls is located on the Little Colorado River at the far eastern edge of the San Francisco Volcanic Field. Although the Little Colorado River is a major tributary of the Colorado River, the river channel is bone dry most of the year. To see the falls in action, plan your visit for spring runoff in March and April.

The creation of Arizona's largest waterfall is directly linked to volcanic activity nearby. About 150,000 years ago, basalt lava from Merriam Crater flowed as a river of magma for about 7 miles, to where it spilled into the 200-foot-deep canyon of the Little Colorado River. The hot, glowing river of magma lapped up and over the canyon's opposite rim and flowed downstream, following the river channel for 15 miles before running out of steam.

This great mass of lava effectively dammed the river. The river was forced to change course, making a wide horseshoe bend to the east around the margin of the lava. Over time, the river carved a new channel and in the process excavated portions of the lava that filled its old channel. To reach its old channel, the river flows in spectacular fashion over sandstone steps in the Kaibab Formation that once was part of the north wall of the old Little Colorado River canyon. When the river is in flood with spring runoff or flash floods from summer storms, this spectacular cascade comes alive as "Grand Falls."

Trail Guide: To reach Grand Falls, drive north from Flagstaff on U.S. Highway 89. About 2 miles past the Flagstaff Mall, turn right at the traffic light onto the Townsend/Winona Road. Drive east 8.3 miles and turn left onto the Leupp Road. Follow the Leupp Road for 15.3 miles and turn left onto a wide dirt road (Navajo Road 70, signed for "Grand Falls Bible Church") just after the cattle guard that marks the boundary of the Navajo Indian Reservation. The rounded cinder cone on the left is Merriam Crater, the probable source of the lava that created Grand Falls.

The road out to Grand Falls is very dusty with washboard bumps and is met by several other roads. Stay on the largest and most heavily used road. Drive for 8.6 miles and turn left onto a smaller dirt road about 0.7 mile past the junction of Navajo Road 6910, which comes in from the right. If you reach the river, you have missed the turn. Follow this rough road about 0.5 mile and park near the rim of the canyon below the last ramada of the picnic area. The trail, which is not marked, starts downstream (west) about 100 yards from the parking area.

Before leaving the parking area, walk cautiously to the edge of the canyon for an overview of Grand Falls. These impressive falls cascade 200 feet over steps in the opposite wall of the canyon. The muddy, sediment-laden water is snowmelt runoff from the White Mountains and Mogollon Rim region along the southern edge of the Colorado Plateau. The color of a latte, the water is on its way to the Grand Canyon more than 100 miles downstream.

Notice that you are standing on dark volcanic rock. This basalt came from Merriam Crater, a cinder cone that you passed driving here. In contrast, the opposite rim is composed of horizontal layers of sandstone in the Kaibab Formation, the same formation that makes up the rim of the Grand Canyon. The Kaibab was deposited by a shallow tropical sea about 250 million years ago during the Permian. These resistant layers form the dramatic steps as the water cascades to the canyon bottom.

From this vantage point, you can see that the dark basalt continues downstream to the west (left) where it flowed as a hot, glowing tongue of magma following the river canyon. Where you are standing was once part of this 200-foot-deep river canyon that was filled by lava.

Once you have absorbed the view from the rim, look for a crude trail heading to the west, or downstream, along the rim of the canyon. The first part of the trail is over loose wind-blown cinders that blanket the rim. There are many confusing branches and false turns, so it may take a little exploring to find the right path.

After about 100 yards the trail becomes rocky and descends gradually

Grand Falls formed when a lava flow dammed the Little Colorado River.

over outcrops of basalt. A close look at the rock reveals that it does not contain any visible crystals: the lava cooled quickly and crystals did not have time to grow. The tiny holes in the rock, called vesicles, represent gas bubbles trapped in the molten lava. In some places the vesicles are elongated or lens-shaped because the gas bubbles were stretched as the lava continued to move while it cooled and solidified into rock.

Several hundred yards from the parking area, the trail reaches a wide ledge on the canyon rim. Directly above the river gauging station (a small building), the trail makes a sharp turn back to the right and becomes more rough and difficult as it heads directly toward Grand Falls. Follow the most obvious

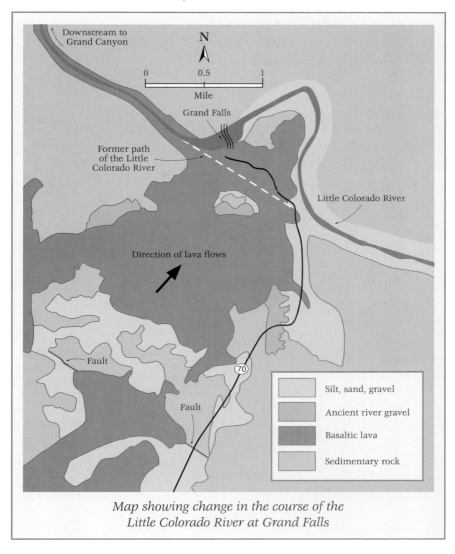

Map showing change in the course of the
Little Colorado River at Grand Falls

route down through the notch in the basalt rock using extreme caution over the difficult spots. On your way down to river level notice the fracture or joint patterns in the basalt that make up the dark right-hand wall of the canyon. Look for columnar patterns, called *columnar joints.* Joints in volcanic rock form because as lava cools it shrinks or contracts, creating cracks in the process.

At river level, a network of worn trails leads closer to the falls. At times the going can get muddy. The view of Grand Falls from below is breathtaking in the spring as the turbulent water kicks up wind and spray. As you soak up the view, notice that to the right of the falls the ledges of Kaibab sandstone end abruptly against the dark basalt. Directly below the picnic area ramada on the left, the basalt is very thin. To the right, the basalt thickens rapidly along a steep boundary that cuts sharply down to the bottom of the canyon. This dramatic *contact* represents the north wall of the old river canyon when the lava filled the canyon and dammed the river. The 200-foot-thick plug of basalt to the right is the lava from Merriam Crater that completely filled the canyon. The thin basalt cap directly beneath the ramada marks where the lava lapped over the rim of the old canyon about 150,000 years ago.

After taking in the spectacle of Grand Falls, carefully retrace your route back to the parking area on the rim.

RED MOUNTAIN

ANATOMY OF A CINDER CONE

Explore Red Mountain, where erosion has cut into the heart of a cinder cone.

DISTANCE ■ **3 miles round trip**

ELEVATION ■ **6760 to 7040 feet**

DIFFICULTY ■ **Easy**

TOPOGRAPHIC MAP ■ **USGS Chapel Mountain and Ebert Mountain, AZ**

GEOLOGIC MAP ■ **5**

KEY REFERENCE ■ **6**

PRECAUTIONS ■ **Please use caution when exploring inside the cinder cone. The cinders become like little ball bearings underfoot. Please stay on established trails; loose cinders are very easily eroded, scarring the landscape.**

FOR INFORMATION ■ **Peaks Ranger District**

About the Landscape: Red Mountain is among the more than 6000 cinder cones within the San Francisco Volcanic Field. Most of these cinder cones

71

are relatively young and only recent additions to the landscape. Erosion, therefore, has not had enough time to cut into the sides of these small and, typically, symmetrical volcanoes.

Red Mountain is an exception. This cinder cone, which formed during eruptions about 740,000 years ago, is older than many of the other cinder cones in the area. Over time, erosion has taken a huge bite out of its northeast flank, exposing the layered internal structure of pyroclastic deposits.

Only a short drive from Flagstaff, this easy hike takes you into the heart of this once explosive volcano.

Trail Guide: To reach the Red Mountain Trail, drive 30 miles northeast from Flagstaff on U.S. Highway 180. At the sign for the Red Mountain Geological Area, turn left onto a well-traveled dirt road and drive 0.3 miles to where it dead-ends at the trailhead.

From the parking area and trail register, the trail follows an old road that winds through a forest of piñon pine and juniper trees. Red Mountain looms on the skyline with its layered internal structure clearly visible through the notch cut into its northeast flank.

Cinder cones are built of tiny fragments of basalt ejected from a central vent during an explosive volcanic eruption. These once-molten blobs of magma were blown to pieces as they rocketed out of the volcano. As they fell through the air, the fragments cooled and solidified before they hit the ground. Eruption after eruption built a loose pile of cinders centered around the vent.

The internal layering of Red Mountain is caused by the differences in the size of material that belched from the vent during the many eruptive epi-

Moon over Red Mountain, an eroded cinder cone in the San Francisco Volcanic Field

sodes. Since a greater amount of cinders accumulated closer to the vent, the layers are slanted away from the vent in the shape of a dome, or *cone*, looking like a giant anthill. Although not obvious, Red Mountain is slightly asymmetrical toward the northeast. Speculation is that the eruptions that built this cinder cone took place as strong winds were blowing from the southwest.

At about the 1-mile point, the old road ends where it meets a dry wash that drains the inside of Red Mountain. Obey the trail signs that point left and follow the wash to the base of the mountain.

All the loose, dusty material underfoot was once molten and ejected from the volcano that built Red Mountain. Had you walked here 740,000 years ago, hot glowing embers would have rained down from the sky. Collectively called *pyroclastics*, the cinders falling from the sky are classified according to size. The smaller particles—which are called *ash* if smaller than 2 mm in diameter and *lapilli* if between 2 to 64 mm in size—would not have been your major concern. Most dangerous would have been the falling rocks larger than 64 mm (about 2.5 inches and up). These are rightly called *volcanic bombs*. The larger rocks along the wash today are all volcanic bombs, some of which are teardrop-shaped, twisted masses of lava. They would hurt coming down, to say the least. Luckily, the volcano is now extinct, so there is little threat of an eruption during your hike today.

An artificial rock dam, scaled easily by the short ladder provided, marks the natural entrance to the interior of the volcano. Once above the dam, take a close look at the fluted outcrop of rock to the right of the trail.

Although from a distance Red Mountain looks like it is made of a crumbly and easily eroded pile of cinders, the mountain is in fact made up of an assortment of rock fragments—ash, lapilli, and volcanic bombs—held tightly together. Notice the tiny holes within the rock fragments, called vesicles, formed by gas bubbles trapped in the lava as it cooled.

The natural glue or *cement* that binds the rock together is a mineral coating that probably formed from hot water and steam that percolated through the cinders, perhaps only shortly after they accumulated. The reddish yellow color is caused by the oxidation of iron-bearing minerals in the cement. Since most of the rock fragments within the rock are actually gray, it is this cement that gives "Red" Mountain its color.

The main trail disappears inside the volcano's impressive interior amphitheater. Erosion has artistically sculpted the cliff that towers more than 900 feet above the floor. As you marvel at the domes and spires worn smooth by wind, water, and time, look for a spur trail to the right that leads to a short, slot canyon carved into the rock.

After you are done exploring and soaking in the fiery essence of this once-explosive volcano, return to the trailhead by the route you came.

Chapter 3
THE GRAND CANYON

There is no place on earth quite like the Grand Canyon. Looking down on a mile-deep gash in the earth, this is in-your-face geology. Here, you are forced by the sheer vastness of the landscape to question the beginnings of life—and time.

The Grand Canyon is the bottom rung of the Colorado Plateau's famed *Grand Staircase.* It is the last step that takes you all the way down into the ancient core of the North American continent. Hidden in the shadows of the canyon's deep abyss are the basement rocks that date back almost 2 billion years, to a time when the continent was first being assembled by plate tectonic actions. Stacked on top of the basement rocks are sedimentary layers one on top of another, with the oldest on the bottom. Recorded within the canyon's colorfully striped walls are the shallow seas, lazy rivers, and great desert dunes that swept across the Colorado Plateau over time.

Rocks revealed in the Grand Canyon read like a highlight film through geologic time. Just imagine Precambrian continents colliding to form the twisted igneous and metamorphic roots of the continent. These rocks include the Vishnu Schist and Zoroaster Granite, which are part of the ancient 1.7-billion-year-old basement rocks that underlie the Colorado Plateau.

On top of the "older" Precambrian basement rocks, primordial oceans flooded the emerging continent, leaving behind primitive life forms (stromatolites of algae in the Bass Limestone and Dox Formation) in a great stack of sedimentary rock more than 2 miles thick. These "younger" Precambrian rocks are known as the Grand Canyon Supergroup. They range in age from about 1.2 to 0.8 billion years old, and include the 1-billion-year-old Cardenas Lavas in the middle of the stack. A rifting event tilted and faulted these rocks, and then a long period of erosion followed, which stripped off many of the older layers and flattened the landscape. The erosion surface is known as the *Great Unconformity* because so much time is missing there from the rock record.

Then about 550 million years ago, waves of the advancing Cambrian sea crashed against dark cliffs in the basement, as the continent was once again flooded. The Paleozoic era had begun. Waves, tides, and currents worked sand along a shoreline in the Tapeats Sandstone, while offshore trilobites crawled in the mud of the Bright Angel Shale. As the first multicellular life forms exploded in the world's oceans, the seas advanced and retreated many times.

Then darkness comes to the screen—missing from the Grand Canyon's geologic highlights are rocks of the Ordovician, the Silurian, and most of the Devonian, a span of nearly 150 million years! What happened during this time gap is one of the great mysteries of the Colorado Plateau's geologic history.

We do know, however, that the ocean flooded the continent again about 350 million years ago during the Mississippian, leaving behind hundreds of feet of lime mud chock-full of fossils in the Redwall Limestone, which forms the prominent cliff halfway down into the canyon. As the sea retreated once again, erosion cut canyons into the top of the Redwall, which are filled with sediments in the Surprise Canyon Formation. Lazy, meandering rivers punctuated by seasonal floods dumped tons of mud, sand, and gravel across a broad coastal plain to form the colorful red layers in the Supai Group. Then, giant dunes of wind-blown sand marched across a desert landscape to become the white Coconino Sandstone, one of the Grand Canyon's most conspicuous layers. The Coconino dunes interfinger with vast tidal flats that border the Toroweap sea, which advances and

Moon over the South Rim from Horseshoe Mesa

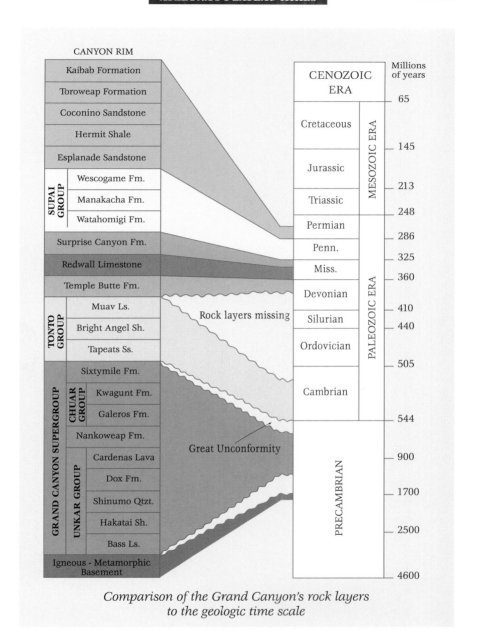

*Comparison of the Grand Canyon's rock layers
to the geologic time scale*

retreats many times. The highlight reel ends with an endless expanse of blue-green water in the tropical Kaibab sea, which will become the Grand Canyon's rimrock.

Hiking in the Grand Canyon is like experiencing this highlight film through time. As you pause on the trail to admire a spectacular view, or to catch your breath, listen for the call of the canyon.

CARVING THE GRAND CANYON

Somewhere along the way the Grand Canyon was carved into the many rock layers of the Colorado Plateau. And it all has to do with the still mysterious history of the Colorado River.

Although some details are well known, geologists continue to debate exactly how the Grand Canyon came to be. They agree, however, that the canyon is a youthful landscape and a relatively recent addition to the Colorado Plateau.

Much of the evidence about the canyon's age has been pieced together from rocks in the western Grand Canyon area. Basalt lava flows 7.5 to 6 million years old found on both sides of the canyon overlie gravel deposits derived from the south and, therefore, show no evidence that a canyon existed at that time.

By about 5.5 million years ago, plate tectonic actions opened the Gulf of California and initiated the formation of a "lower" Colorado River. The sudden appearance of Cretaceous fossils derived from the Rocky Mountains, found in sediments west of the Grand Canyon, indicate that a through-flowing river existed no earlier than 5 million years ago.

To complete the picture, lava flows spilled over the rim in the Vulcan Throne area near Toroweap Point in the western Grand Canyon, documenting that the canyon was cut to near its present depth by 1 million years ago.

Geologically speaking, then, the canyon is a "young" feature and was carved in a mind-boggling 5 million years or less.

HISTORY OF THE COLORADO RIVER

Many questions about the history of the Colorado River remain. What was the route of the "upper" Colorado River following its inception as tectonic forces vaulted the Rocky Mountains skyward during the Laramide orogeny about 65 million years ago? And how did the Colorado River come to flow across the Kaibab Plateau and through the Grand Canyon?

One idea envisions the upper or ancestral Colorado River flowing south through Marble Canyon, then turning to the southeast along the Little Colorado River to eventually reach the Gulf of Mexico. A modification of this idea suggests that the river followed this general southeast route, but instead of continuing south, it simply spilled its water and sediment into an ancient lake, Lake Bidahochi, which once existed in northeastern Arizona. An even more radical, but less well received, twist on this idea proposes that the Grand Canyon was carved only after Lake Bidahochi filled to its brim and began to "spill over" the Kaibab Plateau, draining into the "lower" Colorado River on its way to the Gulf of California.

Perhaps the most popular idea holds that the river originally flowed across the Kaibab Plateau when it was still buried deeply by Mesozoic sedimentary layers. The river then turned to the northwest and drained into lakes that existed in western Utah and eastern Nevada. The present arcuate path of the Colorado River across the uplift is seen as a relict of the ancient course of the river.

All these ideas involve the dastardly deed of *stream piracy* by the lower Colorado River. Following the opening of the Gulf of California, the lower Colorado River extended its length by *headward erosion* toward the western edge of the Colorado Plateau. As it cut deeper and deeper into the higher, upstream regions of its drainage basin—which may have included the Kaibab Plateau—the river worked its way "headward" until it captured the flow of the upper Colorado River.

And, somehow in the process, the Grand Canyon was carved.

The Colorado River has carved deeply through the Colorado Plateau's "geologic layercake." View from Toroweap Point.

HORSESHOE MESA

HIKE THROUGH TIME BELOW THE SOUTH RIM

Hike down the Grandview Trail to Horseshoe Mesa and gaze into the Grand Canyon's Inner Gorge, where rocks as old as 1.7 billion years are exposed.

DISTANCE ■ **8 miles round trip**

ELEVATION ■ **7400 to 4900 feet**

DIFFICULTY ■ **Strenuous**

TOPOGRAPHIC MAP ■ **USGS Grandview Point and Cape Royal, AZ; Trails Illustrated #207**

GEOLOGIC MAP ■ **6**

KEY REFERENCE ■ **7**

PRECAUTIONS ■ **Hiking down into the Grand Canyon can be deceiving—it is farther and steeper than it looks from the rim. Carry plenty of water, wear sturdy hiking boots, and watch every step. Old mine shafts are dangerous and radioactive. A backcountry permit is required for overnight backpack trips. Please camp only in designated sites.**

FOR INFORMATION ■ **Grand Canyon National Park**

About the Landscape: As viewed from Grandview Point, the giant arms of Horseshoe Mesa stretch outward into the middle of the Grand Canyon. Horseshoe Mesa is located along the Grandview Trail about halfway down through the canyon's geologic layercake of Paleozoic sedimentary layers. The steep and rugged walls of the canyon give way to a surprisingly gentle landscape worn on top of the Mississippian Redwall Limestone. It is a refuge of sorts, with geology everywhere on display from the many overlooks that edge the mesa. The canyon's buttes and monuments rise like mountains toward the rims against the skyline. And you can hear the distant roar of the Colorado River as it carves the canyon ever deeper.

Dizzying views from Horseshoe Mesa look down into the twisted and contorted Precambrian metamorphic basement rocks of the Inner Gorge below the Great Unconformity. To the east, the Colorado River is in view where it cuts into the faulted and tilted "younger" Precambrian sedimentary rocks. Turning to the west, erosion has etched the canyon walls into an infinite variety of shapes that become silhouetted with the setting sun. As an added bonus, historic ruins of the Last Chance Mine provide a glimpse of the Grand Canyon's colorful mining history dating back to the late 1800s and early 1900s.

Hiking into the Grand Canyon is like climbing a mountain in reverse, starting at the summit. Keep in mind that it is much steeper climbing up (out of the canyon) than it appears when hiking down (into the canyon). Be prepared and know your limits. Although this is a good but long day hike (except in the heat of summer), it also makes an easy, and perhaps a more sensible, overnight backpack trip (requires a backcountry permit).

Trail Guide: The Grandview Trail is located along the Desert View Drive on the Grand Canyon's South Rim. From the Grand Canyon Village area off Arizona State Route 64, drive about 10 miles east and turn left to Grandview Point. From Desert View, drive about 12 miles west and turn right to Grandview Point. The trailhead is located just below the information kiosk near the main overlook.

Note: Visitor transportation arrangements in the park change from year to year. Reaching some overlooks may require taking a shuttle bus. Inquire at the park entrance for current policies.

Before starting out down the trail, take a moment to absorb the view from the rim. The horizontal layers or *formations* that make up the canyon walls extend as far as the eye can see. Together, stacked one on top of another with the oldest layer nearly 5000 feet below, these Paleozoic sedimentary rocks record over 300 million years of geologic time. But from this lofty view you can barely make out the oldest of the rocks—the

dark, 1.7-billion-year-old Precambrian basement rocks—which lie hidden in the Inner Gorge at the bottom of the canyon. For a better look at the canyon's hidden secrets, a hike below the rim is in order.

Like all trails in the Grand Canyon, the Grandview Trail starts out by switchbacking steeply down through the Permian Kaibab Formation, the canyon's hard and resistant cap rock. In places the trail follows narrow ledges, so use extreme caution while hiking.

The Kaibab Formation is composed of tan to gray layers

Agave and Redwall Limestone, Horseshoe Mesa

of limestone, dolomite (like limestone but with magnesium added), and sandstone deposited on the floor of a warm, shallow sea about 250 million years ago. In places, these rocks contain abundant marine invertebrate fossils including brachiopods, crinoids, and sponges. The sponges are important because their skeletons originally contained silica, which after they were buried dissolved to become *chert,* a finely crystalline variety of the mineral quartz. Chert forms the abundant lenses and nodules characteristic of the Kaibab Formation, strengthening the formation into a hard and resistant rimrock. Without chert, the walls of the canyon may have eroded more rapidly and the Grand Canyon would undoubtedly look much different than it does today.

As the trail continues to switchback down, the Permian Toroweap Formation forms the stepped ledges of sandstone and dolomite below the steep Kaibab cliffs. The exact boundary or *contact* between the two formations is difficult to locate along the trail. Like the Kaibab, the Toroweap was also deposited in a shallow sea but much closer to shore. Together, the Kaibab and Toroweap Formations represent a series of sea level changes during the Permian when a sandy shoreline shifted back and forth across the region that would become the Colorado Plateau.

About 0.5 mile below the rim, the trail passes beneath an overhanging ledge near the base of the Toroweap, then makes a long switchback to the east as it approaches the top of the Coconino Sandstone. The Coconino Sandstone is one of the most prominent formations in the Grand Canyon, forming a conspicuous white to cream-colored cliff from one end of the canyon to the other. The Coconino Sandstone displays sweeping sets of giant cross-beds, the slanting layers indicating that giant wind-blown dunes swept southward across the region during the Permian. Reaching a maximum thickness of over 600 feet, the Coconino records a vast Sahara-like desert that became flooded by the ocean when the Toroweap and Kaibab Formations were laid down.

Below the Toroweap, the trail steps down through layers of cross-bedded Coconino Sandstone to a prominent saddle. Look through the saddle toward the rim and note the tilted layers of the "Sinking Ship" along the Grandview Monocline. Also, a fault slices the saddle, which becomes obvious when you continue along the trail and once again meet the Toroweap Formation. This normal fault has slid the rock layers down to the north and has created a zone of weakness that is more easily eroded to form the saddle.

Once across the saddle, the trail again follows along the base of the Toroweap Formation to the top of the Coconino Sandstone. Here it begins to switchback steeply down to another saddle, called Coconino Saddle. This second saddle is also formed by erosion along a fault. Note how the normally massive, cliff-forming Coconino Sandstone is here highly fractured and broken apart. As the trail makes a long switchback down toward the saddle, look for *slickensides*, which are polished or striated surfaces caused by friction along the fault. A good example is found about knee-high on the right. A series of very steep and tight switchbacks complete the descent to the Coconino Saddle (marked by a sign), a popular rest stop about 1 mile below the rim.

Below the Coconino Saddle, the trail makes much longer switchbacks as it reaches the soft, easily eroded slope-forming layers in the Hermit Shale (which is mostly hidden from view by debris from the overlying Coconino). Only by looking along the canyon walls can you catch a glimpse of the Hermit Shale, which is Permian in age.

The next *outcrops* or rock exposures along the trail are in the red and maroon layers of the Supai Group. After traversing a series of long switchbacks, the trail eventually begins to contour more gently all the way to Horseshoe Mesa.

A *group* is a collection of formations, and the Supai Group includes four formations. These are, in ascending order from youngest to oldest (top to bottom), the Esplanade Sandstone, and the Wescogame, Manakacha, and Watahomigi Formations. All are Pennsylvanian in age, except for the Esplanade, which is Permian.

The colorful formations of the Supai Group represent a variety of coastal and shallow marine environments, locally swept by wind-blown sand dunes and crossed by sluggish rivers and tidal channels. The trail passes through layers and boulders of many different sedimentary rock types, from shale, siltstone, and cross-bedded sandstone to limestone and minor conglomerate, reflecting the varied environments of deposition of the Supai Group.

Ultimately the trail leaves behind the red rocks of the Supai Group and reaches the top of the Redwall Limestone at Horseshoe Mesa about 3 miles below the rim. As you may have already noticed, the limestone rock in the Redwall is really gray but is stained by iron-oxide minerals washed down from the Supai Group. Underfoot along the trail, the top of the Redwall appears mottled with olive and green, probably the result of long periods of weathering before the Supai was deposited. The Redwall, which forms the imposing cliffs that rim the mesa, is a major barrier to hiking routes everywhere in the Grand Canyon.

As the trail continues winding down-slope onto Horseshoe Mesa, notice how the rock layers are tilted down to the north onto the mesa. This is most obvious when looking at the canyon walls both east and west of the mesa. The tilt to the layers defines the trace of the Grandview Monocline, the same structure that tilted the "Sinking Ship" up near the rim.

Hand samples of copper ore from the Last Chance Mine on Horseshoe Mesa. The colorful minerals are malachite (green) and azurite (blue).

As the trail reaches Horseshoe Mesa it passes a prominent yellow and rust colored outcrop on the right. These are the altered and mineralized rocks of the Grandview breccia pipe. *Breccia pipes* are unique features exposed in the Grand Canyon region where rocks deep underground collapsed in on themselves. The collapses probably initiated where rocks started falling into caves dissolved in the Redwall Limestone. While still buried deep underground, the rocks continued to collapse, originating from younger and younger rock layers above. The result is a collection of large, angular broken rocks or breccia that acted as a pipe or conduit for fluids. Over time, the fluids have left behind altered rocks and, in some cases, rich mineral deposits now exposed at the surface by erosion.

Farther down the trail you will see mine tunnels of the Last Chance Mine. Copper was discovered here in 1890, and the Grandview Trail was originally constructed to haul the rich ore to a mill on the rim. Please resist the temptation to collect the colorful mineral specimens; leave the brilliant green and blue copper ore (malachite and azurite) lying scattered in the tailing piles for others to see.

You know you have arrived on Horseshoe Mesa when you pass the junction to Page Springs to the right (located at the base of the Redwall down a steep, cliffy trail). The next junction is with the Cottonwood Creek Trail off to the left. The campsite trail splits off to the right at the old stone building (toilet facility 100 yards away!). The last junction leads to the group campsite on the right (and another toilet facility).

Whether you are day hiking or camping overnight, from here you are free to explore Horseshoe Mesa on your own. You might want to explore the well-worn trail to the left past the group campsites out to a great over-look located at the extreme end of the mesa's west arm, about 1 mile be-yond the campsites. From there you will have breathtaking views up the canyon, and down into the ancient basement rocks of Inner Gorge.

Enjoy the peace, solitude, and dramatic geologic overlooks that Horse-shoe Mesa offers. But don't forget to leave plenty of time for the hike out—climbing back up to the rim you will become intimately familiar with each and every rock layer.

NORTH VS. SOUTH RIM

There is a big difference between the North and South Rims of the Grand Canyon. The South Rim—in addition to being far more acces-sible and, therefore, more crowded—is relatively straight and drops steeply to the Colorado River. Inner canyon hikes are best attempted from the South Rim. In contrast, the North Rim is more irregular, deeply dissected, and farther away from the river. It is also more remote with fewer people.

The North Rim is the erosional edge of the *Kaibab Plateau* (pro-nounced "ki-a-bab"), which is part of the broad Kaibab Uplift that arched upward about 65 million years ago during the Laramide orog-eny. Over the eons that followed, erosion stripped off thousands of feet of Mesozoic sedimentary layers (layers that are preserved else-where on the Colorado Plateau). Today the marine limestone and sandstone of the Kaibab Formation lie exposed at the surface. The hard and resistant layers of the Kaibab cap the plateau and form the rimrock of the Grand Canyon. Amazingly, it has been during "only" the last 5 to 6 million years that downcutting by the Colorado River breached the very heart of the Kaibab Plateau, forming the Grand Canyon and separating the North and South Rims.

Because of the gentle southward tilt of the rocks across the Kaibab Uplift, erosion has created different drainage patterns on the North and South Rims. Rain or snowmelt on the North Rim flows toward the canyon, while water on the South Rim flows away from the can-yon. The result of this difference in drainage has caused deeper and more extensive erosion of the canyon's North Rim. On the North Rim, many long promontories extend far out into the canyon, providing broad panoramas and excellent opportunities to study the canyon's geologic layers from lofty perches.

CAPE FINAL

NORTH RIM VIEW OF THE GRAND CANYON SUPERGROUP

From the North Rim's easternmost point, look down on tilted Precambrian sedimentary layers in the Grand Canyon Super-group exposed beneath the Great Unconformity.

DISTANCE ■ 4 miles round trip

ELEVATION ■ 7847 to 8000 feet

DIFFICULTY ■ Easy

TOPOGRAPHIC MAPS ■ USGS Walhalla Plateau, AZ; Trails Illustrated #207

GEOLOGIC MAP ■ 6

KEY REFERENCE ■ 7

PRECAUTIONS ■ Use extreme caution when you reach the cliff-edged view-point. Overnight stays require a backcountry use permit.

FOR INFORMATION ■ Grand Canyon National Park

About the Landscape: This easy hike to Cape Final, the North Rim's easternmost point, leaves the crowds behind and offers a bird's-eye view of the eastern Grand Canyon.

Exposed in the depths of the abyss are thick sequences of Precambrian sedimentary layers called the *Grand Canyon Supergroup.* Found beneath the Great Unconformity in the eastern Grand Canyon, the Grand Canyon Supergroup, also known as the "younger Precambrian," is largely absent in other parts of the canyon where the formations were removed by erosion before deposition of the Cambrian Tapeats Sandstone. These ancient rocks are exposed only in the Grand Canyon and nowhere else on the Colorado Plateau.

At Cape Final, located at the far end of a long finger jutting off the Walhalla Plateau, the uppermost part of the Grand Canyon Supergroup can be observed from a lofty perch 5000 feet above the Colorado River.

Trail Guide: To reach the Cape Final trailhead, drive north for 3.5 miles from the North Rim Visitor Center off Arizona State Route 67 to the junction with the Cape Royal/Point Imperial park road. Turn right, drive 6.4 miles to a Y-junction and bear right (toward Cape Royal). Then drive about 14 miles to the trailhead parking area on the left.

The trail begins by climbing gently uphill through a forest of towering ponderosa pine trees. After about 0.75 mile, the trail crests a ridge, then continues to wind over the gently rolling plateau through the forest.

At about the 1.25-mile point, the trail approaches the plateau's rim. A short spur trail to the left leads to a spectacular view through an opening in the trees. In view to the north, beyond the foreground ridge that includes Siegfried Pyre, is Saddle Mountain, which lies along the trend of the East Kaibab Monocline.

Continuing past the viewpoint, the trail turns south for about 0.5 mile where it eventually follows above a shallow ravine on the left. Ultimately, it reaches a junction with a faint trail that splits off to the left—if you start winding through scrubby trees you have missed the junction.

For the last 0.25 mile to Cape Final, follow the trail to the left downhill across the ravine, then climb the slope that leads to the canyon's rim. The last part of the trail becomes indistinct as the route steps up onto broken ledges in the Kaibab Formation. If you lose your way, simply continue toward the highest point, but use caution as you approach the edge. Cape Final is marked by survey benchmarks at the edge of a precipitous cliff.

The view from Cape Final was described in the late 1800s by pioneering geologist Clarence Dutton as "the most interesting spot on the Kaibab." And no wonder, for here the layercake of the Grand Canyon's Paleozoic sedimentary rocks falls away sharply from the rim. The sweeping vista looks into Marble Canyon to the north. To the east, the edge of the Marble Platform is broken by the sheer-walled gorge of the Little Colorado River. To the south, the Grand Canyon's South Rim is in view. The scene is punctuated by artistic landforms that capture the imagination, like Vishnu Temple. These buttes and mesas are protected from erosion by remnants of resistant rock, such as the Kaibab and Toroweap Formations, and the Coconino Sandstone.

Much of the eastern Grand Canyon is cut from sedimentary rocks in the "younger" Precambrian Grand Canyon Supergroup. The Grand Canyon Supergroup includes the Unkar and Chuar Groups Taken together, these layers add up to over 2 miles of sedimentary rock, and some volcanic rock, and provide important clues about the evolution of primitive life on earth (the Bass Limestone contains billion-year-old *stromatolites,* fossils formed by mats of microscopic blue-green algae). In other areas of the canyon, these rocks are mostly eroded away and the Paleozoic Tapeats Sandstone is found directly overlying the "older Precambrian" igneous and metamorphic basement rocks.

At river level to the south, the rounded layers are in the reddish Dox Sandstone (look for the big bend in the Colorado River visible at Unkar Delta). The Dox Sandstone is part of the Unkar Group and is just over 1 billion years old. Along with the rest of the Grand Canyon Supergroup, these rocks are tilted gently (about 10 to 15 degrees) toward the northeast. Just above river level these tilted layers meet the flat-lying brown ledge of the 550-million-year-old Tapeats Sandstone above. This is known as the Great Unconformity, which in the eastern Grand Canyon forms an angular unconformity—because the layers meet at an angle.

To the east, the vast undulating landscape in Chuar Valley is cut from gray sedimentary layers of the Chuar Group's Galeros Formation. Notice the low, dark butte near river level. These dark rocks are the Cardenas Lavas, the uppermost formation in the Unkar Group, and provide evidence of a volcanic episode that occurred about 1 billion years ago. Toward the mouth of the Little Colorado, notice the upturned (folded) and broken (faulted) layers along the Butte Fault. This fault underlies the East Kaibab Monocline and is exposed here by the deep erosion of the Colorado River.

Before retracing your steps to the trailhead, look at the rocks along the canyon's rim where you are standing. These gray and tan sandstone and

Looking down on the Coconino Sandstone from Cape Final

dolomite layers in the Kaibab Formation, which caps the Kaibab Plateau and forms the rimrock all across the Grand Canyon region, are hard, resistant rocks representing ancient ocean floor sediments deposited 250 million years ago during the Permian. Farther west, the Kaibab is composed mostly of limestone that contains abundant fossils, such as brachiopods and bryozoans. But here in the eastern part of the canyon, the Kaibab is dominated by sandstone, suggesting conditions very close to shore.

A close look at the rock underfoot reveals rust-stained, irregular nodules. These nodules are composed of chert, a finely crystalline variety of the mineral quartz, derived from siliceous sponges common in the Kaibab. The rounded, popcorn-like chert nodules formed where quartz replaced the mineral gypsum. Gypsum forms in sediment when seawater becomes supersalty as it evaporates in warm, tropical environments.

It is hard to imagine that the rocks along the Grand Canyon's rim were once submerged beneath the sea. Today they are lying 8000 feet above sea level—and are still slowly rising along with the rest of the Colorado Plateau.

Take your time, soak in the view, and enjoy the walk back to your vehicle.

POWELL PLATEAU

NORTH RIM'S ISLAND IN THE SKY

Hike 9

Cross the Crazy Jug Monocline and Muav Fault on this overnight hike out to Dutton Point on remote Powell Plateau.

DISTANCE ■ 15 miles round trip

ELEVATION ■ 7549 (Dutton Point) to 6680 feet (Muav Saddle)

DIFFICULTY ■ Strenuous

TOPOGRAPHIC MAPS ■ USGS King Arthur Castle, AZ; Trails Illustrated #207

GEOLOGIC MAP ■ 6

KEY REFERENCE ■ 7

PRECAUTIONS ■ Some routefinding skills are required to make the traverse out to Dutton Point. Carry plenty of water; none is available on Powell Plateau. A high-clearance or four-wheel-drive vehicle is recommended to get to the trailhead. Inquire about current conditions as fallen trees sometimes block the road. Backcountry use permits are required for camping at the Swamp Point trailhead and for backpacking on Powell Plateau.

FOR INFORMATION ■ Grand Canyon National Park

About the Landscape: Powell Plateau, named after famed geologist and explorer John Wesley Powell, is one of the most remote sections along the

88

Grand Canyon's North Rim. Dutton Point, the destination of this hike, named after the pioneering geologist Clarence Dutton, projects far out into the middle of the canyon, offering one of the best views of the Colorado River anywhere on the North Rim.

Powell Plateau is separated from the rest of the North Rim by the Muav Saddle, a deep notch more than 800 feet below the rim. The saddle was cut by erosion along the Crazy Jug Monocline and Muav Fault, a major north–south trending structural zone with movement dating back to Precambrian time. Of particular significance here are the bent and broken layers displayed in the walls of the canyon below the saddle. These disrupted layers provide clues about the Laramide orogeny and the recurrent history of motion along faults and folds in the Grand Canyon.

The Powell Plateau hike, which starts from the North Bass trailhead at Swamp Point, is an ideal overnight backpacking trip.

Trail Guide: To reach the North Bass trailhead at Swamp Point, drive 2.8 miles from the North Rim Visitor Center off Arizona State Route 67 to the sign for the Widforss Trail. Turn left onto this dirt road and follow it past the Widforss trailhead (on the left) and then bear left at the first Y intersection. Continue following the main dirt road (ignoring any side tracks that split off to the left) to a T-junction 12.2 miles from the pavement. Turn right at the sign toward Kanabownits (left goes to Point Sublime). Follow this road, which becomes rough and rocky in places, bearing left after 3 miles at the first Y-intersection, then left again after 5.3 miles at the next intersection and sign for North Bass Trail. Drive 8 miles to the trailhead parking area at the end of the road.

This hike starts out with a series of long, steep switchbacks down the North Bass Trail. This rugged trail leads you down through the Kaibab and Toroweap Formations, the youngest rock layers at the Grand Canyon. These craggy, gray limestone layers are very resistant to erosion and everywhere form the protective cap on the highest parts of both the North and South Rims.

The rocky ledges below the rim are chock-full of marine fossils. Take a close look to see the crescent moon outlines of brachiopods, disc-shaped stems of crinoids, and round nodules of chert cored by the skeletons of siliceous sponges. These organisms flourished in the warm, shallow seas that washed North America's coastline 250 million years ago during the Permian.

As the trail continues to wind down toward the saddle it passes through the Coconino Sandstone. Typically a sharp, cliff-forming layer, the Coconino here along the Muav Fault is highly fractured and easily eroded. After making a sharp switchback to the right, look for slanted layers or crossbeds in the sandstone along the trail. These inclined partings in the rock represent the steep, advancing faces of ancient sand dunes frozen in the rock. Scanning along the cliff face away from the saddle, cross-beds in the Coconino Sandstone are over 10 feet thick, suggesting they were originally part of giant sand dunes like those found in the Sahara desert today.

Once at the saddle, at about the 1-mile point and more than 800 feet below Swamp Point, the trail crosses the Muav Fault (hidden from view) and reaches a triple junction. The North Bass Trail continues to the left. A short spur trail to the right leads to historic Teddy's Cabin, only a 25-yard detour. Built in 1925, this patrol cabin is named for President

View of Muav Saddle sliced by the Muav Fault and tilted by the Crazy Jug Monocline

Theodore Roosevelt who in 1903 hunted mountain lions on Powell Plateau. Take the middle fork, straight ahead, to continue to the plateau.

Because of the eastward tilt of the Kaibab and Toroweap layers along the Crazy Jug Monocline, the climb up to Powell Plateau follows a gentle grade. Once on top, about 2 miles from the trailhead, the trail generally follows the east rim of Powell Plateau out to Dutton Point. The trail is easy to follow for about the next 1 mile as it winds through an impressive forest of ponderosa pine trees.

The trail becomes more difficult to follow once it meets the first large downed tree. This is when your routefinding skills are called into action. Cross the ravine down to the right and, with luck, you will again find the trail. This scenario of losing the trail then finding it again will continue all the way to Dutton Point. When in doubt, always hike parallel to the rim, keeping it on the left.

About 5.5 miles from the trailhead, the route comes to Dutton Canyon, the deepest ravine encountered on the hike. Before scrambling down through the scrub oak trees, look ahead to see where the trail leads up the other side. Once across Dutton Canyon, the last 2 miles to Dutton Point is fairly open but there is no real trail. Stay close to the rim whenever possible to avoid all the downed trees in the old burn areas.

Ultimately, you will run out of real estate and reach the spectacular viewpoint at Dutton Point. It may take some scrambling around to find the best spot, but once you do, a long section of the Colorado River will be in full view looking upstream toward Bass and Serpentine Rapids. Below in the foreground lies a long, arching formation of Supai Group red rocks called the Masonic Temple, and down and to the right, sits the isolated butte of Redwall Limestone called Fan Island.

Before leaving the viewpoint, find a perch where you can look up Muav Canyon to the saddle. On the left side of the saddle above, notice how the Coconino Sandstone and the overlying Kaibab and Toroweap Formations have been faulted downward and do not match up with the rocks on the right. But the story is not that simple.

The Crazy Jug Monocline formed when the Precambrian Muav Fault was reactivated about 65 million years ago during the Laramide orogeny. The monocline formed where overlying rock layers draped over a step in the Precambrian basement, which is a reverse fault pushed up on the west side. At a much later time, perhaps as recently as 10 to 25 million years ago, the west side dropped down as a normal fault. The end result is a structure with several events needed to explain its origins.

After enjoying a pleasant night camping on Powell Plateau, return to the trailhead by the route you came. As best you can, that is!

TOROWEAP POINT

WESTERN GRAND CANYON'S LAVA CASCADES

View Vulcans Throne from Toroweap Point and see where lava flows spilled over the canyon's rim and dammed the Colorado River many times in the "recent" past.

DISTANCE ■ 3 miles round trip

ELEVATION ■ 4520 to 4560 feet

DIFFICULTY ■ Easy

TOPOGRAPHIC MAP ■ USGS Vulcans Throne, AZ

GEOLOGIC MAP ■ 7

KEY REFERENCE ■ 7

PRECAUTIONS ■ Toroweap Point is remote. Access is over rough dirt roads, which are subject to flash flooding and may be impassable after heavy rains. A four-wheel-drive vehicle is recommended but not required. Tire damage from sharp rocks is common: inspect your tires and check your spare. Carry plenty of extra water. At Toroweap Point use extreme caution hiking along the rim, and avoid stepping on the delicate black cryptobiotic soils.

FOR INFORMATION ■ Grand Canyon National Park

About the Landscape: Only a short hike from Toroweap Point, the drama of the Grand Canyon's fiery past is displayed in the canyon walls. As if frozen in time, Vulcans Throne and numerous other cinder cones cling to the rim. Black rivers of basalt lava spill over the edge of the canyon all the way down to the river. No stretch of the imagination is necessary to picture what happened here.

More than one hundred fifty lava flows have poured into the western Grand Canyon over the last 1.5 million years. Some of these flows stretch for over 80 miles downcanyon from their source. Perhaps as many as twelve times, great dams of lava were constructed in the canyon bottom, effectively blocking the flow of the Colorado River and forming a temporary lake. As the lake behind the dams overflowed, an incredible waterfall spilled downstream carving a new gorge and leaving only remnants of basalt clinging to the walls of the canyon. Later eruptions built new dams, which in turn were also breached and destroyed by the power of the Colorado River.

Trail Guide: Toroweap Point, a remote viewpoint in the far western section of Grand Canyon National Park, can be reached from Arizona Highway 389 near Fredonia or Colorado City, Arizona, or from St. George, Utah. No matter what route you take, it is a long drive of 60 miles or more over rough roads to get to the trailhead. Take your time. The view is well worth the effort.

The most reliable access to Toroweap Point is from Fredonia, Arizona. Drive 7 miles west on Arizona Highway 389. Turn left at the sign for Toroweap Point. Follow the signs 61 miles to the campground and viewpoint at the end of the road.

There is no official trail for this hike, which simply follows west along the canyon rim from the campground and parking area at Toroweap Point. Begin the hike by walking about 0.25 mile to the first viewpoint west of the parking area.

You will notice immediately that the western Grand Canyon has a strikingly different profile than eastern sections of the canyon. The rimrock of the Kaibab and Toroweap Formations, along with the underlying Coconino Sandstone and Hermit Shale, has retreated back from the river and forms an outer rim of cliffs on the skylines on both sides of the river. Erosion beneath these layers has formed a broad expanse of sandstone called the Esplanade Platform, for which the Supai Group's Esplanade Sandstone is named. Here at Toroweap Point the Esplanade Platform forms a red rock rim for the inner gorge of the Colorado River, which has carved a chasm 3000 feet deep and 1 mile wide. Exposed on the sheer-walled cliffs below are the formations of the Supai Group, as well as the Redwall, Temple Butte, and Muav Limestones.

From this first viewpoint lies an incredible view looking down the Colorado River to Lava Falls rapid and beyond. On the right hand, or north side, dark flows of basalt lava reach over the edge of the canyon all the way down to the river. Vulcans Throne is the largest cinder cone above the river on the right. Here, a sea of black lava has engulfed the entire north rim of the canyon.

All this volcanic action has taken place along the Toroweap Fault, one of the major faults in the western Grand Canyon. The fault runs down the length of Toroweap Valley from the north, through Vulcans Throne, and across the river into Prospect Canyon. The fault is in plain view where the rim of the canyon along the Esplanade Platform is down-dropped to the west on both sides of the river. The offset is about 700 feet.

As you can see, great eruptions of lava have taken place along this fault, filling both Toroweap Valley and Prospect Canyon with lava, building cinder cones above the rim on both sides of the Colorado River, and spilling lava over the edge down into the Grand Canyon. Lava even erupted right in the middle of the Colorado River. If you look carefully straight down you might catch a glimpse of Vulcans Anvil, a volcanic plug that sticks up in the middle of the river. An important note is that Lava Falls was not created by the action of the lava flows, but rather was created by boulders

and rock debris delivered by flash floods down Prospect Canyon to the Colorado River channel.

Once you have taken in the first viewpoint, backtrack a short distance and follow the canyon rim to the north, then around to the west to the far sandstone promontory towards Vulcans Throne. As you get closer notice the volcanic rocks littering the ground. These pyroclastics fell from the sky during the volcanic eruptions. Once at the far point, the lava cascades are in full view.

Across the river in Prospect Canyon, see if you can pick out the thick wedge of black lava reaching more than 2000 feet above the river. This is part of the Prospect Canyon dam, the oldest and tallest lava dam in the Grand Canyon. To the right, a small cinder cone is perched along the rim. Amazingly, behind the Prospect Lava dam a lake 2000 feet deep flooded the Grand Canyon, backing up the river beyond where Glen Canyon Dam is today.

What happened here is easy to imagine. Picture red-hot lava oozing from the base of Vulcans Throne. Curtains of fire fill the sky. Glowing cinders fall out across the Esplanade Platform rimming the canyon. Slowly rivers of lava approach the rim, then spill over the edge and cascade in a glowing avalanche down to meet the cold water of the Colorado River in a thunderous explosion of steam. The lava pools in the canyon bottom, then begins to flow downstream. As the eruption continues over days and perhaps weeks, the cooling lava of repeated flows constructs a dam that eventually blocks the flow of the river. The lava dam grows taller and a lake is born.

Geologists estimate that the Prospect Dam lake took more than twenty years to fill with water. An incredible waterfall must have formed as water spilled over the lava dam. Over the thousands of years that followed, erosion by the rushing water undercut the softer river sediment beneath the lava dam, and also plucked and carried away the jointed lava itself. With time, the waterfalls got higher and higher as they eroded upstream toward the dam. Ultimately, a new gorge was eroded through the lava dam, leaving only the remnants of the basalt clinging to the walls of the canyon.

The remnants of the black lava seen here at Toroweap Point provide a key nugget of information about the absolute age of the Grand Canyon. A date from a lava flow in the bottom of the canyon indicates that 1.2 million years ago the Grand Canyon was almost as deep as it is today. From other evidence in the western Grand Canyon we know that there was no Grand Canyon 6 million years ago. Amazingly, it appears the Colorado River carved the Grand Canyon in less than 5 million years!

Once you have taken in all the views and pondered the significance of the Grand Canyon's fiery past, retrace you steps back to the parking area.

Colorado River view from Toroweap Point

Chapter 4
THE PAINTED DESERT

The Colorado Plateau's Painted Desert includes classic Southwest landscapes. This is the land of legends and the old "wild west" of Hollywood movies. The region includes such spectacular landscapes as Monument Valley, Canyon De Chelly, and the Petrified Forest found along famed Route 66.

This chapter includes parts of Arizona's northeast corner that extend beyond the Painted Desert, and includes much of the area covered by both Navajo and Hopi Tribal lands. Simply venturing out across this remote and wide-open desert can be an adventure in itself.

The Painted Desert and surrounding region is a parched landscape of stepped cliffs and colorful badlands carved from Mesozoic sedimentary layers. These same layers once covered the Grand Canyon region but were stripped away by erosion. These rocks range in age from about 248 to 65 million years and chronicle the beginning of the age of the dinosaurs and their demise at the end of the Cretaceous.

The brick-red siltstones and sandstones of the Moenkopi Formation, and the pastel hues within the overlying Chinle Formation, typify the Painted Desert landscape. The Chinle's purple, blue-gray, and maroon layers represent deposition across a broad floodplain dotted by lakes and crossed by rivers that carried sand, gravel, and the logs of trees that would one day become the petrified wood found in Petrified Forest National Park.

Other highlights of the area include the mesas and buttes of Monument Valley, and the maze of canyons within Canyon De Chelly. In these dramatically scenic places, erosion along the Monument and Defiance Uplifts has exposed Permian desert sands of the De Chelly Sandstone, which is found nowhere else on the Colorado Plateau. Other hidden surprises are Coal Mine Canyon, where bizarre landforms are carved in uniquely colored Jurassic strata, and the exhumed desert dunes in the Navajo Sandstone at Coyote Buttes along the Paria Plateau.

EROSION AND LANDFORMS

Rocks exposed at the Earth's surface are subject to *weathering,* a destructive process that breaks rock down into loose particles, which are then moved by *erosion.* Water, wind, and ice are the principle agents of weathering, superimposing their effects on the geologic fabric of the Colorado Plateau.

Differential erosion describes the way rocks vary in their rates of weathering and erosion. Hard or resistant rocks, like limestone and sandstone, erode more gradually than softer, less resistant types such as mudstone and shale.

On the Colorado Plateau, hard and soft rocks are often found layered in alternating fashion. Differential erosion of such flat-lying sedimentary layers results in a common pattern of stair-stepped canyons and plateaus. As a layer of soft rock erodes into a slope, the overlying hard rock layer may break off, forming a steep cliff. Thus, the stair steps of the plateau may alternate between the steep cliffs and crumbled slopes that their rock compositions dictate. As another example of differential erosion, hard layers of limestone, sandstone, and volcanic rock typically form resistant caps on buttes, mesas, and plateaus, shielding soft, underlying rocks from rapid erosion.

Weathering and erosion along fault and fracture zones influence the orientation of cliffs and canyons, as well as the formation of arches, fins, spires, and other scenic landforms.

The artistic forces of weathering and erosion apply the finishing touches on the geologic masterpiece that is the Colorado Plateau.

Differential erosion has worked its magic in Monument Valley on the Arizona–Utah border.

BLUE MESA

STONE TREES IN PETRIFIED FOREST NATIONAL PARK

Walk through pastel-colored hills where a treasure trove of petrified wood is being unearthed by erosion of the Triassic Chinle Formation.

DISTANCE ■ 1 mile round trip

ELEVATION ■ 5600 to 5525 feet

DIFFICULTY ■ Easy

TOPOGRAPHIC MAP ■ USGS Petrified Forest, AZ

GEOLOGIC MAP ■ 8

KEY REFERENCE ■ 8

PRECAUTIONS ■ Federal law absolutely prohibits collection or removal of petrified wood, even small pieces. Please remain on the trails and take only pictures. There are no campgrounds within the park. The park road closes at sundown.

FOR INFORMATION ■ Petrified Forest National Park

About the Landscape: Petrified Forest National Park is one of the world's great storehouses of petrified wood. Here in the Painted Desert region of northeastern Arizona lie the remains of 225-million-year-old fossilized trees scattered across a palette of pastel-colored sedimentary rocks in the Triassic Chinle Formation.

The Blue Mesa Trail winds through an otherworldly landscape of badlands in the Chinle Formation, providing easy access to this treasure trove of fossil trees being unearthed by erosion. The petrified wood found here is remarkably well preserved, amazingly colorful, and incredibly abundant. These trees-turned-to-stone tell a tale of lush tropical forests, flood-swollen rivers, and erupting volcanoes at a time when crocodile-like reptiles and small dinosaurs roamed the ancient landscape.

Trail Guide: To reach the Blue Mesa trailhead, take exit 311 off Interstate 40 at the north entrance to Petrified Forest National Park. From the park visitor center and entrance station, drive 10 miles south on the park road to the sign for Blue Mesa. Turn left and drive 3.5 miles to the trailhead.

From its start near the information kiosk, the first 0.25-mile of the trail is paved as it switchbacks down from the top of Blue Mesa. The ledge of white sandstone and conglomerate capping the mesa is called the Sonsela Sandstone Bed of the Chinle Formation. The trail cuts right through this resistant layer, which acts as a protective cap rock for the softer, more easily eroded mudstone beds below.

As the trail makes its way down toward a constructed stone bench at the first switchback, take a close look at the Sonsela Sandstone Bed in outcrops on the right. The upper part of the ledge is composed of cross-bedded sandstone formed by the migration of sandbars in an ancient river channel. The lower part of the ledge is made of conglomerate that accumulated as gravel in a river channel. The small, marble-size pebbles are mostly rounded fragments of Precambrian igneous and metamorphic rocks, along with abundant gray chert from the Permian Kaibab Formation. These pebbles were washed from ancient mountains called the Mogollon Highlands that existed south of here during the Triassic.

Look for the large petrified logs encased by conglomerate in the steep slope left of the trail. Floods swept these logs downstream from the luxuriant tropical forests that flanked the Mogollon Highlands. Most of the petrified wood in the park comes from the Sonsela Sandstone Bed.

Below the Sonsela ledge, the trail enters a stark landscape of white, gray, blue, and lavender mudstone layers in the Petrified Forest Member of the Chinle. Along with the reds and purples seen in other parts of the park, these soft hues are caused by minute amounts of iron, manganese, and organic material trapped within the mud that settled out on floodplains adjacent to the Chinle streams.

The mudstone layers of the badlands are rich in clays—mostly bentonite—derived from volcanic ash. During the Mesozoic, clouds of volcanic ash periodically blanketed the landscape, spewed from a string of volcanoes along North America's west coast. During the Triassic, the land that would become the Four Corners region was still a part of the supercontinent, Pangea, and was enjoying a wet and humid climate close to the equator (about where Panama is located today). Bentonite has the unique property

Petrified wood along the Blue Mesa Trail

of swelling and expanding when wet, then shrinking and cracking as it dries out, creating a crumbly surface that erodes easily into the badlands around you. This property also makes it difficult for plants to gain a foothold, furthering the development of badlands.

Near where the trail begins to level out, the first pieces of petrified wood lie in a ravine to the right. At about the 0.3-mile point, just past these fossil logs, the trail forks and begins a short loop around the base of the badland hills flanking Blue Mesa. Follow the sign pointing right.

From here on out, petrified wood is littered everywhere. The fact that there are no branches or bark preserved on the logs suggests they were transported a considerable distance from where they grew before being buried by floods of sediment deposited by the ancient river system. The majority of these trees grew very tall. Logs found in the park are typically 80 to 100 feet long and 3 to 4 feet in diameter. Larger specimens range up to 200 feet in length and 10 feet in diameter. Although there are no long, intact fossil logs seen on this hike, several sections of fossil wood approach 4 feet in diameter.

The majority of fossil logs in the Petrified Forest are pine-like conifers of the extinct genus *Araucarioxylon*. They were similar to the "monkey-puzzle" trees (*Araucaria*) that today grow natively in the warm, temperate parts of South America, Australia, and New Zealand. Other plant fossils found in the Chinle Formation include a variety of ferns, giant horsetails (which grew to 30 feet tall), and microscopic spores and pollen that tell a great deal about the types of plants living here over 200 million years ago.

As you make your way around the loop, look closely at some of the amazing specimens of fossil wood, some displaying a rainbow of colors. The vivid colors are caused by trace elements trapped in the quartz minerals that "petrified" the original wood. Amazingly, only trace amounts of iron (and in some cases manganese) in the quartz is responsible for the great variety of colors, including red, yellow, brown, and even blue. The great amounts of silica needed for the fossilization process (the critical ingredient for making quartz is SiO_2) was supplied by the volcanic ash that wafted across the Chinle rivers and floodplains during the Triassic. Once the trees were buried by overlying sediment, the silica from the volcanic ash was dissolved into the groundwater, which then soaked into the wood where it precipitated and fossilized the ancient trees.

Notice also the intricate detail preserved in the fossil wood. Look closely to see some of the original concentric banding in the wood. These are growth interruption bands caused by alternating wet-dry conditions of the ancient environment when the tree was growing. These are not annual "tree rings" corresponding to the tree's yearly growth. They cannot, therefore, be simply counted to date the age of the tree.

As you continue around the loop, take time to imagine the vanished Triassic landscape represented by the colorful layers of the Chinle Formation. Listen quietly and picture yourself along the bank of a flood-swollen river carrying logs, sticks, and other debris downstream. Lean up against a driftwood log and enjoy the moist tropical air. But remember to watch out for the giant reptiles and small dinosaurs that plied the Chinle floodplains during the Triassic!

Returning to the present, complete the loop and retrace your steps back to the trailhead.

CANYON DE CHELLY

ANCIENT WIND-BLOWN DUNES AND THE PALEOZOIC–MESOZOIC UNCONFORMITY

Hike through colorful cliffs of Permian De Chelly Sandstone to White House Ruin, an Anasazi cliff dwelling perched at the base of towering cliffs.

DISTANCE ■ **2.5 miles round trip**

ELEVATION ■ **6210 to 5660 feet**

DIFFICULTY ■ **Moderate**

TOPOGRAPHIC MAP ■ **USGS Del Muerto, AZ**

GEOLOGIC MAP ■ **9**

KEY REFERENCE ■ **9**

PRECAUTIONS ■ **Please respect the private property of the Navajo people living and working in the canyon. Avoid this hike in the midday summer heat. Beware of flash floods and quicksand in the canyon bottom.**

FOR INFORMATION ■ **Canyon de Chelly National Monument**

About the Landscape: Canyon de Chelly is known for the beautiful cliff dwellings built by Ancestral Puebloan people (Anasazi), and for the bottomland that has been home to generations of Navajo people who still live and work in the canyon today.

Canyon de Chelly (pronounced "de-shay") is a sinuous chasm carved from the Permian De Chelly Sandstone along the western flank of the Defiance Plateau, a broad anticline in northeastern Arizona that has a long history of uplift, most recently during the Laramide orogeny. Displayed in the towering cliffs of De Chelly Sandstone are large, sweeping cross-beds that mark the advance of giant wind-blown dunes about 260 million years ago. This is the same salmon red sandstone found to the north in

Monument Valley. Like all "red rocks," the color of the rocks is caused by the iron-oxide stain, similar to rust, that coats each individual quartz grain.

The abrupt and sheer cliffs of Canyon de Chelly owe their existence to erosion beneath the Shinarump Conglomerate, which is the lowest member of the Triassic Chinle Formation. This hard and resistant conglomerate made of dark maroon sand and gravel represents 200-million-year-old stream-channel deposits that form a hard cap rock, protecting the more easily eroded sandstone underneath from rapid erosion.

The trail to White House Ruin winds down through steep cliffs to the canyon bottom. Along the way, you step across an unconformity, or erosion surface, between the De Chelly Sandstone and the Shinarump Conglomerate. In one step you cross a threshold of time where a mind-boggling 60 million years of the rock record is either missing or was never deposited.

Trail Guide: To reach the White House Trail, turn east off U.S. Highway 191 onto Navajo Highway 7 in downtown Chinle, Arizona (near the high school). About 2.7 miles from the intersection, bear right just past the visitor center and follow the South Rim Drive 5.3 miles to the White House Overlook. Turn left and drive to the parking area. Signs mark the trailhead, located down the paved walkway and to the right.

The trail begins by following the rim of the canyon for about 100 yards, where it meets the entrance to a constructed tunnel. Signs mark the entrance to the tunnel that leads down below the rim.

Below the tunnel, a series of switchbacks wind through layers of purple and maroon Shinarump Conglomerate, the basal member of the Triassic Chinle Formation. This resistant layer forms the cap rock for the towering cliffs of Canyon de Chelly, and is a widespread layer across much of the Colorado Plateau.

Take a close look at the fallen Shinarump boulders along the trail on the right, just after the first switchback. The coarse-grained sand, pebbles, and cobbles represent deposition in northwest-flowing stream channels which carried rounded pebbles of igneous and metamorphic Precambrian basement rock, along with Paleozoic sedimentary rock. The main source for this sediment was eroding highlands to the southeast where Texas is today. Tributary streams also supplied sediment from the volcanic Mogollon Highlands to the south, and also from the Ancestral Rocky Mountains in western and central Colorado.

At the second switchback, the trail begins winding down through the underlying De Chelly Sandstone. The boundary (or *contact*) between the Shinarump above and the De Chelly below is exposed above the trail to the left. Follow this contact with your eyes to see the dramatic relief along this erosion surface or unconformity. About 200 million years ago, sand

The DeChelly Sandstone streaked with desert varnish above White House Ruin

and gravel in the Shinarump streams filled channels cut into the top of the De Chelly Sandstone. About 50 yards down the trail from the switchback, a Shinarump channel meets the trail.

Along the trail you can put your hand right on the contact of the two formations, an unconformity which represents a gap in the rock record of about 60 million years. Go ahead, touch it.

Here in Canyon de Chelly, the De Chelly Sandstone is exposed by deep erosion along the western flank of the Defiance Plateau. The Defiance

Plateau, in fact, is a very old structure dating back to uplift of the Ancestral Rockies about 300 million years ago. Across this ancient structure, called the Defiance Uplift, the De Chelly Sandstone rests directly on top of the Precambrian Basement. Any older Paleozoic sedimentary rocks once present here were completely stripped off the top of the uplift by erosion. This unconformity, however, is not exposed at the surface.

What we do see exposed at the surface is the Triassic Chinle Formation resting directly on top of the Permian De Chelly Sandstone. Missing here are Permian layers present at the Grand Canyon, including the Toroweap and Kaibab Formations and the overlying Triassic Moenkopi Formation. These layers are missing because they were stripped off by erosion along the Defiance Uplift prior to deposition of the Shinarump, or perhaps they were never deposited.

Farther down the trail, right before the next constructed bench, the contact between the two formations changes to vertical. Here, the De Chelly Sandstone is on the left and Shinarump Conglomerate is on the right. A short distance down the trail, the De Chelly is on the right and the Shinarump is on the left. What's going on? This is an ancient narrow slot canyon where the Shinarump sand and gravel filled a deep channel cut into the top of the De Chelly. This steep-walled channel is more obvious when viewed from a distance from other points on the trail.

At about the 0.25-mile point, the trail switchbacks sharply to the right. Below, the trail has been chipped into the De Chelly Sandstone. At the switchback, there is an impressive view looking along the cliff face at the large, sweeping cross-beds that mark the advance of the ancient dunes. About 260 million years ago, the sand was transported southward by parched Permian winds from the floodplains of streams to the north. These streams drained sediments eroded from the Uncompahgre Uplift of the Ancestral Rocky Mountains.

After about 0.5 mile, the trail leaves behind the *slickrock* portion of the trail—where it crosses worn, bare-rock surfaces—and continues its decent through sandy areas of modern-day dunes which the wind has piled against the cliff base. After passing through another tunnel cut through the sandstone, the trail reaches the canyon bottom at about the 1-mile point from the rim. For the last 0.25 mile the trail follows along the base of a sheer cliff, crosses a metal bridge, then follows a two-track road to White House Ruin.

White House Ruin is perched on a ledge near the base of a spectacular 600-foot-high wall of De Chelly Sandstone. Streaks of desert varnish paint the cliff face, forming a beautiful tapestry of rock and mineral.

Once you have breathed in the coolness of the canyon bottom, return to the trailhead by the route you came.

Hike 13

COAL MINE CANYON

GHOSTS AND PAINTED SPIRES

Sandstone and coal beds in the Cretaceous Dakota Sandstone cap other-worldly badlands carved from Jurassic sedimentary rocks.

DISTANCE ■ **2 miles round trip**

ELEVATION ■ **5820 to 5460 feet**

DIFFICULTY ■ **Easy (except for the steep entry)**

TOPOGRAPHIC MAP ■ **USGS Tuba City SE, AZ**

GEOLOGIC MAP ■ **9**

KEY REFERENCE ■ **10**

PRECAUTIONS ■ **Do not try this hike after a recent rain; it is treacherous when muddy. The short, steep route off the rim may prevent the less adventurous from attempting this route. Please respect the private property nearby. Note: At the time of publication this trail was temporarily closed to protect active raptor nesting sites. Call for current information before planning this hike.**

FOR INFORMATION ■ **Hopi Parks and Recreation Department**

About the Landscape: Coal Mine Canyon is a hidden gem on the Hopi Indian Reservation in northeastern Arizona's Painted Desert. Indeed, even as you approach the canyon, it remains out of sight until the very last moment.

Etched into the edge of Coal Mine Mesa, the badlands of Coal Mine Canyon are carved from colorful Jurassic sedimentary rocks. Exposed in the walls of the canyon are rocks of the San Rafael Group, including the Cow Springs Sandstone, a member of the Entrada Formation, and the underlying Carmel Formation. The rim of the canyon is capped by Cretaceous rocks in the Dakota Sandstone, which includes sandstone, conglomerate, and thin seams of coal that have been mined periodically, giving the canyon its name.

This short but timeless hike takes you below the rim while *hoodoos,* or freestanding spires, dance on the skyline above. As you will discover, these bizarre landforms continue to keep the legend of the ghost of Coal Mine Canyon alive, especially if you linger at dusk.

Trail Guide: To find Coal Mine Canyon, drive 15.2 miles east from Tuba City on Arizona Highway 264. At the point where you see a windmill on the skyline ahead, turn left onto an unmarked dirt road. Drive about 0.5 mile from the highway to continue straight ahead at the first junction, bear right at the second junction, then proceed straight ahead again at the third junction (which is a crossroad that leads to the windmill now on the right). The canyon does not come into view until the last moment when you reach the picnic area perched on its rim.

Park near the fence and begin your hike by walking east through the picnic area. The unmarked trail starts just before you reach the last picnic table closest to the rim. Bear left down a gentle slope to the red hills below. Although the route into the canyon here continues to the right, take a moment to walk down to the left to view the coal beds exposed beneath the prominent red-capped point.

These thin coal seams were formed more than 100 million years ago along the coast of the advancing Cretaceous seaway. *Coal* is formed by the accumulation and burial of dead trees and plants in swampy areas. After burial, the deposits of organic carbon are converted into coal by compaction and pressure over time. This is a very poor, low-grade coal and was only mined for short periods of time, though still visible is the terrace cut into the rim of the canyon to dig out the coal.

The contorted-looking red rocks above the coal seams are a strange type of rock that formed when some of the coal beds caught fire and burned while underground. Called *clinker,* these red rocks formed when the sandstone and shale surrounding the coal was oxidized as they were "cooked" by the burning coal. The burning is a natural process sparked by lightning when coal beds lie at or near the surface. Erosion has now exposed the clinker at the surface. Today, coal beds are burning underground nearby on the Kaiparowits Plateau in Utah.

Retrace your steps back upslope and then drop down slightly, following an excavated terrace to the east. After about 50 yards, look for a worn path that heads across a soft slope down to a gray rock ledge only a short distance below. Along the slope look for fragments of fossil oyster shells that are weathering off the rocks that cap the rim. These oysters lived in mixed fresh and saltwater estuaries along the coast of the Cretaceous seaway.

This rock ledge is the lowermost sandstone unit in the Dakota Sandstone, and represents the base of Cretaceous-age rocks. The gray sandstone was deposited in streams that cut channels into the underlying Jurassic sandstone, draining into the coal swamps near the coast. A close look at this sandstone reveals that it is chock-full of black carbonized fragments of wood and plant material. The base of this layer represents the Jurassic-Cretaceous boundary and is an unconformity, because beneath this ledge there is a gap in the geologic record where older rocks were removed by erosion before the sandstone was deposited on top.

Although there is no distinct trail, the route into the canyon drops

The Jurassic Entrada Sandstone is particularly colorful in Coal Mine Canyon.

steeply down the slope to the left of the ledge. It is not as dangerous as it looks, but please use caution. At the base of the slope a clear, well-traveled trail appears and continues its steep descent through a narrow canyon.

The walls of the canyon are carved in the Jurassic Cow Springs Sandstone (a member of the Entrada Sandstone), which is the white sandstone below the Dakota. Below the Cow Springs are the colorful Entrada and Carmel Formations. Although obscured by weathering, slanting layers or *cross-beds* provide clues that the Cow Springs and lower Entrada are wind-blown layers of sand representing ancient desert sand dunes.

Notice how the red of the Entrada Sandstone is patchy and does not necessarily follow the orientation of the layering within the rock. The red color of the rock is caused by minute amounts of iron which coated the sand grains as groundwater percolated through the rock while it was deep underground. The prominent color horizons may represent variations in ancient water tables.

After about 50 yards, the trail levels and then contours along the west side of the canyon. The walking becomes much easier from here on out, and the canyon becomes more beautiful and intriguing with each step. About 0.25 mile below the rim, a short spur trail to the left leads to a viewpoint at the top of a low ridge.

At this point, the canyon begins to open up and the artistry of erosion is displayed in all its magnificence. The walls of the canyon appear as though they are melting. It is obvious that here the sand grains are not cemented together as tightly as in the other, more resistant sandstone layers that form sheer cliffs. The more resistant Dakota Sandstone above influences the erosion pattern. Notice that the rim of the canyon and many of the hoodoos have a protective cap on top. Once this harder sandstone layer is eroded or falls off, the softer sandstone below weathers more rapidly into badlands. Also notice the window in the cliff on the opposite canyon wall. The top of the window is held up by a channel deposit in the Dakota Sandstone.

The main trail drops steeply now to follow the wash for about 50 yards and then meet another trail that climbs up and to the left. Take the high road. If you continue following the wash you'll come to a drop-off that must be scaled using a rope left behind by climbers.

Once above the wash, the trail contours down the canyon with great views in all directions. In a few places it drops and climbs steeply for short distances where it crosses small tributaries. Notice the haunting shapes of rock formations on the skyline to the left.

About at the 1-mile point below the rim, another spur trail splitting off to the left leads up to a viewpoint. Here, you are standing at the junction of two canyons. As you can see, it is possible to walk for miles downcanyon. This viewpoint, however, is the turnaround point for this hike. If you have the time and energy, you may want to explore the western arm of the canyon before retracing your steps back to the rim. But if you are afraid of ghosts, be sure to exit the canyon before dark. Also keep in mind that this is the "scene of the crime" in a Tony Hillerman murder mystery!

MONUMENT VALLEY

Hike
14

RED ROCK BUTTES AND MESAS

Hike the short North Window Trail for a spectacular view of landforms carved from Permian red rocks along the Monument Uplift.

DISTANCE ■ **0.5 mile round trip**

ELEVATION ■ **5280 to 5320 feet**

DIFFICULTY ■ **Easy**

TOPOGRAPHIC MAP ■ USGS Mitten Buttes, AZ

GEOLOGIC MAP ■ 9

KEY REFERENCE ■ 11, 12

PRECAUTIONS ■ Except for short hikes at several of the overlooks along the self-guided scenic drive, hiking in Monument Valley requires a local Navajo guide. This is a hot place during summer. Beware of afternoon thunderstorms and sudden blowing sandstorms. Please respect the privacy of the people who live here.

FOR INFORMATION ■ Monument Valley Tribal Park

About the Landscape: Monument Valley offers some of the all-time classic geologic views in the Southwest's canyon country, and is one of the Colorado Plateau's most photographed spots outside the Grand Canyon. The colorful buttes, mesas, and spires of Monument Valley are legendary, made famous by John Wayne and Hollywood filmmakers.

Erosion along the crest of the Monument Uplift has sculpted layered sedimentary rocks into a variety of spectacular landforms carved from the Permian De Chelly (pronounced "de-shay") Sandstone. This scenic formation is another one of the great piles of ancient wind-blown sand on the Colorado Plateau. Where the De Chelly Sandstone has been stripped away by erosion, the softer, underlying Organ Rock Shale weathers into the brilliant red desert landscape that stretches as far as the eye can see.

This short hike from the North Window offers an outstanding panorama. The drive to the trailhead alone is worth the time and effort.

Trail Guide: Monument Valley straddles the Arizona–Utah state line along U.S. Highway 163, and is located about 24 miles north of Kayenta, Arizona, and about 21 miles south of Mexican Hat, Utah. Turn at the sign for the Monument Valley Visitor Center, and drive 4 miles east to the spectacular rim of the valley where the visitor center is located.

After paying the required entrance fee, follow the scenic drive for 8 miles to the North Window turnoff. Turn right and drive 0.5 mile to the

109

View through North Window, Monument Valley

trailhead parking area. The scenic drive is bumpy and dusty but passable—except when wet—for most vehicles.

This short hike follows a well-worn path that contours along a slope beneath the towering cliffs of Cly Butte. You don't have to walk very far to witness one of the grandest views in all of Monument Valley.

As you pass through the North Window (a gap between Elephant and Cly Buttes), the immense scale of Monument Valley emerges before you. Most prominent, East Mitten and Merrick Buttes rise over 800 feet above the valley floor. In the distance, spires and buttes shape the skyline.

The spectacular cliff-edged landforms of Monument Valley are carved from the Permian De Chelly Sandstone. Ancient winds piled this sand into a vast dune field about 260 million years ago, at a time when Cutler Formation rivers were washing immense quantities of sediment from the northeast off the Uncompahgre Highland of the Ancestral Rockies.

Looking northward, the buttes of Monument Valley end abruptly. This is because the De Chelly Sandstone thins in this direction and ultimately disappears, or pinches out, near the San Juan River. In addition, the rock layers are more deeply eroded near the crest of the Monument Uplift, and any buttes that may have once existed have been stripped away by erosion. On the far skyline the cliffs of Cedar Mesa are not made of De Chelly Sandstone, but rather are cut from Cedar Mesa Sandstone. Coincidentally, Cedar Mesa Sandstone, which is still Permian but older than De Chelly Sandstone, pinches out south toward Monument Valley.

The colorful ledges and slopes below the De Chelly Sandstone cliffs are mudstones and siltstones in the Organ Rock Shale, the same rocks of the trail where you are standing. Permian in age, these rocks are river and coastal plain deposits that correlate directly with the Hermit Shale in the Grand Canyon region (the De Chelly Sandstone is absent in the Grand Canyon). The Organ Rock Shale forms the terraced foundations for all the monuments in the valley.

The stepped ledges sitting on top of the De Chelly Sandstone cliffs are sandstones and siltstones in the Triassic Moenkopi Formation (pronounced "mo-n-kopi"). Thus, the time boundary between Paleozoic and Mesozoic rocks occurs almost everywhere near the top of the buttes and mesas in Monument Valley. Similar to the Organ Rock, the brilliantly colored Moenkopi layers were also deposited across a broad coastal plain.

Capping many of the buttes and mesas in Monument Valley is a ledge of sandstone and conglomerate in the Shinarump Member of the Triassic Chinle Formation. These rocks were deposited in channels of an extensive river system that extended across the entire Colorado Plateau over 200 million years ago. The Shinarump is a very important layer because it acts as a hard, resistant cap protecting landforms from rapid erosion.

Before turning around to return to the parking area, take a moment to ponder the forces of uplift and erosion that have shaped Monument Valley.

Turn the clock back 65 million years to the beginning of the Laramide orogeny, when forces in the earth buckled these rock layers into the Monument Uplift. At that time, the area that would become Monument Valley was still buried under thousands of feet of younger sedimentary rocks. Although erosion etched at the landscape for millions of years following this event, it was not until the last 10 million years or so that things really got serious. Even though the exact timing remains a subject of debate, this is when many geologists agree that the Colorado Plateau began its slow push skyward. This uplift invigorated the streams and rivers that swept across the region, spawning a time of intense downcutting and headward erosion that continues today. Following a similar geologic story to that of the Grand Canyon, the fabulous landforms of Monument Valley are, like the Grand Canyon, relatively young features of the Colorado Plateau landscape.

Hike

15

COYOTE BUTTES

EXHUMED DESERT SAND DUNES

Explore a hidden wonderland of colorful cross-beds eroded in the Jurassic Navajo Sandstone.

DISTANCE ■ **7 miles round trip**

DISTANCE ■ **5000 to 5400 feet**

DIFFICULTY ■ **Strenuous**

TOPOGRAPHIC MAP ■ **USGS Coyote Buttes, AZ**

GEOLOGIC MAP ■ **10**

KEY REFERENCE ■ **13**

PRECAUTIONS ■ **This hike is not for beginners. A trail is evident for only the first mile, so the hike requires routefinding ability. Bring a topographic map and compass. Do not attempt this hike in the summer heat—there is little shade, no dependable water, and sections of deep sand to cross. To help protect this popular and fragile area, hikers must purchase a permit in advance, and camping is prohibited. The access road to the trailhead may be impassable when wet.**

FOR INFORMATION ■ **Arizona Strip Land Office, Paria Canyon–Vermilion Cliffs Wilderness**

About the Landscape: Lying astride the Arizona–Utah border, the Paria Canyon-Vermilion Cliffs Wilderness is a colorful landscape of unusual rock formations. From its headwaters in Utah's high plateaus, the Paria River has carved, on its way to meet the Colorado River at Lees Ferry, Arizona, an intricate network of canyons along the flank of the East Kaibab Monocline.

Hidden within this maze of cliffs, canyons, and buttes is a destination unlike any other on the Colorado Plateau. Here, in an area called simply "The Wave" of Coyote Buttes, there exists a fanciful microcosm of sensuously sculpted sandstone worn smooth by wind, water, and time.

Trail Guide: This hike begins at the Wire Pass trailhead in Utah, one of four trailheads providing access to Paria Canyon. To reach the Wire Pass trailhead, drive 35.6 miles west from Page, Arizona, on U.S. Highway 89 and turn sharply left onto a dirt road (no sign) located at the big bend in the highway 5.2 miles past the Paria Canyon Ranger Station. Then drive 8.9 miles south to the trailhead parking area on the right (sign and toilet).

The trail to Coyote Buttes begins on the opposite side of the road near the Buckskin Gulch Trail register. The trail follows the Buckskin Gulch Trail for about the first 0.5 mile.

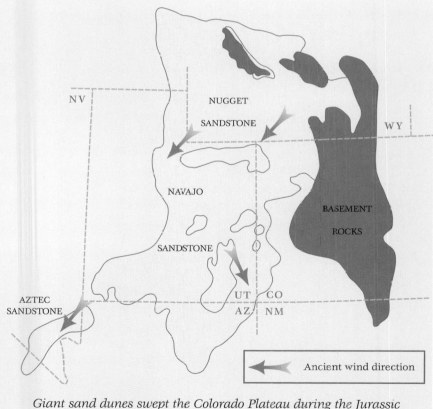

Giant sand dunes swept the Colorado Plateau during the Jurassic

From the trailhead, the trail immediately crosses Coyote Wash, then parallels the wash for about 0.25 mile before ultimately merging with the wash. About 0.5 mile from the trailhead, the Coyote Buttes Trail splits off from the wash to follow an old road up a steep hill on the right. A sign for the Buckskin Gulch Trail, which continues straight ahead following the wash, marks the junction.

From the Coyote Buttes Trail register at the top of the hill, the Coyote Buttes Trail follows the old road as it crosses a sand dune area for about the next 0.5 mile. The old road ends where it meets a small tributary wash that flows along a ridge of Navajo Sandstone directly ahead.

Note: From this point on there is no longer a trail and you must follow directions carefully. Ignore any footsteps that continue straight ahead across the wash. That is the "long" route.

From the point where the old road meets the wash, turn right and follow the wash upstream for about 100 yards. Just past a small tooth-like projection of rock above on the left, begin climbing up the slickrock ridge left of the wash. This is one of the steepest parts of the hike. At the top of the ridge, there is a sweeping view of the Paria Canyon country.

From the ridge top, hike to the right (south) about 50 yards to where the ridge meets a steep slickrock slope that curves off to the left. From here the route is a little tricky but not unsafe. The route contours along this steep slope for about the next 0.25 mile, following a subtle bench where large cross-beds meet in the sandstone. Try your best to maintain elevation, and avoid stepping on any loose rocks or boulders. Friction here is your friend. The going becomes much easier at the point where the route meets a subtle divide. Before continuing, take a moment to get your bearings. Look south toward the mesa on the far skyline. Although you can not see it, The Wave is located below the prominent dark, vertical "crack" in the cliff above a sand dune that climbs the lower portion of the cliff (at a compass bearing of about 160 degrees, or south 20-degrees east, from where you stand).

Continue by traversing slightly downhill across a small sand dune to a broad sandstone bench. Walking south, continue along this bench toward the mesa with the vertical crack, keeping the cliffs always to your right. The going is easy for about the next 0.5 mile. Notice the interesting polygonal joints in the sandstone underfoot and the large-scale cross-beds high on the cliffs to the right.

Before reaching the sand dune that climbs up the opposite side of the canyon toward the dark, vertical crack, the route eventually crosses a broad, sandy wash. On the opposite side of the wash, look for the well-worn path in the sand dune near the solitary juniper tree. This path leads steeply up the dune until it meets bare rock in a small wash. Continue climbing uphill, following the wash to where it meets another sandy area. At the upper end of this next sandy stretch, head toward the opening in the slickrock cliff directly ahead. This is the entrance to The Wave.

Exploring a fanciful landscape

The intricate layers in the rock are composed of giant dunes deposited about 150 million years ago during the Jurassic. At this time, the region that would become the Colorado Plateau was part of a vast Sahara-like desert along the west coast of North America. As the dunes were buried under more and more sand, they became saturated with groundwater. Slowly, groundwater minerals cemented the sand grains together, turning the dunes to stone. These ancient dunes later became known as the Navajo Sandstone, the most prominent and widespread rock layer exposed by uplift and erosion on the Colorado Plateau.

As you enter the smoothly sculpted sandstone canyon, the patterns in the rock walls create a three-dimensional puzzle for the eyes. Let your imagination run wild!

The thin slanting lines in the rock, called cross-beds, represent the steep faces of sand dunes as they advanced downwind. The cross-beds are strikingly colorful. The amazing palette of colors is the result of minerals once carried by the groundwater that saturated the rock as it lay buried. The colors are caused by subtle differences in the chemical states of the minerals, principally iron and manganese, which stained the individual sand grains and the binding cement. Notice that the colors do not necessarily follow each individual cross-bed layer, in places creating complex and abstract patterns at angles to the cross-beds.

As you follow the main canyon higher, there are places where the once perfect cross-beds are wildly contorted. These disruptions in the layers formed before the sand became rock. The weight and pressure of sand piled on top of the buried dunes, coupled with the water pressure between the sand grains, caused the layers to flow, a process called *soft sediment deformation.*

If you have the time and energy, it is worthwhile to explore along the cliffs and ledges above The Wave. Notice the clusters of hummocky, turtle-like rock formations created by weathering and erosion of contorted sandstone layers deformed by soft sediment deformation. Also notice the strange and wonderful lichens underfoot which cause the surface of the sandstone to peel and curl. Please be careful not to crush these delicate structures underfoot as you explore.

As the shadows in the canyons grow longer, it will soon be time to retrace your steps back to the trailhead. Be sure to leave enough time for routefinding before darkness falls on this amazing landscape.

Half moon over Fisher Towers

Part 2
UTAH'S PLATEAU HIKES

Chapter 5
THE SLICKROCK COUNTRY

Utah's slickrock country is a land sculpted in stone. Here, in the haunts chronicled by writer Edward Abbey in his classic *The Monkey Wrench Gang,* is a vast expanse of red rock cliffs, intricate canyons, and scenic mesas. This is the very heart of the Southwest's Colorado Plateau, where more national parks and monuments are found than anywhere else in America.

The *slickrock* landscape is a sandstone wilderness that sprawls over almost all of southeastern Utah and rises to meet Utah's High Plateaus to the west. It is a region carved from the Colorado Plateau's layered stack of colorful sedimentary rocks by the Colorado River and its many tributaries—the Escalante, Dirty Devil, Green, Paria, and San Juan to name a few. Sadly, Glen Canyon, the mother of all slickrock canyons, is presently submerged beneath Powell Reservoir (also called Lake Powell). But in the viewpoint of geologic time, the lake is only a temporary feature on the landscape. One day Glen Canyon will be reclaimed by the forces of nature (and Seldom Seen and Hayduke will cheer from their graves).

Utah's slickrock country is a desert landscape where the old bones of the earth are revealed. Nearly flat layercakes of sediments were bent upward to form upright folds called monoclines 65 million years ago during the Laramide orogeny. Erosion has sculpted the monoclines into long spines of sandstone standing on end. They include some of the most prominent landforms of the Colorado Plateau, like Waterpocket Fold, the San Rafael Swell, the Cockscomb, and Comb Ridge.

Topping the "who's who" list of the slickrock formations in the Navajo Sandstone are the massive cliffs in Zion National Park, the majestic domes along Capitol Reef's Waterpocket Fold, and the twisting Escalante Canyonlands of the Grand Staircase–Escalante National Monument. The sandstone fins and arches in Arches National Park, the bizarre hoodoos of Goblin Valley, and the curious sandstone pipes of Kodachrome Basin are all worn from another marquee name—the Entrada Sandstone. And there is also the prominent Wingate Sandstone, known for expansive sheer cliffs that edge many of the mesas, including Canyonlands' Island in the Sky. All three of these formations are part of the Jurassic "sand pile" of wind-blown dunes that swept the Colorado Plateau between about 200 and 175 million years ago.

But perhaps the most surprising aspect of slickrock country is the ranges of majestic mountains that pierce the landscape. The La Sal, Abajo, and Henry Mountains are the remains of great blisters of magma, called *laccoliths,* which squeezed between the Colorado Plateau's sedimentary layers between about 31 and 20 million years ago. Erosion has now exposed the hard, resistant cores of igneous rock and left them standing high above the surrounding desert landscape. While forays into these mountains provide welcome relief from the heat in the canyon country and forests grow on their slopes, the views from 10,000 feet of the surrounding endless expanse of sandstone are awe-inspiring.

And although it would take many lifetimes to explore all the nooks and crannies that Utah's slickrock country has to offer, even a short day hike into this sandstone wilderness opens a whole new universe of discovery.

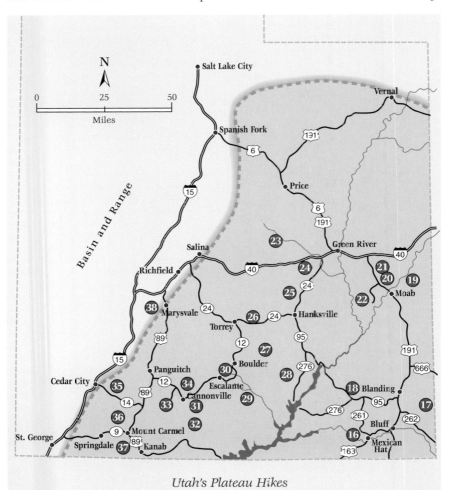

Utah's Plateau Hikes

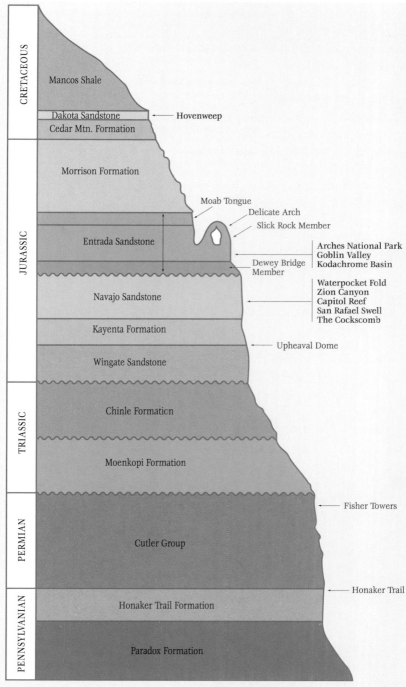

Simplified geologic column showing rock layers of Utah's slickrock country

LACCOLITHS—ISLAND MOUNTAINS OF THE COLORADO PLATEAU

The Colorado Plateau is punctuated by a number of isolated mountain ranges that give form to the landscape. These include the Abajo, La Sal, Ute, and Henry Mountains, and Navajo Mountain. But unlike the volcanic mountains that rim the edge of the Colorado Plateau—among them Arizona's San Francisco Peaks, Colorado's San Juan Mountains, New Mexico's Jemez Mountains, and Utah's Tushar Mountains—these island mountains are not volcanoes as geologists originally suspected. Instead, they are all the eroded cores of a special style of igneous intrusion.

Following his exploration of the Henry Mountains in 1875-76, pioneering geologist G.K. Gilbert proposed a geologic process never before described to explain the origin of these unique mountains, which he called *laccoliths.*

The igneous core of the Henry Mountains rises above the colored layers of the Morrison Formation.

Gilbert envisioned that each mountain range was formed by molten rock that pushed upward through the Colorado Plateau's geologic
layercake. As magma forced its way upward, it bent back the overlying sedimentary layers like opening a trap door. Away from the center
of the main intrusion, the magma squeezed out laterally forming

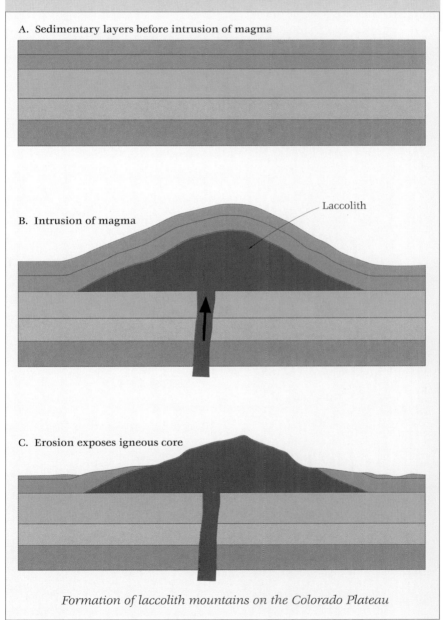

A. Sedimentary layers before intrusion of magma

B. Intrusion of magma

Laccolith

C. Erosion exposes igneous core

Formation of laccolith mountains on the Colorado Plateau

sills of igneous rock between the once flat-lying sedimentary layers.

Over time, the magma pooled below the surface, hardening into mushroom-shaped intrusions of the crystalline rock diorite. This process happened over and over in a series of multiple intrusions. Like giant pistons, each younger intrusion pushed the older intrusions upward, forming giant blisters in the landscape above. Some of the rock was pushed upwards almost 2 miles by the magma thrusting from below.

Recent studies generally confirm Gilbert's groundbreaking ideas about the origins of laccoliths, although slight modifications have been suggested. Modern techniques date this action to Oligocene time, between about 31 and 20 million years ago.

As the Colorado Plateau has been uplifted over the last 10 million years, erosion has gradually worn away the overlying dome of softer sedimentary strata that encased the laccoliths, exposing the igneous rocks that core the intrusions. It is the hard internal cores of these laccoliths that stand tall above the landscape today.

HONAKER TRAIL

Entrenched Meanders of the San Juan River

Hike down the Honaker Trail to the San Juan River and discover fossils with every step.

DISTANCE ■ 5 miles round trip

ELEVATION ■ 5160 to 4150 feet

DIFFICULTY ■ Strenuous

TOPOGRAPHIC MAP ■ USGS The Goosenecks, UT; Trails Illustrated #706

GEOLOGIC MAP ■ 11

KEY REFERENCE ■ 14

PRECAUTIONS ■ This is a rugged hike and not for the faint of heart. Be sure to carry plenty of water and watch every step. A high-clearance vehicle is recommended for driving to the trailhead.

FOR INFORMATION ■ San Juan Resource Area

About the Landscape: The goosenecks of the San Juan River are a series of entrenched meanders featured in many geology textbooks. Here, downcutting by the river has dissected the crest of the Monument Uplift, a broad dome that buckled during the Laramide orogeny some 65 million years ago.

As the Colorado Plateau has uplifted slowly over the last 10 million years, the San Juan River has tirelessly deepened its channel, originally establishing its lazy meandering pattern while cutting through softer Mesozoic sandstone layers. Already set in its ways, the river continued to chisel its way deeper and deeper into the older, more resistant Paleozoic limestone layers below.

Revealed today in the layered canyon walls are the 300 million-year-old rocks of Pennsylvanian age, some of the oldest sedimentary rocks found anywhere in southern Utah's slickrock country. These rocks were deposited in the Paradox Basin, a deep sag or *downwarp* that developed along the front of the Uncompahgre Uplift during uplift of the Ancestral Rocky Mountains.

Situated near Utah's Goosenecks State Park, Honaker Trail is a famous Colorado Plateau locality for geologists. It was along this historic trail that some of the early detailed studies were done on Pennsylvanian-age limestone rocks. From this work, the trail became known as the "type locality" for the Honaker Trail Formation, and it is also the most accessible place to study the famous Ismay, Desert Creek, Akah, and Barker Creek limestone cycles found in the underlying Paradox Formation. Geologists are interested in these rocks because they produce prolific amounts of oil in the giant Aneth field east of Bluff, Utah. Even today geologists still flock here; don't be surprised if you run into some of them during your hike.

Trail Guide: To reach the trailhead for the Honaker Trail, drive 4 miles north from the small town of Mexican Hat on U.S. Highway 163 and turn left onto Utah State Route 261. Drive 1 mile and turn left again at the sign for Goosenecks State Park onto SR 316. After 0.5 mile, turn right onto a graded dirt road (San Juan County Road 244) and drive for 2.2 miles to another dirt road on the left marked by a water tank and a low, rusting metal sign that says "Honaker." From this point, follow the sandy two-track road 1.4 miles to the canyon rim.

At the rim bear left and drive 0.25 mile, looking for a faint road off to the right that leads about another 0.25 mile down to a lower rim where the trailhead is located. A tall rock cairn marks the trailhead.

Standing at the trailhead you can see the tops of the buttes of Monument Valley peeking out across the river to the south. Cedar Mesa looms on the skyline to the north. All these Permian red rock layers have been stripped back by erosion across the Monument Uplift. The Honaker Trail was constructed in 1893 as a supply route down to the river for gold prospectors. Although the route proved too rugged for pack animals and the gold rush was short-lived, the trail has endured the test of time.

The trail begins by stepping down through a gray limestone ledge near the top of the Honaker Trail Formation. Just below the rim is the number 147 painted in yellow on the cliff left of the trail. You will see yellow numbers on rocks here and there all the way down to the river. Geologists painted these numbers, unsightly as they are, in preparation for a major field symposium conducted along the Honaker Trail in 1952. Over time, some of the numbers have worn off. Those that remain have become part of the folklore of Colorado Plateau geology and are useful points of reference.

This first ledge is composed of limestone chock-full of fossil marine organisms that lived in a shallow sea about 300 million years ago during Pennsylvanian time. A close look at the rock reveals tiny disc-shaped fossils called crinoids and an assortment of other shell fragments. The slanting lines weathering out along the face of the rock are cross-beds, which represent the inclined faces of submerged dune forms washed by currents moving fossil fragments along the sea floor.

Below the rim the trail makes a series of long switchbacks. Pennsylvanian-age rocks are known for their *cyclic* sequences, which leave alternating layers such as those seen here along the Honaker Trail. As you descend, notice that the Honaker Trail Formation is composed of a series of hard gray limestone ledges, which alternate with softer slope-forming layers of red siltstone and sandstone. This relationship is more clearly seen looking laterally along the canyon wall. These cycles were related to the advance and retreat of ancient sea levels, which geologists attribute to the waxing and waning of glaciers in the polar regions during this time.

As you continue down the trail, look closely at any of the gray rocks scattered along the trail and notice they are full of fossils. In particular, look for a gray limestone ledge marked 130 and study the rock up-close with your hand lens. The rock is packed together with fossil fragments.

As the trail contours below layer 130, notice the red, irregular nodules of chert exposed along the base of the cliff. *Chert* is a micro-crystalline variety of the mineral quartz. The red color is caused by minute amounts of iron trapped within the quartz. Red chert is also called jasper. In some of the fallen blocks below the cliff, look for fossils that themselves have been replaced by the chert. The fossils are mostly *brachiopods*, shelled organisms that lived on the sea floor. Also exposed in some of the fallen rocks are branching trails and burrows of worm-like animals that lived in the sea floor. These remnants are called *trace fossils* because only traces were left behind, not the hard parts of the animal body like a true fossil.

The trail continues winding down through more limestone ledges. At about the 1-mile point, the trail meets the top of the Paradox Formation. The Paradox Formation is Middle Pennsylvanian in age and famous for its oil-bearing zones called *cycles* or *stages*. In descending order these are

the Ismay, Desert Creek, Akah, and Barker Creek cycles. These cycles were deposited in the Paradox Basin as worldwide sea levels fluctuated in response to glacial intervals. In the center of the Paradox Basin, the Paradox Formation is a thick sequence of *evaporite* minerals (like salt and gypsum) crystallized out of super-salty seawater trapped in the basin. At the same time, the limestone cycles of the Paradox Formation formed in shallow-water environments that rimmed the edge of the basin.

The top of the Ismay cycle is another gray limestone ledge like that in the Honaker Trail Formation above. Although there is a limestone ledge marked "Ismayand" in big yellow letters and the number 102, this is reportedly incorrect. The actual top of the Ismay is unmarked and located in the stepped ledges below.

Below the false top of the Ismay, a series of switchbacks leads down to a prominent point of rock called The Horn at about the 1.5-mile point. The Horn is in the lower part of the Ismay cycle. Look under your feet. You cannot take a step without stepping on fossil brachiopods that litter the surface. There are spectacular views from The Horn looking both up and down river.

Continuing below The Horn to the river is not for the faint of heart. The trail immediately cuts steeply down through a crack in a thick ledge of dark gray limestone (layers 82–79). The boundary with the next cycle, the Desert Creek, occurs at the top of the next switchback marked 74, where there is an obvious horizon of black chert. The trail switchbacks steeply through cliffs and ledges of the Desert Creek to the top of the Akah cycle, which lies below another darker horizon of chert at the base of layer 68.

From this point, the trail contours along a ledge following the black chert bed. In places you can see layers of black shale along the trail. This is the Chimney Rock Shale, which marks the boundary between the Desert Creek and Akah cycles. This organic-rich rock is one of the source-rocks for oil in the Paradox Formation. If you break this rock open it smells like crude oil.

Finally, after following the ledge at the top of the Akah cycle for about 0.5 mile, the trail switches back and cuts down steeply through ledges of Akah limestone. The trail contours again along another ledge (below 36) until it ultimately winds down steeply to river level. The lowermost ledges are in the Barker Creek cycle (17 and below), the oldest cycle of the Paradox Formation.

Along the river, a confusing network of trails worn by river rafters leads back and forth along the riverbank. It's time to soak your feet in the river! Once you are revived, follow your footsteps back up through the cyclic layers to the canyon's rim.

Pennsylvanian limestones in the Paradox Formation are exposed along the San Juan River.

TWIN TOWERS

STONE RUINS IN HOVENWEEP NATIONAL MONUMENT

The Cretaceous Dakota Sandstone caps a cliff-edged canyon sheltering the remains of structures built by Ancestral Pueblo peoples.

DISTANCE ■ **2-mile loop**

ELEVATION ■ **5200 to 5150 feet**

DIFFICULTY ■ **Easy**

TOPOGRAPHIC MAP ■ **USGS Ruin Point, UT**

GEOLOGIC MAP ■ **11**

KEY REFERENCE ■ **15**

PRECAUTIONS ■ **All archaeological sites are protected by law, so please remain on the established trails and leave all artifacts in place. Avoid the heat of summer and beware of afternoon thunder and lightning storms.**

FOR INFORMATION ■ **Hovenweep National Monument**

About the Landscape: Lying astride a remote area along the Colorado–Utah border, Hovenweep National Monument harbors the remains of a unique cluster of round, square, and D-shaped towers of stone. This area was inhabited by peoples of the Ancestral Puebloan culture more than 500 years ago. The ruins are located within the upper reaches of Little Ruin Canyon, which is part of a network of shallow canyons that dissect Cajon Mesa.

Constructed on, within, and around ledges and boulders of sandstone, the ruins at Hovenweep (a Paiute/Ute word meaning "deserted valley") are unique among archaeological sites in the Southwest. As with all cliff dwelling sites, they are constructed of local materials, in this case rocks from the Cretaceous Dakota Sandstone. These structures, which have been stabilized but not rebuilt, have stood the test of time and are the main attraction for exploring the Dakota Sandstone one of the most widespread of all the sedimentary layers on the Colorado Plateau. The Dakota Sandstone marks the westward advance of the Cretaceous seaway about 100 million years ago, and today it forms the resistant cap rock on many of the mesas and plateaus in the region.

The Twin Towers Trail follows along the rim of Little Ruin Canyon where the stone ruins are located, then winds down through the cliffs, crosses the canyon bottom, and climbs back to the rim to complete the loop. Along the way, observe a variety of sedimentary rocks from sandstone and conglomerate to shale and coal.

Trail Guide: Not so long ago, the roads to Hovenweep were dirt and gravel, and dusty—making getting there a real adventure. Today, the route is paved and signs point the way.

To reach Hovenweep from Utah on U.S. Highway 191, travel east on Highway 262 about 8.8 miles and turn left onto San Juan County Road 414. Drive 16.5 miles, bearing right at Hatch Trading Post, and then turn left again onto San Juan County Road 413. Drive another 6.2 miles to Hovenweep National Monument and turn right.

From Colorado along Highway 160/666, 3 miles south of Cortez, follow the McElmo Canyon Road east into Utah. About 3.5 miles past the Ismay Trading Post, turn right onto San Juan County Road 401. After 3.7 miles, turn right again onto San Juan County Road 413 and continue 6.2 miles to the monument entrance on the right.

There are two places to begin the Twin Towers Trail: at the ranger station and at the campground. Although it makes no difference where you start, this description begins from the campground.

The trail from the campground begins opposite the interpretive kiosk, then follows west along the canyon rim. Note the huge boulders of Dakota Sandstone that have broken away from the cliff, exposing cross-beds along their sides. Cross-beds are also exposed on the slickrock surface underfoot as swooping lines like furrows in the rock. That the cross-beds change direction and are at angles to one another suggests they formed along

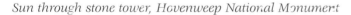

Sun through stone tower, Hovenweep National Monument

beaches and sandbars in a coastal marine environment where the strength and direction of currents changed often. The sands that would become the Dakota Sandstone shifted with tides, waves, and currents during the advance of the Cretaceous seaway across the Colorado Plateau region.

At the intersection with the trail from the canyon bottom, continue straight ahead following the canyon rim. Soon, the first ruins come into view. At Stronghold House Ruin, the Twin Towers Trail crosses the paved trail from the visitor center on the right. The trail continues along the canyon rim, passing numerous other ruins, perhaps the most impressive being Hovenweep Castle. Dominating the horizon to the southeast is Sleeping Ute Mountain. Like other mountains that punctuate the Colorado Plateau landscape, Sleeping Ute Mountain is a unique intrusion of igneous rock called a laccolith that domed the overlying sedimentary layers upward. Erosion has now stripped back the sedimentary rock, exposing the resistant igneous core.

After the trail rounds the head of Little Ruin Canyon, and about 0.25 mile past the Twin Towers on the south side of the canyon, the trail cuts down through the cliff, crosses the canyon bottom, then climbs back to the rim on the north side of the canyon.

As the trail descends through the layers of Dakota Sandstone, take a close look at the coarse-grained nature of the sand grains and the pebble layers deposited within this shoreline sequence. Geologists read these clues as evidence of deposition by water in a high-energy environment such as a stream or tidal channel affected by changing currents.

As the trail climbs out of the canyon bottom, the first rocks along the way are massive ledges and boulders of conglomerate in the Burro Canyon Formation. This mix of rock types was deposited in a river system. Note the crude cross-beds formed by some of the pebble layers, indicating currents strong enough to form sand and gravel bars in an ancient river channel. The roundness (as opposed to angular shapes) of the clasts indicate that they were transported a long distance. The source of this sediment was a mountain range rising to the west, called the Sevier Highlands. The Burro Canyon Formation lies directly below the Dakota Sandstone, along an unconformity where considerable erosion took place prior to the advance of the Cretaceous seaway about 100 million years ago.

As the trail continues to climb to the canyon rim, it crosses a slope of dark gray shale covered with large boulders of Dakota Sandstone. This organic-rich shale and the thin beds of coal represent plant material that accumulated in swampy, backwater environments along the ancient coastline.

Once back on top of the canyon rim, you have come full circle. Turn right to return to the campground, or head left to reach the visitor center.

NATURAL BRIDGES

The Bridges of White Canyon

Hike through a canyon oasis and view three impressive natural bridges hewn from the Cedar Mesa Sandstone.

DISTANCE ■ 8.6-mile loop (or 6.25 miles one way with shuttle)

ELEVATION ■ 6200 to 5850 feet

DIFFICULTY ■ Moderate

TOPOGRAPHIC MAP ■ USGS Moss Back Butte, UT; Trails Illustrated #703

GEOLOGIC MAPS ■ 11, 12

KEY REFERENCE ■ 16

PRECAUTIONS ■ This is a long, hot hike during summer, despite shade trees and seasonal pools of water. Get an early start or, better yet, save this hike for spring or fall. The canyons are prone to flash floods—avoid this hike when thunderstorms are expected. The first part of the hike climbs down well-placed ladders into the canyon bottom. Remember that all archeological sites are fragile and protected by law. There is no backcountry camping permitted along the trail.

FOR INFORMATION ■ Natural Bridges National Monument

About the Landscape: Often overlooked by travelers on their way to somewhere else, Natural Bridges National Monument is one of the jewels in Utah's canyon country. Here, hidden in White Canyon and its tributary, Armstrong Canyon, are three spectacular natural bridges—Sipapu, Kachina, and Owachomo. Sculpted from the Permian Cedar Mesa Sandstone, each span of rock illustrates a different stage of bridge development.

This pleasant hike below the canyon rim threads its way under all three bridges. Cliff dwellings built on ledges and pictographs painted on the canyon walls by Ancestral Puebloan peoples add further intrigue.

Trail Guide: The hike begins at the Sipapu Bridge trailhead in Natural Bridges National Monument. The monument is located about 40 miles west of Blanding, Utah, or 95 miles east of Hanksville, Utah, along State Route 95. At the sign for Natural Bridges National Monument, turn onto SR 275 and drive 4.7 miles to the visitor center. Then continue on Bridges View Drive for another 2.6 miles to the Sipapu Bridge Trailhead.

From the parking area, the Sipapu Bridge Trail winds down from the canyon rim through white sandstone with prominent cross-beds. White Canyon is carved through the Cedar Mesa Sandstone, a thick pile of sand that accumulated along the shores of an ancient sea about 270 million years ago during the Permian.

131

Sipapu Natural Bridge is carved in the Permian Cedar Mesa Sandstone.

Unlike the more familiar and widespread Navajo Sandstone, which is Jurassic in age and much younger, Cedar Mesa Sandstone is found only locally on the Colorado Plateau. It stretches from its namesake, Cedar Mesa, north into the Canyonlands region around Moab. And make no mistake—the buttes of Monument Valley are in the De Chelly Sandstone (also younger but still Permian), not in the Cedar Mesa Sandstone.

Geologists debated for decades the source of the sand in the Cedar Mesa, and whether it was blown into dunes by the wind or washed along the coast by tides and currents. Certainly the large-scale cross-beds and uniform, fine grain size along the trail just below the rim suggest a wind-blown origin. These slanting lines in the rock formed along the face of a tall dune that was advancing downwind. Indeed, most geologists now agree that the Cedar Mesa Sandstone is predominantly a wind-blown deposit.

The Cedar Mesa is equivalent in age to the Cutler Formation stream sediments washed from the Uncompahgre Highland to the east. But Cutler sediments are feldspar-rich arkose deposits, and Cedar Mesa Sandstone contains only very little feldspar. Apparently, much of the feldspar had weathered away by the time the sand got this far downstream.

Below the first switchback and the large cross-beds, the trail follows along a ledge before stepping down a well-constructed metal staircase. Notice the red siltstone to the left of the trail, which has weathered out to form this ledge. Many of the localized springs or seeps in the canyon occur along these layers because the water percolating down through the more porous white sandstone can't infiltrate the less permeable red siltstone layers.

From the base of the metal staircase, the trail follows the ledge to a wooden ladder and another ledge below. In the rock steps below the ladder, look for a red slab of siltstone with well-preserved ripple marks on the surface.

The trail follows this next ledge for several hundred yards, passing a large overhang or alcove. Notice that the walls are streaked with mineral stains called desert varnish.

About 0.25 mile from the trailhead, a ledge widens out and there is an excellent view of Sipapu Bridge. The largest of the three natural bridges you will see on this hike, Sipapu Bridge rises 220 feet above the canyon bottom and spans 268 feet. Notice the abandoned canyon that winds up and to the right of the bridge. This is the old meander channel where water flowed before the stream bored its way through the wall of sandstone to form the bridge, altering the course of the stream.

A series of metal railings and two more wooden ladders take you down to the canyon floor. A trail register is located in the cool, shady bottom directly under the bridge, and a wooden sign points left to Kachina Bridge.

The trail from Sipapu Bridge to Kachina Bridge follows the canyon bottom downstream for 2.3 miles. Depending on the time of year and how recently it has rained, there may or may not be pools of water in the streambed. The well-worn trail crosses back and forth over the channel, but mostly follows along the bank. Where the trail forks, take the "high road," but all trails seem to merge again anyway. If you get led astray, be sure to retrace your steps and follow another track.

Along the way, look for evidence of high water, such as debris wrapped around trees above the riverbank, and think about the walls of water that have cascaded down the canyon during flash floods. You may even see chunks of petrified wood carried downstream from the younger, Mesozoic Chinle Formation exposed in the cliffs above White Canyon.

About 1 mile downstream from Sipapu Bridge, just upstream of the junction with Deer Canyon entering from the right, look for hand pictographs under a large alcove to the right of the trail. Downstream of the Deer Canyon junction, Horse Collar ruins are located on a ledge across the wash to the right. The Ancestral Puebloan people utilized a natural bench eroded along one of the red rock layers as a safe place to build their dwellings and small storage structures (granaries).

House-size boulders and large cottonwood trees shading pools of water make the approach to Kachina Bridge particularly picturesque. With its blocky appearance and impressively thick rock span, Kachina Bridge is considered the youngest of the three natural bridges. Its size is deceptive— the bridge is 210 feet high and 204 feet across. Notice that the stream channel is still working to undercut its base on either side of the channel. Erosion along the prominent red rock layer just above the canyon floor will also help to widen the bridge.

Kachina Bridge is located at the confluence of White Canyon and Armstrong Canyon, which comes in from the left. The trail passes directly beneath the bridge and then bears left upstream into Armstrong Canyon to the Kachina Bridge Trail, which climbs out of the canyon bottom. Look for a trail marker on the left bank of the wash. If you miss it, the trail dead-ends at a high ledge that spans the canyon a few hundred yards upstream.

After climbing steeply above the canyon bottom on the Kachina Bridge Trail, the trail to Owachomo Bridge is marked by a sign pointing to the right. To the left, the trail climbs out of the canyon to the Kachina Bridge trailhead. From the sign, the trail winds down to a slickrock ledge, then continues upstream in Armstrong Canyon for about 3 miles to Owachomo Bridge.

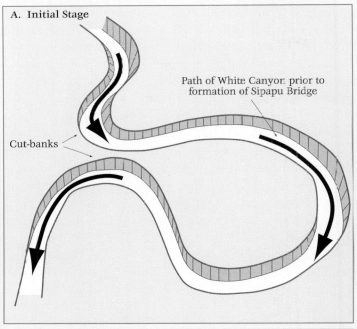

A. Initial Stage

Path of White Canyon prior to formation of Sipapu Bridge

Cut-banks

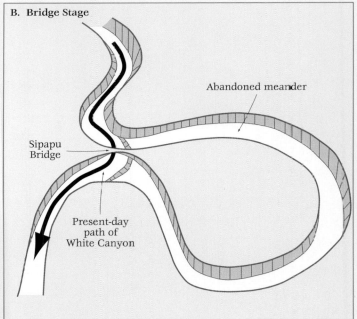

B. Bridge Stage

Abandoned meander

Sipapu Bridge

Present-day path of White Canyon

Sipapu Bridge evolution

As you pass the pour-over, notice the impressive potholes carved by swirling boulders during flash floods.

Beyond the ledge, the trail to Owachomo Bridge follows the canyon bottom until the last mile before the bridge. At this point the trail climbs the left bank, then levels out along another wide ledge. A trail sign with an arrow marks the point where the route leaves the stream.

And finally, just when you begin wondering if there really is a third bridge, Owachomo Bridge comes into view. This delicate natural rock structure is 106 feet high and spans 180 feet across the canyon, and appears as though it could collapse at any minute. In fact, the bridge is only 9 feet thick at its thinnest point. It's interesting to note that in contrast to the other two bridges, Owachomo Bridge was not carved by a major drainage but by a small side stream draining into Armstrong Canyon from the left.

The trail up to the canyon rim passes under Owachomo Bridge, then climbs up to the left. Once at the rim, it's another 2.1 miles via the Mesa Trail to complete the loop back to your vehicle parked at the Sipapu Bridge trailhead. But your feet will be happy if you had thought ahead and arranged to leave a shuttle vehicle at the Owachomo Bridge overlook parking area.

NATURAL BRIDGES—HOW THEY FORM

In contrast to natural arches, which form by frost action and erosion by moisture and wind, natural bridges are formed by the action of running water.

A *natural bridge* is formed as a stream undercuts the neck of a large bend or meander along its course. Armed with tons of grit (i.e., sand, silt, and boulders), the stream continues its work undermining the canyon wall. Over time the river breaks through the canyon wall, creating a "shortcut" downstream and abandoning the old meander loop, leaving it high and dry. Slowly, with the help of continued undercutting by the stream and erosion by moisture from within the rock, the opening in the canyon wall is enlarged, and a bridge is formed.

But as with arches, natural bridges are only temporary features of the landscape. Ultimately, gravity wins the battle. In what must be a thunderous and catastrophic event, the bridge will one day come crashing down under its own weight. Hopefully this will not happen when you are walking underneath!

FISHER TOWERS

RED ROCK TOWERS OF CONGLOMERATE

Hike among sediments in the Permian Cutler Formation shed from the Ancestral Rocky Mountains.

DISTANCE ▪ 4.4 miles round trip

ELEVATION ▪ 4720 to 5400 feet

DIFFICULTY ▪ Moderate

GEOLOGIC MAP ▪ USGS Fisher Towers, UT

GEOLOGIC MAP ▪ 13

KEY REFERENCE ▪ None

PRECAUTIONS ▪ Look for rock cairns that mark the main trail. Watch for falling rocks if climbers are above you.

FOR INFORMATION ▪ Moab District Office

About the Landscape: In a region dominated by such marquee destinations as Arches and Canyonlands National Parks, Fisher Towers are known mostly by rock climbers and Hollywood producers. Indeed, more than two dozen westerns have featured these red rock pinnacles as a scenic backdrop, and climbers flock here on weekends to test their skill on the crumbling spires of sedimentary rock.

Fisher Towers are located along the Colorado River northeast of Moab, Utah. These artistically sculpted spires, pinnacles, and balanced rocks are carved from sandstone, shale, and conglomerate in the Permian Cutler Formation. This thick pile of sediment was shed from the Ancestral Rocky Mountains into the Paradox Basin that flanked the Uncompahgre Highland more than 300 million years ago.

The Fisher Towers Trail winds along the base of these towering rock sculptures, culminating with a panoramic view of Castle Valley and the Colorado River.

Trail Guide: To reach the Fisher Towers trailhead, drive 2 miles north from Moab, Utah, on U.S. Highway 191 to the intersection with Utah State Route 128. Turn right and follow this winding road along the Colorado River 21 miles to the signed turn for Fisher Towers. The trailhead is located at the parking area above the campground at the end of this 2.2-mile-long dirt road.

From the trail register, the well-worn trail steps gently down from the parking area and begins its sinuous route along the base of the intricately carved towers that dominate the skyline. The rocks underfoot are in the Permian Cutler Formation.

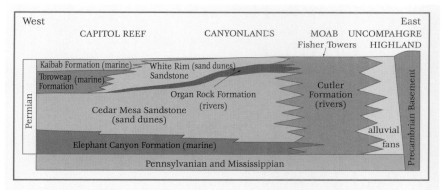

Permian-age rock layers in Utah's slickrock country

This thick sequence of colorful sedimentary rock was shed from the Uncompahgre Highland, the western range of the Ancestral Rocky Mountains which began to vault skyward more than 300 million years ago. The Paradox Basin adjacent to the rising mountains sagged, creating a deep, down-faulted trough which became the dumping ground for huge fan-shaped piles of sediment—called *alluvial fans*—where the Cutler layers accumulated.

Within the red and purple outcrops along the trail are marble, baseball, and even bowling ball–size rounded rocks embedded in the sandstone and conglomerate layers of the Cutler Formation. These rock fragments were derived from Precambrian metamorphic and granitic basement rocks that formed the core of the Uncompahgre Highland to the east. This coarse-grained sediment was washed from the mountains by raging rivers, resulting in sedimentary rock called arkose because of its dominant feldspar content.

As the trail winds around the base of the towers, it climbs over slickrock ledges and crosses narrow side canyons. Well-positioned rock cairns mark the route ahead of you. At one point, you will use a short metal ladder (not to worry) to scale a rock ledge otherwise difficult to negotiate. Along the way, the views looking up at the towers are breathtaking. It is like walking through a series of red rock cathedrals whose walls are fluted with pipe organs reaching skyward.

Just over 1 mile from the trailhead (about halfway to the overlook at the end of the trail), there is an area where boulders stand on raised-rock pedestals. Here, large sandstone boulders from the Triassic Moenkopi Formation (the rock layer directly above the Cutler Formation) have fallen from the cliffs above. Over time, erosion has removed the softer Cutler layers from around the boulders—which are harder and more resistant to erosion. Meanwhile, the boulders have protected the rocks directly under-neath, resulting in boulders raised on their own pedestals. In a similar way, the Moenkopi Formation, which caps the uppermost portion of some of Fisher Towers, may have played an important role in the creation of the towers by being a resistant cap rock, allowing erosion to work its magic carving the magnificent steep-walled spires and pinnacles below.

The last 0.25 mile of the trail traverses a gentle gradient over slickrock, then switchbacks steeply up to a divide. From this vantage point, you have a panoramic view looking back down the trail (north) at Fisher Towers, as well as into Onion Creek ahead (south). For an even better view, fol-low the trail along the ridge to the right (west) to where it emerges along a rocky promontory. Before you lie great views of Castle Valley to the west and the Colorado River to the north.

After lingering for awhile and marveling at the rock formations, follow the same route back to the parking area. Watch carefully for the cairns that mark the main trail.

Fisher Towers are part of the eroded remains of the Ancestral Rocky Mountains.

DELICATE ARCH

SANDSTONE ICON IN ARCHES NATIONAL PARK

Hike to the geologic shrine of Delicate Arch for sunset.

DISTANCE ■ **3 miles round trip**

ELEVATION ■ **4300 to 4780 feet**

DIFFICULTY ■ **Strenuous**

TOPOGRAPHIC MAPS ■ **USGS The Windows Section and Big Bend, UT; Trails Illustrated #211**

GEOLOGIC MAP ■ **14**

KEY REFERENCE ■ **17**

PRECAUTIONS ■ **Avoid this hike in the midday heat during the summer months (there is no shade). The last 200 yards of the trail traverses a narrow rock ledge. Use caution when scrambling along the steep slickrock at the arch viewpoint. Delicate Arch and the trail to it are not the places to be during a thunderstorm.**

FOR INFORMATION ■ **Arches National Park**

About the Landscape: The short but strenuous hike to Delicate Arch in Arches National Park leads to one the most photographed spots on the Colorado Plateau. Delicate Arch is Utah's trademark, appearing on the state's license plates and road sign logos. But despite its popularity and crowds during the high season, witnessing the sunset here is not to be missed. The suspense builds during the hike because Delicate Arch does not come into view until the very end of the hike.

Delicate Arch could just as easily have been called "Perfect Arch." It is a freestanding sandstone sculpture clinging precariously to the sloping lip of a large stone amphitheater. Like other arches in the park, Delicate Arch is constructed in the colorful wind-blown layers of the Jurassic Entrada Sandstone. But unlike other arches, Delicate Arch stands alone, with no flanking sandstone fins remaining to protect it.

Situated high above Cache Valley—a collapsed salt anticline—and set against the perfect background of the La Sal Mountains—a laccolith—the view from Delicate Arch is a shrine for geologists and photographers alike.

Trail Guide: The trail to Delicate Arch departs from the Wolfe Ranch parking area in Arches National Park. To reach the entrance of Arches National Park, drive 5 miles north from Moab, Utah, on U.S. Highway 191 and turn right at the signed entrance to the park. From the entrance station and visitor center, follow the park road 11.7 miles and turn right at the sign for Wolfe Ranch and Delicate Arch. Drive 1.2 miles to the parking area on the left.

The first 0.5 mile of the trail is relatively easy, traversing over flat to gently inclined terrain in the Morrison Formation. The Morrison Formation overlies the Entrada Sandstone, the arch-bearing rock layer that forms the sloping ridge on the skyline ahead. The rocks were broken and tilted by down-faulting along the margin of Cache Creek Valley, a graben that formed when the Cache Creek salt anticline collapsed.

Only 50 yards from the parking area the trail passes the historic Wolfe Ranch cabin on the left. The trail then crosses a bridge over Salt Wash. An outcrop of sandstone and conglomerate located left of the trail just before the bridge was deposited as sand and gravel in an ancient Morrison stream channel about 150 million years ago during the Jurassic. The pastel-colored green and purple shale in the slope on the right after the bridge represents mud that accumulated in the floodplain adjacent to the Morrison streams. The Morrison Formation is famous for dinosaur bones; some are found not far from here in Rabbit Valley near the Utah–Colorado border.

Beyond the bridge, at about the 0.25-mile point, the trail makes a switchback up through the sandstone and shale layers in the Morrison, then levels out before it winds down again. The large, irregular boulders

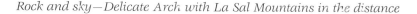

Rock and sky—Delicate Arch with La Sal Mountains in the distance

along the trail are blocks of chert, a micro-crystalline variety of the mineral quartz, formed as silica-rich waters derived from volcanic ash permeated a rock layer. These colorful rocks, also called *agate* where brightly colored (look closely for red and yellow), are weathering out of conglomerate layers in the Morrison Formation.

As you leave the chert boulders behind, the trail begins its steep climb up a slickrock surface in the Entrada Sandstone. For about the next 0.5 mile, rock cairns mark the route. As you stop to catch your breath, take in the great views of Cache Valley to the south. The steep red rock cliffs across the valley are in the massive Wingate Sandstone, the lowestmost Jurassic wind-blown sandstone layer on the Colorado Plateau. The red slope along the base of the cliff is in the Triassic Chinle Formation. Notice the soft, hummocky gray-yellow hills in the center of the valley. These are marine rocks of the Cretaceous Mancos Shale that were down-dropped about 2500 feet when the Cache Valley salt anticline collapsed. Peeking above the cliffs on the skyline is the first glimpse of the La Sal Mountains.

After the steep climb, the trail eventually levels out where it crosses sand and rock of the ancient Entrada sand dunes. This section of trail either passes cross-beds exposed in sandstone pedestals or steps on cross-bedded surfaces underfoot. These intricate patterns preserved in the rocks are the products of winds that blew about 160 million years ago during the Jurassic. This sandstone "garden" is decorated with twisting trunks of piñon pine and juniper trees.

You are closing in on the Delicate Arch viewpoint when the trail begins its traverse along a narrow rock ledge (sounds worse than it is). Ultimately, the trail ends at the top of the ridge as Delicate Arch finally comes into view.

The geologic vista before you could not be more dramatic. Delicate Arch artistically frames the symmetrical peaks of the La Sal (meaning "the salt" in Spanish) Mountains, a laccolith which formed when magma intruded through the sedimentary layers of the Colorado Plateau between 25 and 28 million years ago. As the Colorado Plateau has slowly uplifted over the last 10 million years, these resistant igneous rocks have been revealed by erosion as the overlying sedimentary strata have worn away.

Delicate Arch is a miracle of erosion. It originally formed in a continuous sandstone fin. Gradually over time, the sandstone on either side fell away until only the arch remained. Today, only the rock layer that caps the arch, which is slightly harder and more resistant to erosion than the layers below, protects the arch from washing away.

But as with all arches, Delicate Arch is only a temporary structure. Note that the left leg of the arch is thinner where it is weathering more rapidly.

As weathering continues, the leg will become thinner and thinner. Ultimately it will break, and the arch will catastrophically collapse.

The wind- and water-sculpted sandstone amphitheater below the arch reveals sweeping cross-beds. During the magic hour before sunset, this scene is baked gold until only the last rays of the setting sun highlight Delicate Arch.

After paying silent homage to this geologic shrine, carefully make your way back to the trailhead. If you have lingered until sunset, as you should, please take extra care negotiating the slickrock in the diminishing twilight.

SALT TECTONICS OF THE COLORADO PLATEAU

Around 300 million years ago during Pennsylvanian time, up to 4000 feet of *salt* (mostly the minerals halite and gypsum) accumulated by the evaporation of seawater in the Paradox Basin, in an area that later became part of the Colorado Plateau. The Paradox Basin was a large basin that formed adjacent to the Uncompahgre Highland, the western range of the Ancestral Rocky Mountains. As the salt deposits were buried by sediments eroded from the rising mountains—called the Cutler Formation—the salt oozed from below, pushing upward on the overlying rock layers and arching them into elongate ridges called *salt anticlines*.

The upward migration of salt continued for perhaps 150 million years, from the late Pennsylvanian to the late Jurassic. This process—called *salt tectonics*—profoundly affected the thickness of many of the overlying sedimentary layers. Many of the Triassic and Jurassic formations thin across the upturned and truncated edges of older formations disrupted by the salt movement. These structural features were later enhanced by compression about 65 million years ago during the Laramide orogeny, which shaped the rock layers into true anticlines and bent the adjacent areas into synclines. Some minor collapse along the crest of the structures occurred when the Laramide "squeeze" ended.

Over the last 10 million years, as the region along with the rest of the Colorado Plateau slowly uplifted, younger sedimentary layers that entombed the salt structures were eroded off the top. As the structures were breached, surface water eventually found its way inside these salt-cored anticlines and dissolved a portion of the salt. This caused major collapse of the salt-cored anticlines along a series of normal faults.

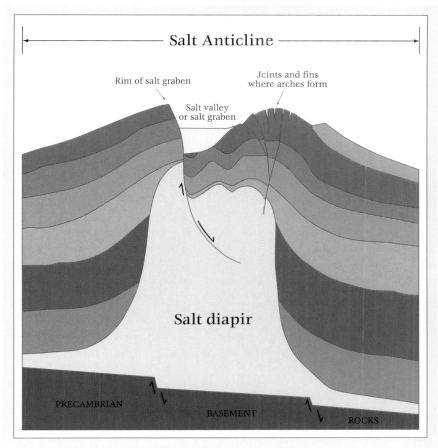

Salt tectonics of the Colorado Plateau

Over time, continued erosion ultimately formed a series of elongated valleys, with the walls of the valleys held up by Triassic and Jurassic sedimentary layers along the upturned limbs of the anticlines. In all, seven major valleys were formed on the Colorado Plateau near the Colorado–Utah border. Today, several of these valleys are cored with gypsum, recognized at the surface in a jumbled heap (the halite having been dissolved). In places, the thickness of the salt from the upward flowage exceeds 10,000 feet.

In Utah, Salt Valley in Arches National Park is a classic salt-cored anticline formed by salt tectonics. In Colorado, the Dolores River flows across two valleys formed by salt tectonics—Gypsum Valley and Paradox Valley—the latter being the largest of the seven salt anticlines formed in this way.

DEVILS GARDEN

STANDING STONES IN ARCHES NATIONAL PARK

Hike among standing walls of stone to view seven natural arches including Landscape Arch, one of the world's longest.

Hike 21

DISTANCE ■ 7.2 miles round trip (includes side trails)

ELEVATION ■ 5180 to 5480 feet

DIFFICULTY ■ Moderate

TOPOGRAPHIC MAPS ■ USGS Mollie Hogans, UT; Trails Illustrated #211

GEOLOGIC MAP ■ 14

KEY REFERENCE ■ 17

PRECAUTIONS ■ Extreme (hot!) temperatures are a real danger during summer months. Carry plenty of water and hike early or late in the day. Use caution when traversing the more difficult slickrock sections of the trail beyond Landscape Arch. Please stay on established trails and follow the rock cairns. Arch formation (and destruction) is an ongoing process—beware of falling rocks.

FOR INFORMATION ■ Arches National Park

About the Landscape: The Devils Garden Trail, the longest maintained trail in Arches National Park, winds through a fanciful landscape of standing stones where a high concentration of natural arches are found in the Jurassic Entrada Sandstone. Hidden in this maze of narrow corridors and canyons between vertical walls of sandstone are the seven arches viewed on this hike—including Landscape Arch, one of the longest arches in the world.

Trail Guide: The Devils Garden trailhead is located at the far end of the paved road in Arches National Park. To reach the entrance of Arches National Park, drive 5 miles north from Moab, Utah, on U.S. Highway 191 and turn right at the signed entrance to the park. From the entrance station and visitor center, follow the park road 18 miles to the trailhead located on the one-way loop at the end of the road (just past the picnic area and entrance to the Devils Garden Campground).

From the parking area, the trail passes through a narrow corridor between towering walls of colorful Entrada Sandstone. The Entrada is a widespread pile of wind-blown sand that accumulated around 160 million years ago during the Jurassic, when Sahara-like dunes swept the Colorado Plateau landscape. On the wall to the right of the trail, notice the cracks cutting vertically through the rock. Called *joints,* these aligned fractures extend through the rock for miles. Over the eons weathering has eroded and

Sandstone fins in the Devils Garden

widened the joints, creating an artistic display of narrow rock slabs, called *fins,* where the arches are found.

At about the 0.25-mile point, an intersection with a side trail to the right leads to Tunnel and Pine Tree Arches, the first arches of the hike. The main trail (heading toward Landscape Arch) climbs gradually toward a rock pinnacle standing in a gap between sandstone fins. Visible on the face of the sandstone fin on the right before the pinnacle are gently sloping layers in the rock, which are highlighted by subtle streaks of gray. These inclined layers are large-scale cross-beds that formed as a giant Entrada sand dune migrated downwind during the Jurassic.

After passing through the gap, the trail climbs a series of constructed steps to reach a crest where you can look back through the gap. Beyond the sandstone fins rise the La Sal Mountains, a massive igneous intrusion or *laccolith* that blistered the sedimentary layers of the Colorado Plateau between 25 and 28 million years ago.

From this point, the trail traverses over the undulating tops of sand dunes to Landscape Arch. Indeed, the very sand that once made up the Entrada Sandstone is being recycled into modern-day dunes. Ahead, the tilt (to the east) of the Entrada Sandstone layers is very noticeable in the dissected fins on the skyline. Devils Garden is located along the tilted northeast flank of Salt Valley, a collapsed salt anticline.

As the trail heads down-slope, Landscape Arch is before you. Sharp eyes can also pick out Partition Arch, the fourth arch of this hike, located high along the same fin to the right.

The best view of Landscape Arch is located about 100 yards beyond the junction with the primitive trail on the right. With a span measured at 306 feet, this masterpiece of erosion appears tenuous, as if it could come crashing down at any moment. At its thinnest point, the ribbon-like expanse of solid rock is a mere 11 feet thick. That the arch remains at all is a miracle in itself—marvel at it while it lasts! As a precaution, the spur trail that climbs under the arch has been closed since 1991, when a 70-foot-long slab of rock fell from above.

Beyond Landscape Arch the trail changes dramatically, becoming more strenuous as it follows through narrow slots in the fins, and climbs up and over the fins themselves another 1.2 miles to Double O Arch. Rock cairns mark the route where the trail crosses slickrock surfaces.

As the sandstone walls close in on either side, the next arch is Wall Arch,

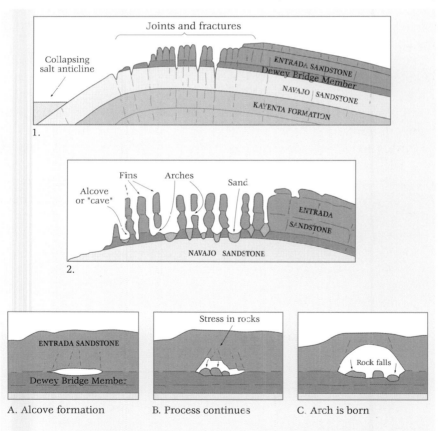

Formation of natural arches in Arches National Park

located on the right less than 0.25 mile from the Landscape Arch viewpoint. The large blocks of rock along the trail have fallen from the arch, leaving no doubt that this window to the sky is actively widening.

Beyond Wall Arch, the trail follows along narrows in the jointed sandstone as it climbs to the intersection with the side trail leading to Partition (0.2 mile) and Navajo (0.3 mile) Arches off to the left (easy and worthwhile side trips if you have time).

From the intersection, the main trail skirts across the tops of sandstone fins and, at one point, actually climbs up on top along a narrow stretch of naked stone. Do not fear, a series of stone steps cut into the rock lead you back down. Be sure to stop and breathe in the dramatic views.

Double O Arch, the seventh and final arch along this hike, is located about 2 miles from the trailhead (without side trips) where the sandstone fins give way to an open area between the next set of standing stones in the distance. Rock cairns lead you carefully down the last slickrock section of the trail. Formed by two arches stacked one on top of another, Double O is now in view in the next sandstone wall to the west. To get to the arch, the trail winds between a number of large boulders.

Although Double O Arch is the destination for this hike, a strenuous primitive trail continues to a standing stone pinnacle called the Dark Angel, then makes a 1-mile loop back to Landscape Arch. This alternate route is for experienced hikers only and should only be attempted with plenty of water.

For the rest of us, carefully follow the same route back to the trailhead.

NATURAL ARCHES—HOW THEY FORM

Natural arches are most common in sedimentary rocks, typically sandstone, which are plentiful on the Colorado Plateau.

Three primary ingredients are required for the formation of *natural arches*—defined as natural openings or rock spans with at least three feet of uninterrupted space through which light can pass.

First, the rocks must erode into narrow vertical walls, or *fins*. Second, the rocks involved must be strong enough to support their own weight if the underlying rocks to the sides are removed. And third, arches typically form where a porous sandstone layer overlies a less permeable shale or siltstone layer. In Arches National Park, the 300-foot-thick Slick Rock Member of the Entrada Sandstone overlying siltstone in the Dewey Bridge Member meets these requirements.

Landscape Arch, one of the longest natural arches in the world

The most important agent in the "carving" of arches is weathering. Weathering works both by chemical processes, such as water seeped into the rock dissolving the natural cement that binds grains of sand together; and by physical processes, such as the freezing and expansion of water in cracks in the rock. Water percolating through the sandstone can't infiltrate the less permeable siltstone below. This helps to weaken the base of the sandstone layer. Other forces—such as gravity, running water, and wind—then work together to dislodge and remove the loosened sand grains and tiny rock fragments. Natural arches are different than natural bridges, which form by the erosion and undercutting of rock walls by flowing streams.

As the process continues over thousands of years, the sandstone fin thins until it finally breaks through. At first, just a small window opens. As the opening slowly enlarges grain by grain and block by block, an arch is created, unique and never to be duplicated.

As you might expect, the same processes that create arches ultimately destroy them. Since 1977 at least five arches in the park have come crashing down. As recently as 1991, a huge slab of rock fell from Landscape Arch. These are good facts to keep in mind when hiking the geology of Arches National Park.

UPHEAVAL DOME

Hike 22

SALT DOME OR METEORITE IMPACT CRATER?

Hike along the upturned rim of Upheaval Dome and ponder its origin.

DISTANCE ■ 2 miles round trip

ELEVATION ■ 5680 to 5800 feet

DIFFICULTY ■ Easy

TOPOGRAPHIC MAPS ■ USGS Upheaval Dome, UT; Trails Illustrated #210

GEOLOGIC MAP ■ 15

KEY REFERENCE ■ 18, 19

PRECAUTIONS ■ This hike can be very hot during the summer months. Use caution when scrambling along the slickrock rim, and beware of afternoon thunderstorms.

FOR INFORMATION ■ Canyonlands National Park

About the Landscape: Upheaval Dome is a huge, gaping hole or *crater* in the Colorado Plateau that has puzzled geologists for generations. Millions of years of erosion have stripped off overlying layers to reveal a circular structure of upturned sedimentary rock layers surrounding a deep, central crater. Triassic and Jurassic sedimentary rocks have weathered in a concentric pattern stepping away from a chaotically arranged inner core that reaches down to the Permian-age rocks.

Upheaval Dome sits atop a high mesa called Island in the Sky within Canyonlands National Park. Island in the Sky is constructed from resistant flat-lying layers of Mesozoic sedimentary rocks that rise 2000 feet above the canyons of the Colorado and Green Rivers. These two great rivers have dissected the Colorado Plateau's "geologic layercake" into a bold landscape of deep canyons, cliff-walled mesas, and artistically sculpted buttes and pinnacles.

But at Upheaval Dome something special has happened to upset the stack. What caused this local disturbance of the otherwise flat or gently folded rock layers? The two most popular—and highly debated—explanations are the "salt dome" and "meteorite impact" theories. The hike provides excellent views into the heart of Upheaval Dome, offering the opportunity to ponder its origin.

Trail Guide: To reach the Upheaval Dome trailhead in Canyonlands National Park, drive 8.5 miles north from Moab, Utah, on U.S. Highway 191 to the turnoff for Canyonlands and Deadhorse Point (State Route 131). Turn left and drive 25 miles to the entrance of Canyonlands National Park.

Follow the park road past the visitor center for 5 miles and turn right at the sign for Upheaval Dome. The trailhead is located at the end of the road 5.3 miles from the turnoff.

The Upheaval Dome Overlook Trail begins by winding through sandstone ledges in the purple and lavender Kayenta Formation on the fringe of Upheaval Dome. About 25 yards from the trailhead, the trail meets the junction with the signed Syncline Loop Trail, which splits off both to the right and left and completely circumnavigates Upheaval Dome. Continue straight ahead on the Overlook Trail.

As the trail climbs up an easy grade, notice that the Kayenta rock ledges are tilted—they slant to the south away from the center of Upheaval Dome. The trail comes to another junction 0.5 mile from the trailhead. Straight ahead is an overlook of Upheaval Dome only 25 yards away. To the left, a 0.5-mile side trail leads along the rim to another overlook offering spectacular views of the deep crater.

At the first overlook, interpretive signs detail the two most popular explanations for the origin of this 2-mile-wide hole in the earth. You are standing on the Wingate Sandstone, a thick pile of wind-blown sand that accumulated about 200 million years ago during the Jurassic. The Wingate, which lies below the stream-deposited Kayenta Formation, forms

Upheaval Dome is thought to be the eroded remains of a meteorite impact feature.

the sandstone rim that nearly encircles the dome. The rim, which is cracked and broken in places by faults and fractures that formed as the rock was bent back to create the dome, is breached on the west side by a canyon that drains all the way to the Green River.

It is well known that a thick layer of salt (evaporated seawater from the 300-million-year-old Paradox Basin) underlies the Canyonlands region of southeastern Utah and southwestern Colorado. Under pressure deep below the surface, this salt has flowed plastically over time, pushing upward on the overlying rock layers and bending them into salt anticlines. Later, these features collapsed where a portion of the salt was dissolved by groundwater—like Salt Valley in Arches National Park nearby.

At Upheaval Dome, geologists speculate that salt flowed upward through the rock layers as a bubble or mushroom-shaped "salt dome," rather than along an elongate structure like a salt anticline. In this case, the salt disrupted a very localized area of the layered rock as it rose vertically—like an air bubble rising through thick molasses. They envision that the present surface of Upheaval Dome is now the pinched-off stem below the long since eroded mushroom of salt. The fundamental problem with this explanation is that there is no evidence that salt ever flowed through the sediments that core the crater.

An alternative explanation, and the one I favor, involves a meteorite impact. In this case, geologists envision that Upheaval Dome is the eroded core of an impact structure that formed when a meteor hit the earth millions of years ago during the Jurassic. Many geologists favor the impact theory since the arrangement of the rocks rimming the crater is similar to proven impact structures (like Arizona's Meteor Crater). Although the exact age of the event has not been determined, we know that it is at least younger than the Navajo Sandstone (which is about 175 million years old), since the Navajo is the youngest formation deformed by the impact. The fundamental problem with the meteorite impact theory is that no fragments of the meteor have been found, presumably removed by erosion long ago. Until a smoking gun is found, a meteorite fragment for example, the origin of Upheaval Dome will continue to be debated.

The trail along the crater rim is certainly worth the time and effort. Well-placed rock cairns lead you along the slickrock rim of Upheaval Dome to where it ends at a precipitous drop-off guarded by a chain-link fence. Here there is a great view into the distorted layers that core the dome. Notice the chaotic arrangement of the colorful rocks eroding in the center of the structure. These include the deformed remains of the Chinle (green and purple shale) and Moenkopi (mostly brown) Formations, which are the much softer shale and siltstone layers that underlie the more resistant

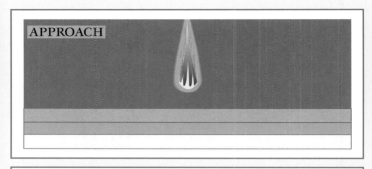

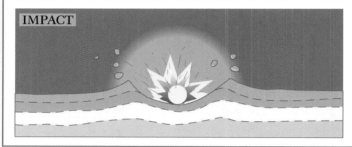

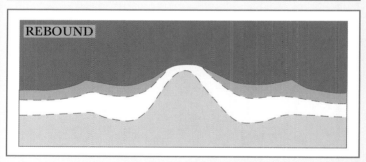

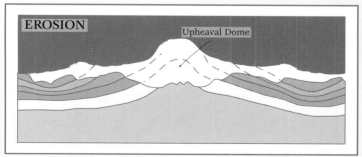

*The "meteorite impact" theory for the origin of
Upheaval Dome, Canyonlands National Park, Utah*

153

Wingate Sandstone along the rim. These once flat-lying Triassic-age layers were disrupted, presumably, by the impact of the meteorite (or alternatively, the upward movement of salt). The light-colored rocks exposed in the crater are bleached and highly contorted Permian-age formations including the White Rim Sandstone and Organ Rock Shale.

Peeking above the east rim of the dome are the highest peaks of the La Sal Mountains. Like other mountain ranges that punctuate the Colorado Plateau landscape, the La Sals are a unique-style intrusion of igneous rock called a laccolith that domed up the overlying sedimentary layers. Erosion has now stripped back the sedimentary rock, exposing the resistant igneous core.

Once you have taken in the drama of the landscape and puzzled about its origin, carefully follow the trail back to the parking area.

LITTLE GRAND CANYON

Hike 23

HEART OF THE SAN RAFAEL SWELL

Hike a remote canyon along the San Rafael River to a small but well-preserved pictograph panel.

DISTANCE ■ **7 miles round trip**

ELEVATION ■ **5150 to 5200 feet**

DIFFICULTY ■ **Moderate**

TOPOGRAPHIC MAP ■ **USGS Bottleneck Peak, UT**

GEOLOGIC MAP ■ **16**

KEY REFERENCE ■ **None**

PRECAUTIONS ■ **Avoid this hike in the heat of summer.**

FOR INFORMATION ■ **San Rafael Resource Area**

About the Landscape: The San Rafael Swell is one of the classic uplifts of the Colorado Plateau. This large dome-like upwarp or *anticline* was formed by compressive forces during the Laramide orogeny about 65 million years ago. Paleozoic rocks that core the structure are exposed in the center of the uplift, where deep erosion has stripped away all the overlying Mesozoic rocks that once arched across the uplift. However, where the familiar Triassic and Jurassic layers still remain, differential erosion has worked its magic, sculpting massive cliffs and rising walls of stone.

The San Rafael River and its tributaries have carved a network of deep canyons across the northern end of the San Rafael Swell, the largest of which has been called by many the "Little Grand Canyon." This hike follows the San Rafael River upstream into the heart of a sandstone wilderness where cliffs of colorful Triassic and Jurassic sedimentary rocks rise steeply above the river.

Trail Guide: If you are looking for a remote hike, this one fits the bill. The trailhead is a long way from the nearest services. Be sure to tank up with gas, food, and water before heading out.

The trailhead can be reached from two directions. Approaching from the south on Interstate 70 between Green River and Salina, take Ranch Exit 129 and drive north on a graded gravel road 19.5 miles to a dirt road on the left. The turn, marked by a sign that reads "Corrals," is 0.4 mile before the bridge over the San Rafael River. Approaching from the north, follow the Buckhorn Wash Road south to the San Rafael River and turn right 0.4 mile after crossing the bridge. Drive 0.9 mile to the trailhead located at the old road (marked by a barricade) left of the corrals.

This hike begins by following an old road to the banks of the San Rafael River. The old road is carved into the soft slopes in the Triassic Moenkopi Formation (pronounced "mo-n-kopi"). Although the Moenkopi is a brick-red color over much of the Colorado Plateau, here the rocks are mostly tan and gray. These thinly bedded layers of shale, siltstone, and sandstone represent sediments that accumulated on an ancient coastal plane or tidal flat bordering a shallow sea that lay to the west more than 225 million years ago. Look for ancient ripple marks in the fallen, flagstone-size blocks of sandstone to the left of the trail. For comparison, look along the riverbank for modern examples of ripple marks.

As the old road continues to follow the river, the canyon opens up with sweeping views upstream. At about the 0.5-mile point you'll see the old remains of a corral against the largest of a number of boulders that have tumbled down from the cliffs on the left side of the trail. These boulders are sandstone of the Moss Back Member of the Chinle Formation, which forms the thick ledge on top of the Moenkopi slopes. The Moss Back Member represents sand and gravel deposited in the channels of ancient Triassic streams. On up the trail you will see that it contains considerable conglomerate and also fossilized logs of petrified wood.

Beyond the Moss Back boulders, the trail leads away from the river as it crosses a flat expanse of bottomland. Look for the remains of an old cabin hidden in the cottonwood trees on the right.

About 1 mile from the trailhead, a sign marks the boundary with a wilderness study area. The trail begins to climb up slopes of the Moenkopi Formation to good views of the river and also of the steep cliffs on the opposite side of the canyon.

This is a good vantage point to pick out the formations that make up the canyon walls. At the base of the cliffs are the now-familiar slopes of the Moenkopi Formation capped by the Moss Back Member of the Chinle Formation. Above the Moss Back cliff are maroon stepped ledges also in the Chinle Formation. The massive shear cliff streaked with desert varnish above the Chinle is the Jurassic Wingate Sandstone, a thick accumulation of wind-blown sand from a time when parched desert conditions swept the Colorado Plateau about 200 million years ago. The layered cliffs above the Wingate are stream-deposited sands in the Kayenta Formation. The canyon walls are capped by the massive cliffs of Jurassic Navajo Sandstone, the most widespread, wind-blown sandstone on the Colorado Plateau.

As the trail follows above the river, the trail is littered with conglomerate boulders from the Moss Back. The trail drops steeply to where it crosses a major wash, and then follows along the bottomland through cottonwood trees. The white crust underfoot is mineral salt that forms as moisture in the soil evaporates.

At about the 2-mile point, the trail once again follows the riverbank with the Moss Back cliff above and to the left. After crossing another wash, look for a large piece (chopping block–size) of petrified wood sitting by itself to the right of the trail. Petrified wood is common in the Chinle

Formation, most notably at Arizona's Petrified Forest National Park. The fossil wood found here was transported in the ancient rivers that deposited the sand and gravel in the Moss Back Member. More fragments of petrified wood are scattered on the ground near the next large Moss Back boulder to the left of the trail. The petrified wood here is black and not as colorful as the specimens at Petrified Forest. (Warning: Much of the petrified wood contains uranium minerals—so don't put a piece in your pocket!)

Little Grand Canyon of the San Rafael Swell

Beyond the petrified wood area, the trail drops down to river level where it soon gets lost in a thicket of tamarisk trees. Continue by following the most well-worn path parallel to the river. The trail emerges from the trees, then winds around a number of large Moss Back boulders, one of which has a small arch worn through it. Here, the river makes a bend to the right (north).

At about the 3-mile point the river turns back to the west and the trail climbs slightly before dropping back down to the river. The Moss Back ledges are now at the level of the river. Note the cross-beds displayed in the cliffs on the left formed by ancient river currents. Ahead, a massive cliff of Wingate Sandstone dominates the horizon. There is a small window through this narrow fin of rock.

After another 0.5 mile, the river makes a sharp bend to the right (north) where a major wash (Cane Wash) comes in on the left. Turn left here and follow the well-worn trail on the left bank to the Moss Back ledge about 50 yards away. Look for the pictographs underneath the overhang. There are also several logs of petrified wood on the ground

Although it is possible to continue exploring this amazing side canyon, the pictographs are the turnaround point for the hike. After enjoying the shade of the overhang, retrace the route downstream and back to the trailhead.

Hike
24

SAN RAFAEL REEF

WORLD OF STANDING STONE

Hike a remote canyon that slices through upturned layers along the east limb of the San Rafael Swell.

DISTANCE ■ 2 miles round trip (about 3.5 miles without a 4WD vehicle)

ELEVATION ■ 4600 to 4720

DIFFICULTY ■ Easy

TOPOGRAPHIC MAP ■ USGS Spotted Wolf Canyon, UT

GEOLOGIC MAP ■ 16

KEY REFERENCE ■ 20

PRECAUTIONS ■ Do not enter old mines, which are dangerous and radioactive. Beware of flash floods.

FOR INFORMATION ■ San Rafael Resource Area

About the Landscape: The rugged and remote San Rafael Swell is a large dome-like upwarp or *anticline* measuring roughly 75 miles long and 30 miles wide. About 65 million years ago, tectonic forces during the Laramide orogeny buckled the Colorado Plateau's originally flat-lying sedimentary

157

layers into this broad fold. The upturned edges or limbs of the San Rafael Swell are not symmetrical. In contrast with its gently inclined western limb, the rocks along the Swell's eastern limb, called the San Rafael Reef, are standing abruptly on end.

This hike explores a remote canyon that slices completely through the San Rafael Reef where the familiar colorful sandstone layers of the Wingate, Kayenta, and Navajo Formations rise to nearly vertical, forming an impressive wall of rock. An old mine tunnel is a reminder of the uranium boom days of the 1950s.

Trail Guide: It is well worth the effort to reach the trailhead of this remote canyon. Although a short, easy hike is described here, there are endless possibilities for longer, more rugged hikes.

The trailhead for this hike is reached by an unmarked dirt road off State Route 24, located about 34.5 miles north of Hanksville, Utah, and 7.8 miles south of Interstate 70. Follow this graded dirt road east for about 6.9 miles (bearing right after 1.9 miles) to a more rugged dirt road on the left. A high-clearance, four-wheel-drive vehicle is recommended for the last 0.7 mile to the trailhead, which is located at the end of the road. Be forewarned that the last 0.25 mile is steep and rocky.

There are great views from the parking area looking along San Rafael Reef, an impressively steep wall of rock stretching as far as the eye can see. From east to west, note the abrupt change in the rocks from horizontal to nearly vertical, then back to horizontal again. This type of fold is called a monocline, and it marks the eastern limb of the San Rafael Swell.

This hike starts out by following an old mining road to the mouth of the canyon. For about 100 yards, the road cuts down through a variety of layers in the Carmel Formation, which is a proverbial grab bag of sedimentary rocks deposited in a variety of nearshore marine and tidal flat environments during the Jurassic. The gray outcrops right of the trail are gypsum layers, which formed by the evaporation of seawater in shallow coastal lagoons. Look to the south across the wash to see how the Carmel layers are tilted steeply against the resistant wall of Navajo Sandstone rising to the sky.

To enter the canyon, climb up the low sandstone ledge on the right. You have entered a world of standing stone. As you walk up the canyon, you are walking backwards through time, from the Jurassic into the Triassic. And, if you choose to continue, you will cross from the Mesozoic into the Paleozoic. But unlike other canyons where great elevation changes occur as you walk back in time, here the rocks are standing on end and you simply walk with little elevation change past each successive layer.

Inside the canyon, towering walls of Navajo Sandstone block out the sun. You may not recognize this familiar wind-blown sandstone as the same

Entrance to old uranium mine, San Rafael Reef

rock that forms towering cliffs in such places as Zion and Capitol Reef National Parks. Here, the Navajo is laced with microfractures and small-scale faults that obscure the formation's characteristic wind-blown cross-beds. Look closely at the rocks to see these small-scale features, called *deformation bands,* that formed in response to the great compressive forces applied to the rocks as they were being bent upright about 65 million years ago during the Laramide orogeny.

Upstream of the sheer walls of Navajo Sandstone, the canyon widens slightly where the layered cliffs of the Kayenta Formation begin. Beyond the Kayenta, the massive Wingate Sandstone towers above the wash, streaked with its characteristic desert varnish. After the Wingate, a dramatic change occurs as you reach the softer, more easily eroded layers of the Chinle Formation that underlies the Wingate. As the canyon walls rapidly recede, look for tilted layers of pastel-colored sandstone, siltstone, and shale.

As you step up, over, and around the boulders that choke the wash, imagine the mighty flash floods that periodically scour the canyon. It took great erosive power to carve this canyon through the sheer walls of rock that make up the San Rafael Reef. And it was the sand and rock underfoot that provided the grit.

As the canyon opens up even more, revealing a hidden valley behind the reef, look on the right for the entrance to an old mine. This uranium mine was dug into stream-deposited sandstone and conglomerate in the

Moss Back Member of the Chinle Formation During the 1950s, the Colorado Plateau was a hotbed of exploration for uranium, spurred in part by government guarantees for the discovery of weapons-grade uranium ore. The bulk of the uranium was found in the ancient streambed sand and gravel of the Chinle and Morrison Formations.

On the skyline to the west are uplifted layers of Paleozoic rocks, including the Permian Black Box Dolomite and White Rim Sandstone. These resistant rock layers, which are equivalent in age to the Kaibab Formation at the Grand Canyon, form the core of the San Rafael Swell where the overlying Mesozoic layers have been stripped away by erosion.

Once you have explored this world of standing stone, return to the trailhead by the route you came.

GOBLIN VALLEY

Hoodoo Playground

No reason to follow a trail here. Let your imagination run wild as you get lost in this bizarre landscape of differential erosion in the Jurassic Entrada Formation.

DISTANCE ■ It's up to you

ELEVATION ■ 4980 to 4920

DIFFICULTY ■ Easy

TOPOGRAPHIC MAP ■ USGS Goblin Valley, UT

GEOLOGIC MAP ■ 16

KEY REFERENCE ■ 21

PRECAUTIONS ■ Don't get lost for too long. Please use care to limit your impact on this fragile area.

FOR INFORMATION ■ Goblin Valley State Park

About the Landscape: Goblin Valley is a strange and wonderful place. Here, water, wind, and time have worked in concert to create an area unlike anywhere else.

This fanciful and bizarre landscape is a masterpiece of differential erosion. Sedimentary layers in the Jurassic Entrada Sandstone accumulated 160 million years ago as local wind-blown sand dunes on a flat coastal plain or tidal flat. The sandstone layers are separated by shale/siltstone layers of tidal-flat origin.

This layering is the perfect setting for weathering and erosion to sculpt hoodoos or *goblins* of all shapes and sizes. The sandstone layers in the Entrada

160

at Goblin Valley are slightly more resistant to erosion than the intervening shale/siltstone layers. Regional fracture patterns help promote goblin formation by providing preferential zones of weakness for erosion to work its magic. Once exposed, weathering attacks and removes angular edges, creating smooth, rounded boulders, a process called *spheroidal weathering.* With time, sandstone cap rocks protect the softer, underlying shale/siltstone beds, creating balanced rocks or "hard hat" pedestals. As with the other red rocks of the Colorado Plateau, the Entrada's reddish hues come mainly from hematite minerals (iron oxide, like rust) that stains the rock.

Goblin Valley is a place of continual change, though at a rate largely slower than human time scale. Old goblins eventually topple over and are destroyed. Look for round boulders lying on the ground next to soft mounds that were once pedestals. Meanwhile, ongoing erosion creates new goblins in their place.

Trail Guide: To reach Goblin Valley State Park, on State Route 24 drive about 17.2 miles north from Hanksville, Utah, or 25 miles south from Interstate 70. Turn at the sign for Goblin Valley State Park and drive 5.3 miles east. Then turn left at the next park sign and drive 6.7 miles south to the entrance station. From the entrance station, drive 0.5 mile, then turn left and drive 0.7 mile to the overlook and parking area.

No trail description is needed at Goblin Valley. From the parking area, follow any of the obvious routes down into the swarm of goblins. From there, get lost on your own. But be careful not to let your imagination get the best of you. And whatever you do, get back to your vehicle before dark. Boo!

Bizarre landforms in the Entrada Formation

RIM OVERLOOK

SANDSTONE CLIFFS OF CAPITOL REEF

Climb high on the cliffs above the Fremont River for outstanding views along Waterpocket Fold, and ponder the curious black volcanic boulders perched high on the canyon walls.

DISTANCE ■ 4.5 miles round trip

ELEVATION ■ 5360 to 6360 feet

DIFFICULTY ■ Moderate

TOPOGRAPHIC MAPS ■ USGS Fruita, UT; Trails Illustrated #213

GEOLOGIC MAP ■ 17

KEY REFERENCE ■ 22, 23

PRECAUTIONS ■ Watch your step while exploring along the cliffs. Avoid being caught on the cliffs during summer thunderstorms.

FOR INFORMATION ■ Capitol Reef National Park

About the Landscape: Waterpocket Fold is one of the major monoclines of the Colorado Plateau, a feature formed about 65 million years ago during the Laramide orogeny. Erosion has unveiled this long stretch of bent, tilted, and broken rock, creating a string of rugged sandstone cliffs that stretch for nearly 100 miles, from Thousand Lake Mountain all the way to the Colorado River in Glen Canyon (now submerged by Lake Powell).

In the heart of Capitol Reef National Park, the Fremont River cuts the largest canyon through the Waterpocket Fold. Capitol Reef gets its name from the rounded, dome-shaped landforms sculpted in the Navajo Sandstone, reminiscent of the rotundas of capitol buildings. The term *reef* was used by pioneers and early geographers and refers to impassable areas of rock.

This hike climbs high above the Fremont River for a grand panorama of Waterpocket Fold. Because the trail follows the natural slope of the rocks, it never gets too steep or strenuous. Along the way, catch a glimpse of Hickman Natural Bridge and walk past large, rounded volcanic boulders of dark basalt that beg the question of how they got here. From the Rim Overlook, look down on the Fremont River as it meanders through the orchards in the historic settlement of Fruita.

Trail Guide: This hike shares the trailhead with the Hickman Bridge Trail. To reach it, drive 2 miles east from the park visitor center on Utah State Route 24 between Hanksville and Torrey. Turn left at the sign for the Hickman Bridge trailhead to arrive at the parking area.

The trail begins by climbing steps constructed along ledges above the

Fremont River. The cliff face left of the trail offers an opportunity to closely examine rocks in the Kayenta Formation.

The ledge-forming Kayenta Formation separates the massive cliffs of the Wingate Sandstone below from the white Navajo Sandstone that adorns the top of Waterpocket Fold. The tan sandstone and purple mudstone layers in the Kayenta were deposited in an ancient river system about 190 million years ago during the Jurassic. Notice how the thick sandstone units, which represent sands in a riverbed, cut down into and scour out the thinner mudstone layers of the adjacent floodplain. In places, slabs of the mudstone were ripped up, turned sideways, and encased in the sands as the river deepened its channel. As you continue to climb the sandstone steps, look for ripple marks formed by the ancient stream currents.

At the top of a series of short switchbacks through the Kayenta ledges, a short spur trail to the right leads to a viewpoint of Navajo Dome. This erosional landform is sculpted in the wind-blown sands of the Navajo Sandstone. The vertical lines in the rock are fractures formed as the rock flexed and bent to form Waterpocket Fold. To the south, directly across the canyon, Pectols Pyramid is another erosional feature carved in the Navajo.

Next, the trail crosses a terrace mantled by round dark boulders of basalt. How did these boulders get here, perched so high above the Fremont River? Ponder this question as you continue walking and we will revisit this question on up the trail.

At 0.25 mile, a sign points to Hickman Natural Bridge Trail splitting off to the left, a worthy side trip if you have the time and energy. Continue to the right toward the Rim Overlook. The trail from this point starts climbing gently, following the tilt of the layers along Waterpocket Fold. For its entire length, the trail traverses the ledges in the Kayenta Formation.

The large, round volcanic boulders continue to lie scattered on top of the sandstone. Then, at about 0.75 mile from the trailhead, the boulders suddenly disappear from the trail. Retrace your steps until you find the last accumulation of boulders. These round black boulders of basalt are from the 20 million-year-old lava flows that cap Boulder and Thousand Lake Mountains, part of the High Plateaus that mark the western boundary of the Colorado Plateau. Since the lava flows probably never did cover Capitol Reef, they must have been transported from their source on Boulder Mountain about 30 miles away. Presumably, catastrophic floods and debris flows washed the boulders down from the High Plateaus of Boulder Mountain at a time when the Ice Age glaciers were melting.

Rounded from miles of rolling and tumbling, these enigmatic boulders lie in terraces high above the present-day Fremont River. This suggests that the river has greatly deepened its channel since the boulders were deposited; the river could not have placed these boulders where you find them today, no matter how great the floods or debris flows. Recent studies using sophisticated dating techniques suggest that the terraces of black basalt boulders range in age from around 60,000, 100,000, and 150,000 years ago. These dates correspond to times when the glaciers were at their maximum extent. Curiously, however, the dates did not identify a terrace from the last glacial interval that ended around 12,000 years ago.

Beyond the last basalt boulders, the trail traverses slickrock marked by small cairns. At about the 1-mile point on the hike, a sign points to the left to a view of Hickman Natural Bridge hidden in the canyon below.

Hickman Bridge is a span of rock carved from a sandstone layer in the Kayenta Formation. But in fact it is not a true natural bridge at all; it is misnamed. It is an arch carved from a fin of Kayenta Sandstone by two small washes running parallel to one another on the two sides of the "bridge." The washes cut into the sandstone, creating a hole through the fin, which over time has widened into the majestic arch we see today.

Basalt boulders stranded by catastrophic Ice-Age floods and debris flows high above the present-day Fremont River, Waterpocket Fold

For the next mile to the Rim Overlook, the trail climbs higher and higher on ledges in the Kayenta Formation, making a series of large bends to skirt minor side canyons. Notice the sweeping patterns of cross-beds in the cliffs above the trail to the right. These features were left by swirls of ancient winds in the white Navajo Sandstone.

The Rim Overlook presents a dizzying view along the Wingate cliffs and down to the Fremont River where it flows through the historic settlement of Fruita. Although the trail continues on for another 2 miles to the Navajo Knobs, this is the turnaround point for this hike.

Toward the western skyline and Boulder Mountain, the colorful Mesozoic layers have all been stripped away by erosion. The Fremont River has carved a deep gorge through the oldest layers of Waterpocket Fold. Exposed in the gorge are ancient Paleozoic rocks, including the Kaibab Formation—the same rock that rims the Grand Canyon. To the east the Henry Mountains, a string of igneous intrusions called laccoliths, rise above the domes and pyramids that adorn the top of Waterpocket Fold.

Once you have enjoyed the view, carefully follow the trail back to the parking area.

STRIKE VALLEY OVERLOOK

TILTED ROCKS ALONG WATERPOCKET FOLD

Experience the drama of upturned rock layers extending as far as the eye can see.

DISTANCE ■ **1 mile round trip (6 miles without a 4WD vehicle)**

ELEVATION ■ **5850 to 6000 feet**

DIFFICULTY ■ **Easy**

TOPOGRAPHIC MAPS ■ **USGS Bitter Creek Divide, UT; Trails Illustrated #213**

GEOLOGIC MAP ■ **17**

KEY REFERENCES ■ **22, 23**

PRECAUTIONS ■ **The dirt roads to the trailhead are impassable when wet. Be sure to inquire about current conditions. Please try not to step on the fragile organic (*cryptobiotic*) soils. Watch your step at the overlook and avoid being caught on the ridge top during summer thunderstorms.**

FOR INFORMATION ■ **Capitol Reef National Park**

About the Landscape: Waterpocket Fold is one of the Colorado Plateau's major monoclines and forms the backbone of Capitol Reef National Park. This sinuous ridge of upturned sedimentary layers represents the steep

165

eastern flank of the Circle Cliffs Uplift, a broad dome that arched upward about 65 million years ago during the Laramide orogeny. Erosion along the fold has stripped away softer rocks, leaving a rugged barrier of cliffs, or *reef,* standing high above the landscape. Waterpocket Fold extends from Thousand Lake Mountain south to the Colorado River east (now submerged under Lake Powell)—a distance of nearly 100 miles.

The tilted layers exposed along Waterpocket Fold are highlighted by impressive cliffs and canyons sculpted in the Wingate, Kayenta, and Navajo Formations. Strike Valley Overlook offers a dramatic view of these tilted layers along the length of Waterpocket Fold.

Trail Guide: The trailhead for Strike Valley Overlook is located in the remote southern section of Capitol Reef National Park, and is also the trailhead for Upper Muley Twist (a more strenuous 4-mile loop).

To reach the trailhead, drive 8.9 miles east from the park visitor center on Utah State Route 24 between Hanksville and Torrey. At the park boundary, turn right (south) onto the Notom–Bullfrog Road, which is paved for only the first 15 miles. Drive 33.8 miles and turn right at the junction with the Burr Trail. Drive 3.2 miles up the Burr Trail, which switchbacks straight up the Waterpocket Fold, then turn right at the sign for Upper Muley Twist. The trail register is located 0.5 mile off the Burr Trail. If you have a high-clearance or four-wheel-drive vehicle, continue driving another 2.5 miles, winding through the rocky wash, and park at the end of the "road."

The trailhead is located along a wash eroded in the softer sandstone layers in the Kayenta Formation. The Wingate Sandstone, the rock layer below the Kayenta, forms the red cliffs to the west. The Strike Valley Overlook Trail heads east through the notch between high white cliffs of Navajo Sandstone, which overlies the Kayenta. Both the Wingate and Navajo Sandstones are thick deposits of Jurassic wind-blown sand dunes. The Kayenta Formation represents sediments left behind by a Jurassic river system.

The Strike Valley Overlook Trail starts out by following a small, sandy wash, then crosses the wash after about 200 yards. At the 0.25-mile point, the trail meets a broad, sloping slickrock surface of Navajo Sandstone. From this point on, small cairns mark the route to the top of the ridge. The furrows in the slickrock surface are the eroded edges of large cross-beds, patterns in the rock swirled by ancient winds during the Jurassic. Continue following the cairns to the extreme southern end of the ridge.

You are now standing atop the Waterpocket Fold, some 2000 feet above Strike Valley. The upturned layers that define the fold extend off to the south beyond the far skyline toward the Colorado River. (The term *strike* refers to the trend of the sloping layers.) The resistant backbone of the Navajo Sandstone forms a high ridge weathered into steeply inclined, slickrock surfaces. The rocks here are standing almost completely on end.

The view here reveals the eroded edges of younger, less resistant sedimentary layers, which overlie the Navajo and form stripes extending along the length of Strike Valley. Exposed in the floor of the valley are the remains of shifting environments of ancient oceans, rivers, and deserts stacked up like a layercake turned on its side. Imagine the rocks laid out on edge in the valley instead extending overhead, arching across the sky to the west over the top of Waterpocket Fold and the Circle Cliffs Uplift. All these Mesozoic formations, like a who's who of Colorado Plateau stratigraphy, have now been stripped back by erosion—the Carmel, Entrada, Morrison, Curtis, Summerville, Dakota, Mancos, and Mesaverde.

To the east, the Henry Mountains form a string of rounded summits that follow the trend of Waterpocket Fold. These mountains are the resistant cores of magma blisters that domed up overlying sedimentary layers between 31 to 23 million years ago. The Henry Mountains were one of the last mountain ranges in the west to be explored. In the late 1800s pioneering geologist G.K. Gilbert used the term *laccolith* to describe this cluster of igneous intrusions. The Cretaceous sedimentary rocks that once covered the intrusions now form cliffs that ring the base of the mountains. Erosion has stripped away the highest parts of these softer sedimentary layers, including the Cretaceous-age Mancos Shale and sandstones of the Mesaverde Group, exposing the igneous rocks coring the intrusions.

Once you have taken in the view of Waterpocket Fold, retrace your steps back to the trailhead.

Tilted rock layers along Waterpocket Fold; view from Strike Valley Overlook

MOUNT HILLERS

Hike 28

LACCOLITHS OF THE HENRY MOUNTAINS

Explore upright rock layers flanking one of the igneous intrusions in the Henry Mountains.

DISTANCE ■ **1.5 miles round trip (2 miles without a 4WD vehicle)**

ELEVATION ■ **6400 to 6800 feet**

DIFFICULTY ■ **Moderate**

TOPOGRAPHIC MAPS ■ **USGS Mount Hillers, UT; Trails Illustrated #213**

GEOLOGIC MAP ■ **18**

KEY REFERENCES ■ **24, 25, 26**

PRECAUTIONS ■ **This is a remote area—be prepared and call ahead for weather and road conditions. Avoid hiking in the midday heat of summer.**

FOR INFORMATION ■ **Henry Mountain Resource Area**

About the Landscape: The Henry Mountains stand like a string of islands in a sea of sedimentary rock. Originally referred to by John Wesley Powell as the "Unknown Mountains," this range of isolated peaks was the last in the West to be placed on a map. These remote mountains were made famous by the work of pioneering geologist G.K. Gilbert, who in 1877 proposed that they were not volcanic but formed by the erosion of a special type of igneous intrusion that he called a *laccolith.* Although Gilbert's observations have withstood the test of time, and the Henry Mountains are today featured in textbooks as the "type section" for laccoliths, all five of the Henry Mountains are considered by some geologists to be large and more complex intrusions called *stocks.*

This hike along the southern flank of Mount Hillers explores one of the best areas in the Henry Mountains to view the dramatic structures along the flank of an igneous intrusion. Here you come face to face with remnants of upturned igneous sills and sedimentary layers tilted back during the intrusions that formed the Mount Hillers laccolith.

Trail Guide: To reach the trailhead for this hike, drive about 25 miles south from Hanksville on Utah State Route 95. Turn right onto SR 276, then drive 15 miles and turn right at the sign for "Starr Ranch." Drive 3 miles on this good gravel road to Starr Springs Picnic Area and Campground. Bear left at the intersection just before the campground and drive 1.8 miles. Bear right at the next **Y**-intersection (signed "Horn 25 miles") and drive another 1.1 miles, then turn right onto a small dirt road immediately after crossing a small stream lined with cottonwood trees. If you do not have a high-clearance vehicle, park here and start hiking up the road. A pullout (with campsite) is located 0.25 mile farther up this road on the left.

This hike follows the road to its end, then drops down into a boulder-strewn wash that leads into a steep, narrow canyon that penetrates the upturned flank of Mount Hillers. But before starting out, climb up the low outcrop of yellow sandstone to the right of the road where you parked.

You are standing on the Cretaceous Ferron Sandstone which was deposited about 100 million years ago along a sandy shoreline that bordered the Cretaceous seaway. Look in the distance to the west, where you can follow the Ferron Sandstone cliff as it climbs gently toward Mount Hillers. But it never makes it to the flank of the mountain.

Between where you stand and the edge of the mountain, the Ferron Sandstone was tilted skyward by the force of magma rising from deep within the earth. Originally, it and other sedimentary layers above and below arched over the top of the intrusion, forming a broad dome. Imagine your fist pushing up from underneath a pile of blankets, bending the blankets on top. Over time, the softer sedimentary rocks that once draped over the top of the intrusion (the blankets) have been removed by erosion, leaving the hard igneous rocks that core Mount Hillers (your fist) standing tall above the surrounding landscape.

To further picture how the Henry Mountains formed, look at the mountains to the south. All are examples of laccoliths. Farthest away on the skyline is Navajo Mountain. This perfect dome is still covered by its "blanket" of sedimentary layers arching over the top of the igneous intrusions that pushed up from below. Apparently, the "fist" of molten rock did not push up as high as in the Henry Mountains, and erosion has yet to uncover Navajo Mountain's igneous core.

The closer mountains are the southernmost peaks in the Henry Mountains: Mount Ellsworth is to the west and Mount Holmes is next door to the east. Erosion has exposed the igneous cores of both mountains and you can see how the light-colored sedimentary layers arch upward along the flank of the mountains.

Now look again at the face of Mount Hillers before you. The towering fins of rock along the base of the mountain are the "trap door" layers bent upright by the powerful force of the igneous intrusions that formed the laccolith.

For a closer look at this spectacular geologic landscape, hike to the end of the road. Before you drop down into the wash on the right, note the outcrop of white sandstone on the hillside left of the road. This is what is left of the Cretaceous Dakota Sandstone, which has been bent upright to form a broken spine that extends along the front of the mountain to the east.

Once in the wash, you can't help but notice the boulders of diorite that have tumbled down from Mount Hillers' inner core. This igneous rock is peppered with white feldspar crystals. A close look with your hand lens reveals black needles of hornblende set in a gray, fine-grained matrix. The large crystals in this rock indicate that it cooled slowly beneath its insulating blanket of sedimentary layers.

Carefully boulder-hop into the narrow canyon ahead. The red sandstone plastered against the dark fin on the right is the Jurassic Entrada Sandstone, familiar to you from places like Arches National Park and Goblin Valley. The dark fin of rock is a diorite sill that squeezed into the Entrada before both were turned on end by the forces of later intrusions. As you enter the narrow canyon, the wash brings you face to face with this diorite sill on the left.

Beyond the sill, more red Entrada Sandstone makes up the walls on both sides of the canyon. Below the Entrada (or toward the mountain, since everything is standing on end in a nearly vertical position), the weathered slopes and saddles above on both sides of the canyon are in softer red shale and siltstone layers in the Carmel Formation. Farther up the canyon the massive walls of tan sandstone are in the Navajo Formation, of Zion Canyon fame. Although it is highly fractured, you can still see original layers in the rock and make out cross-beds in this Jurassic wind-blown sandstone.

As you make your way toward the head of the canyon, the going is made increasingly difficult by log and boulder jams; one in particular can be skirted by climbing out of the wash up onto the hillside on the left. But sooner or later, it is useless to continue.

No matter how far you climb, from any high vantage point there is an impressive view of the contorted, upper canyon walls where large slabs of light-colored sedimentary rocks are surrounded by swarms of igneous rock. This is the margin of the mountain's inner core where magma forced its way upward about 29 million years ago. High above, the steep slopes

Close-up of gray feldspar crystals in diorite (a type of igneous rock), Henry Mountains, Utah

of Mount Hillers are made entirely of jagged outcrops of the once-molten diorite. Over time erosion has exposed this hard, resistant inner core of the laccolith to leave it standing high above the surrounding landscape.

Before carefully retracing your steps down the canyon to the road and back to your vehicle, take a moment to also admire the view looking downcanyon. The upright walls of rock flanking Mount Hillers are very dramatic and you can look beyond to the desert landscape along Capitol Reef's Waterpocket Fold.

DRY FORK COYOTE GULCH

SANDSTONE SLOT CANYONS

Explore three different slot canyons carved in the Navajo Sandstone.

DISTANCE ■ From 1 to 12 miles round trip, depending on which slots you explore

ELEVATION ■ 4800 to 4560 feet

DIFFICULTY ■ Moderate

TOPOGRAPHIC MAPS ■ USGS Big Hollow Wash; Trails Illustrated #710

GEOLOGIC MAP ■ 12

KEY REFERENCE ■ 27

PRECAUTIONS ■ There is real danger here of flash floods. Do not enter the narrows after recent rains or if afternoon thunderstorms are building. Avoid this hike in the midday heat of summer. Use caution climbing in slot canyons, and beware of rattlesnakes. The road to the trailhead may become impassable when wet.

FOR INFORMATION ■ Grand Staircase–Escalante Interagency Visitor Center

About the Landscape: The Dry Fork of Coyote Gulch is a major side canyon of the Escalante River within Grand Staircase–Escalante National Monument. The Escalante River and its tributaries have excavated an intricate network of canyons, creating one of the largest areas of slickrock found anywhere on the Colorado Plateau. The maze of canyons are carved into the western flank of the Circle Cliffs Uplift, a broad dome of rock that arched upward about 65 million years ago during the Laramide orogeny. Over time, erosion has stripped away thousands of feet of sedimentary rock exposing vast expanses of the Jurassic Navajo Sandstone where the artistic forces of erosion have worked their magic.

Hidden within this sandstone-lover's paradise are three easily accessible slot canyons: Dry Fork Narrows, and Peek-a-boo and Spooky Gulches. How far you hike depends on how curious—and daring—you are to see what's around the next bend in each of the slot canyons.

Trail Guide: To reach the Dry Fork trailhead, drive 6 miles east from the town of Escalante on Utah State Route 12 and turn right onto the Hole-in-the-Rock Road. Follow this wide gravel road south for about 26 miles to the Dry Fork road on the left. Turn left onto the small dirt road and drive 1.5 miles to the trailhead, bearing left at a Y-junction.

From the trail register, the Dry Fork Trail leads downhill through ledges of sandstone and red beds in the Carmel Formation. After only about 50 yards, the trail reaches the top of the Navajo Sandstone where rock cairns mark the route down a steep slickrock slope. The trail winds across a sandy bench and then switchbacks down into a narrow side canyon leading to Dry Fork of Coyote Gulch.

Once in the main wash, the Dry Fork Narrows begin through the opening in the sandstone cliff to the left. These impressive narrows extend several miles upstream, slicing a cross-section through solid rock that was once sand dunes piled high by Jurassic winds 175 million years ago. Notice the slanting lines indicating cross-beds, and the small, round nodules in the canyon walls. The walls close in with every step, and ultimately the canyon becomes only arm's length wide. At the upper end of the narrows it is

Looking skyward through a slot canyon, Dry Fork Coyote Gulch

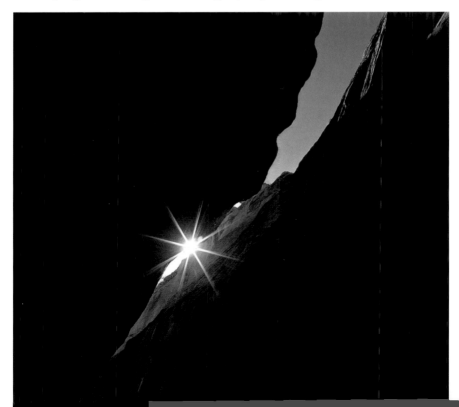

possible to climb out of the canyon for a view of the surrounding landscape.

Once you have explored Dry Fork Narrows to your heart's content, retrace your steps downstream to the main wash. Peek-a-boo Gulch, the next slot canyon to explore, is barely 0.25 mile downstream on the left.

A ledge about 12 feet high guards the entrance to Peek-a-boo Gulch. Imagine the waterfall that must gush out of this canyon during a flash flood. Using the well-positioned hand- and footholds, it is possible to climb up into the entrance of the narrow canyon.

Once inside, a series of plunge pools and fluted ledges make continuing upstream equally challenging. But the main reward for your efforts is close at hand. Immediately above is an artistically sculpted double bridge across the roof of the canyon. Beyond the double bridge, the canyon narrows to where you must pass through two holes worn through the sandstone by the swirling floodwaters. Navigating farther upstream continues to be a challenge. You need to be a contortionist to twist through the tight, slanting walls, and the fluted canyon floor is sometimes not wide enough for your feet. Continue upstream as far as you dare, then retrace your steps back to the main wash of Dry Fork.

To reach Spooky Gulch, the third and final slot canyon explored on this hike, follow the main wash of Dry Fork downstream for about 0.5 mile to where a trail climbs out of the wash on the left. This trail leads through a short, sand-filled side canyon for about 0.25 mile then meets another wash. The entrance to Spooky Gulch is just upstream to the left. As you will soon discover, it is amazing how wide the main wash is considering how narrow Spooky Gulch is. The flash floods that rip through this canyon must be incredibly powerful.

The entrance to Spooky Gulch is very unassuming. It begins with a series of shallow pockets scoured into the canyon walls. When floodwaters flush through the canyon, the sand below your feet becomes the natural grit that grinds away at the canyon walls.

About 50 yards upstream from the entrance, a boulder—or *chock stone*—blocks the passage. This is a good place to drop your pack to crawl underneath. Beyond the boulder, the walls of the canyon close in so tight that you have to squeeze yourself through (which is easier without your pack). This slot canyon is more like a "sliver" canyon. Upstream from the first constriction is a long, straight corridor carved out by water following fractures in the rock. The canyon quickly becomes extremely narrow again—not a place for the claustrophobic. Continue upstream as far as you dare, then retrace your steps back to the entrance.

Once back in the main wash of Dry Fork, return to the trailhead by the route you came.

173

LOWER CALF CREEK FALLS

DESERT OASIS BETWEEN SANDSTONE CLIFFS

Hike past Ancestral Puebloan ruins, rock art sites, and sandstone cliffs to a hidden desert waterfall.

DISTANCE ■ 5.6 miles round trip

ELEVATION ■ 5350 to 5520 feet

DIFFICULTY ■ Moderate

TOPOGRAPHIC MAPS ■ USGS Calf Creek, UT; Trails Illustrated #710

GEOLOGIC MAP ■ 12

KEY REFERENCE ■ 27

PRECAUTIONS ■ Avoid hiking in the midday heat of summer. The rocks around the waterfall can be very slippery.

FOR INFORMATION ■ Grand Staircase–Escalante Interagency Visitor Center

About the Landscape: Lower Calf Creek Falls is one of the most popular destinations in the Grand Staircase–Escalante National Monument. Situated at the head of a scenic canyon where it offers a refreshing desert oasis, Lower Calf Creek Falls plunges over a sheer cliff of Navajo Sandstone 126 feet to the canyon floor.

Calf Creek is a lush, perennial tributary of the Escalante River. This labyrinth of slickrock canyons is carved along the western flank of the Circle Cliffs Uplift. Exposed along the walls of Calf Creek Canyon is the boundary or *contact* with the underlying Kayenta Formation.

Trail Guide: The Lower Calf Creek Falls trailhead is located at Calf Creek Campground, 15 miles east of Escalante on Utah State Route 12 or about 12 miles southwest of Boulder. A sign for Calf Creek Recreation Area marks the turnoff, and trailhead parking is at the picnic area. The trailhead is located in the campground just before the road crosses the creek.

The trail starts out by climbing a series of constructed steps up to the trail register (pick up a trail guide, which points out the locations of ruins, rock art, and other interesting features). Look for ripple marks in the sandstone steps, which are from the Kayenta Formation. Ledges of purple and maroon sandstone in the Kayenta Formation are left of the trail just beyond the trailhead. Small holes and niches have been worn in the friable rock by the action of wind and water.

For most of its length, the trail follows a well-worn sandy track and winds along ledges cut in the Kayenta Formation. Look for small and medium-scale cross-beds produced by currents in the stream channels about 190 million years ago during the Jurassic.

Overlying the ledges of Kayenta Formation is Navajo Sandstone, which forms the massive cliffs along the length of the canyon. Look for sweeping cross-bed patterns along the cliff face. These large cross-beds formed as the faces of advancing sand dunes were buried by sand blown by the Jurassic winds. The Navajo Sandstone is one of the most widespread rock layers on the Colorado Plateau and represents the remains of a vast sandy desert not unlike the Sahara today.

The boundary between the Kayenta Formation and Navajo Sandstone is at the level of the trail at about the 1.75-mile point. The contact is marked by the abrupt change from the purple Kayenta layers under your feet to the white cross-bedded Navajo Sandstone above. Notice that some of the cross-beds near the base of the Navajo are wavy and distorted. This is a result of soft sediment deformation: the weight of sediment piled on top bends underlying sediment before it hardens into stone.

Lower Calf Creek Falls spills through a notch in the Navajo Sandstone.

For the last 0.5 mile to the falls, the canyon narrows. Along this stretch, the walls of the canyon are adorned with particularly impressive streaks of desert varnish. These dark streaks mark where water has trickled down the cliff face, leaving behind a thin chemical coating of mostly iron and manganese oxides. Exactly how desert varnish forms is not well understood. Recent research suggests that organic processes may play an important role.

The thunderous roar of Lower Calf Creek Falls echoes off the canyon walls about 0.25 mile before they come into view. Then finally, as the trail rounds the last bend in the canyon, a notch high in the cliff is filled by a healthy stream of water that cascades down to the canyon floor. The temperature in the canyon drops noticeably as you approach the mist-filled plunge pool where the trail ends.

After soaking up the coolness of this hidden desert oasis, return to the trailhead by the route you came.

KODACHROME BASIN

Hike 31

MYSTERIOUS SANDSTONE PIPES

The origin of Kodachrome Basin's sandstone pipes still puzzles geologists.

DISTANCE ■ **3-mile loop (up to 5 miles if you hike every side loop)**

ELEVATION ■ **5760 to 5920 feet**

DIFFICULTY ■ **Easy**

TOPOGRAPHIC MAP ■ **USGS Henrieville, UT**

GEOLOGIC MAP ■ **See map in key reference**

KEY REFERENCE ■ **27**

PRECAUTIONS ■ **Avoid this hike in the midday heat of summer. To avoid trampling the delicate, organic (*cryptobiotic*) soil, please remain on the established trails.**

FOR INFORMATION ■ **Kodachrome Basin State Park**

About the Landscape: It was researchers on a 1948 National Geographic expedition who named Kodachrome Basin for its colorful landforms (Kodachrome was once a popular Kodak color-slide film). Kodachrome Basin is carved from the wind-blown dune sands of Jurassic Entrada Sandstone. The basin is located at the extreme northern end of the Kaibab Uplift, one of the many Laramide-age uplifts on the Colorado Plateau.

Set aside as a Utah state park, Kodachrome Basin is known for more than just its colorful landforms sculpted from sedimentary rock. For here there is an unusual concentration of sandstone *pipes* whose origin still puzzles geologists. The enigmatic sandstone pipes of Kodachrome Basin are free-standing towers of light-gray to white rock that rise in contrast to the red Entrada Sandstone layers that surround them. A total of sixty-seven sandstone pipes have been identified in Kodachrome Basin.

This hike follows the Panorama Trail past a number of sandstone pipes and red rock spires. Along the way, a close look at one of the tallest and most accessible pipes in the park reveals important characteristics that make these structures unique and also provide clues to their origin.

Trail Guide: To reach the Panorama trailhead, drive 7.2 miles south from Cannonville on the Cottonwood Canyon Road and turn left at the sign for Kodachrome Basin State Park. Drive 1.4 miles on the paved entrance road and park either at the trailhead kiosk on the left or in the larger parking area directly across the road on the right.

From the trailhead, the Panorama Trail follows an old road used for horseback and stagecoach rides. For about the first 0.25 mile the trail winds through low hills in the Jurassic Carmel Formation. The gray rocks scattered on the hillsides are solid layers of the mineral gypsum, which formed by evaporation of salty seawater in a shallow inland sea that 170 million years ago covered parts of the area that would ultimately become the Colorado Plateau.

At about the 0.25-mile point, the first group of rock spires are marked by a sign pointing to "Fred Flintstone Spire" to the right of the trail. These towers of rock are not sandstone pipes. These spires retain the original horizontal layering of the Entrada Formation and are formed by erosion of softer layers beneath a slightly harder and more resistant cap rock. The spires before you are red, not light gray or white like the more mysterious sandstone pipes you will see ahead.

Just past the first spires is a sign for "petrified lightning," pointing to a short spur to the right. The "petrified lightning" was not formed by lightning at all, but rather its name refers to light-colored fractures that zigzag through the red rock cliff.

The first true sandstone pipe is left of the trail at the junction with the "Old Indian Cave," a spur trail leading off to the right. Notice the light-colored rock that fills the pipe in contrast to the surrounding red sandstone layers that still largely encase the pipe. Avoid the temptation to walk off the trail to investigate this pipe. There is a larger and more accessible one up ahead.

The next rock spire to the right of the trail also is not a true sandstone pipe, but merely an erosional remnant of Entrada Sandstone. Note the horizontal layering retained in the red rock that forms this spire.

Nearing the 1-mile point, a sign points to where the Panorama Trail

branches off to the right from the stagecoach road, which continues to the left. Directly ahead is a spectacular sandstone pipe called Ballerina Geyser. Rising like a white rocket ship, this pipe exhibits all the key characteristics that make the sandstone pipes unique. Follow the short spur trail down to the right and up and around to the base of the pipe.

Look closely at the rock that forms this pipe and notice how it differs from the surrounding red sandstone of the Entrada Formation. The pipe itself is composed internally of a chaotic mixture of sand and angular shards of sedimentary rock, in sharp contrast with the still-layered red sandstone that surrounds it. The pipe-filling rock is harder and more resistant to erosion than the surrounding red sandstone. Over time, the surrounding softer sandstone was stripped away by erosion, leaving the pipe standing tall above the landscape.

Theories about how the pipes formed range from geysers and springs to liquefaction triggered by earthquakes. A more recent, and perhaps simpler, explanation suggests that the pipes are the result of over-pressuring of a fluid-filled sediment slurry derived from the Carmel Formation.

In this model, the pipes formed where a water-sand-sediment slurry, under pressure, forced its way upward from the Carmel Formation into the overlying Entrada Sandstone. As the slurry worked its way upward, it scoured out the host rock (Entrada Sandstone) and entrained fragments of the host rock within the slurry. Once created, the pipe acted as a conduit for fluids moving vertically through the rock. These fluids cemented the pipe-filling sediment more tightly than the surrounding host rock, and bleached the pipes in the process. The sandstone pipes are presumed to have formed sometime after the deposition of the Entrada Sandstone. It is speculated that they may have formed during deposition of the overlying Henrieville Sandstone when rivers buried the Entrada sand dunes about 150 million years ago.

Once you have thoroughly inspected the Ballerina Geyser pipe, continue following the Panorama Trail as it winds around this scenic area. Along the way, the pink cliffs of Bryce Canyon loom on the western skyline. You may choose to explore the many side trails, including the short Hat Shop and Secret Passage loops, or the 2-mile-long Big Bear Geyser Trail. A must is the short climb up to Panorama Point for a sweeping view of the entire Kodachrome Basin.

From Panorama Point, a return loop trail winds across the floor of the basin and meets back with the stagecoach road near Fred Flintstone Spire. From there, retrace your steps back to the trailhead.

Enigmatic sandstone pipe at Kodacrome Basin State Park

Hike 32

THE COCKSCOMB

SLOT CANYONS ALONG THE EAST KAIBAB MONOCLINE

Explore a network of sinuous slot canyons sliced into tilted layers of The Cockscomb, the northern extension of the East Kaibab Monocline.

DISTANCE ▪ 3-mile loop

ELEVATION ▪ 5640 to 5500 feet

DIFFICULTY ▪ Easy

TOPOGRAPHIC MAP ▪ USGS Butler Valley, UT

GEOLOGIC MAP ▪ 19

KEY REFERENCE ▪ 29

PRECAUTIONS ▪ There is real danger here of flash floods. Do not enter the narrows after recent rains or if afternoon thunderstorms are building. Avoid this hike in the midday heat of summer. The Cottonwood Canyon Road may become impassable when wet.

FOR INFORMATION ▪ Cannonville Visitor Center

About the Landscape: Southern Utah's Cockscomb is a scenic area of upturned sedimentary layers within the Grand Staircase–Escalante National Monument. The bent, broken, and tilted rocks of The Cockscomb represent the northern extension of the East Kaibab Monocline, a dramatic fold that defines the eastern limb of the Kaibab Uplift. This is one of the Colorado Plateau's major structural features, stretching over 100 miles northward from the Grand Canyon.

A long dirt road, called the Cottonwood Canyon Road, winds through a series of strike valleys developed along the monocline. Differential erosion has created a bizarre landscape of sandstone fins and ridges standing tall against the skyline. The road generally follows a valley cut into softer layers between a ridge of Jurassic Navajo Sandstone to the west and sandstone cliffs to the east in the Cretaceous Strait Cliffs Formation.

This hike explores an easily accessible area of intricate slot canyons carved by Cottonwood Creek through the steep limb of The Cockscomb. Exposed in the walls of the canyons are microscale faults and fractures formed when the rocks buckled to form the East Kaibab Monocline during the Laramide orogeny around 65 million years ago.

Trail Guide: To reach the start of this hike, drive south from Cannonville, Utah, on the Cottonwood Canyon Road. About 12.5 miles past Kodachrome Basin State Park, the road drops steeply into a tight little valley called "Candyland" by local ranchers. As the road levels out in the valley bottom, park in the pullout on the left directly opposite an obvious opening in the wall of sandstone to the right (west) of the road. There is no sign marking the trailhead for this hike.

To reach the trailhead from U.S. Highway 89, drive about 25 miles north on Cottonwood Canyon Road to where the road drops steeply into Candyland Valley. Look for the pullout on the right and park. The red and white "candy" towers near the pullout are upturned layers in the Entrada Formation.

Start the hike by crossing the road and descending into Cottonwood Creek, following a narrow little wash hugging the right (north) side of the opening in the sandstone wall. Once safely down in the canyon, notice the steep tilt or *dip* of the rock layers. In places, the rocks are inclined up to 65 degrees along this section of the East Kaibab Monocline.

Like a rug draped over a step, monoclines on the Colorado Plateau form where layered rocks are bent and warped across faults hidden in basement rocks deep below the surface. The East Kaibab Monocline is one of the rare monoclines on the Colorado Plateau that has had its faulted basement revealed by erosion in the Grand Canyon.

Flash flood–transported log wedged high in a sandstone slot canyon, The Cockscomb

The upright wall of white sandstone where you entered the canyon is the Page Sandstone tongue of the Carmel Formation. This Jurassic wind-blown sandstone is bounded above and below by layers of red siltstone and shale that is more easily eroded. The Navajo Sandstone, also wind-blown sand of Jurassic age, is the massive upturned sandstone layer below the Carmel Formation.

Although the main route of this hike follows the canyon downstream to the left and then loops back to your vehicle along the road, take time to explore the narrow canyons upstream.

The first upstream slot canyon is carved into the Navajo Sandstone. The walls of the canyon are riddled with an assortment of thin white lines. Although they look similar to mineral-filled veins, these lines are microscale faults and fractures formed in response to the Laramide compressional forces that buckled the rocks to form the monocline. Look closely to see where the layers in the rock are actually offset along these tiny faults. Faults of all types—normal, reverse, and thrust—are represented here in miniature, all of which formed to accommodate the extreme bending of the rocks.

Above this first slot canyon, the wash widens out where it has carved through red beds in the Carmel Formation. These softer rocks were literally crushed and smeared between the sandstone layers as the rocks were upturned to form the monocline. In places the red siltstone is a chaotic jumble smashed together. In other places, it has been squeezed up into the overlying sandstone. After a couple hundred yards, the wash bends to the right and enters another slot canyon, this time cut into the Page Sandstone, which underlies the Carmel.

Be sure to continue upstream to where there is a log wedged 20 feet above the wash, a testament to the depth of the walls of water that fill these slot canyons during major flash floods. Armed with sand, rocks, and other debris, the floods scour away the rock to form the sculpted canyon you see today.

After reaching the log, retrace your steps back to the opening where you entered the canyon, then follow the wash downstream. Sheer walls of Navajo Sandstone rise steeply on either side. The thin, slanting lines throughout the rock walls are cross-beds, which represent the preserved, downwind faces of advancing sand dunes.

For most of its length, the wash is sandy-bottomed. However, near the end, large boulders block the wash and you must scamper up and around to the left before dropping back down into the main wash.

After about 1.5 miles, the wash spits you out into the main strike valley where the road is located. Look for a worn trail marked by a cairn to the left just after passing under the powerline. Climb uphill to the main road, turn left, and walk north back to your vehicle.

Chapter 6
THE HIGH PLATEAUS

The Colorado Plateau's western edge is defined by a series of high, flat-topped mountains known as the *High Plateaus*. Capped by the colorful pink cliffs that rim Bryce Canyon, Cedar Breaks, and the Table Cliffs Plateau, the High Plateaus are the last step in the famed Grand Staircase—they are the proverbial icing on top of the Colorado Plateau's "geologic layercake."

Named by geologist Clarence Dutton in his pioneering survey of the region in the late 1800s, the High Plateaus contain a wealth of information about the geologic evolution of the western margin of the Colorado Plateau. These forested tablelands also offer refreshingly cool air during the summer when the surrounding canyon country is a virtual furnace.

One reason that the High Plateaus are indeed so high is because a veneer of volcanic rock has protected the Colorado Plateau's thick stack of sedimentary rocks from more widespread erosion. In addition, regional uplift has taken these rocks on a ride from sea level to above 10,000 feet in elevation in a time span of about 65 million years. Working in concert, this has left the High Plateaus standing high along the Colorado Plateau's western skyline.

The fireworks on the High Plateaus began with explosive eruptions in the Tushar Mountains between about 30 and 19 million years ago. Originating from a cluster of tall composite or stratovolcanoes where at least five calderas formed, these eruptions spewed tremendous volumes of predominantly rhyolite and andesite tuff and breccia across a preexisting landscape of sedimentary rock. This fiery episode subsided with more tame outpourings of molten basalt lava between 7 and 3 million years ago. These later eruptions smothered the landscape farther east and south of the Tushar Mountains. The probable source for these later basalt eruptions may have been fissures and dikes of similar age and composition now exposed by erosion in the San Rafael Swell and Capitol Reef areas. Presumably this volcanic cap was originally much more widespread than it is today and has been removed by erosion.

Critical to the expression of today's landscape, this veneer of hard, resistant volcanic rock protects softer, underlying sedimentary layers from

Bristlecone pine at Cedar Breaks National Monument on Utah's High Plateaus

rapid erosion. Perhaps most significantly it has helped preserve the Tertiary Claron Formation, the layer that forms the pink cliffs of Bryce Canyon and Cedar Breaks, and also fringes the lofty Table Cliffs Plateau. Where not protected under this volcanic veneer, the Claron Formation has almost completely disappeared from the adjacent canyon country.

The modern High Plateaus landscape emerged as uplift continued to raise Utah's High Plateaus, along with the rest of the Colorado Plateau, in some places more than 11,000 feet above sea level. Erosion continued to dig deeper into the rocks, while at the same time a series of major north–south trending normal faults dissected the western edge of the Colorado Plateau about 15 million years ago. These faults, which down-dropped the rock layers to the west and were associated with the pulling apart or *extension* of the Basin and Range, were also active during the Laramide orogeny, and perhaps date as far back as the Precambrian. They extend far to the south where they have also strongly influenced the evolution of landforms in the western Grand Canyon region. These faults include, from east to west, the Paunsaugunt, Sevier, and Hurricane Faults. Erosion along these major zones of weakness has dissected the volcanic-capped High Plateaus into at least seven distinct plateaus—including the Fish Lake, Awapa, Aquarius, Table Cliffs, Paunsaugunt, Markagunt, and Sevier.

Ice Age glaciers that scoured higher elevations during the Pleistocene provided the finishing touches to the High Plateaus. Evidence of glaciation—including striations and moraines—can be seen on the Aquarius Plateau (Boulder Mountain), in the Fish Lake area, and in the Tushar Mountains, particularly Bullion Canyon (see Hike 38).

THE GRAND STAIRCASE

It was Major John Wesley Powell who in 1869 first described the ascending cliffs of the Colorado Plateau as the *Grand Staircase*. The recently designated Grand Staircase–Escalante National Monument pays homage to Powell's description of this spectacular geologic landscape.

The Grand Staircase is a series of cliffs or *escarpments* formed by erosion of the Colorado Plateau's "geologic layercake." At the bottom of the stack are the Chocolate Cliffs of the Triassic Moenkopi Formation. The next step is the Vermilion Cliffs of the Jurassic Kayenta and Moenave Formations, with the White Cliffs of the Jurassic Navajo Sandstone and the Gray Cliffs of the Cretaceous Straight Cliffs Formation above. At the top, the icing on the cake are the pink cliffs of the Eocene Claron Formation, which paint the colorful rocks of Bryce Canyon, Cedar Breaks, and the Table Cliffs Plateau.

The Grand Staircase has been sliced and diced by the Hurricane, Sevier, and Paunsaugunt Fault zones. This action has created a series of plateaus—namely the Markagunt, Paunsaugunt, and Table Cliffs—that step upward from west to east in a similar fashion to the Grand Staircase.

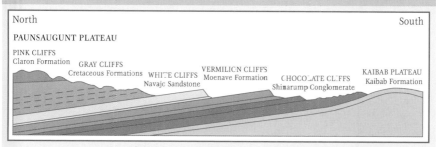

Cliff layers of the Grand Staircase

BRYCE CANYON

FAIRYLAND OF HOODOOS

Hike below the rim and explore this masterpiece of erosion carved in the Tertiary Claron Formation, the youngest layer at the top of the Colorado Plateau's Grand Staircase.

DISTANCE ■ 3-mile loop

ELEVATION ■ 8000 to 7400 feet

DIFFICULTY ■ Moderate

TOPOGRAPHIC MAPS ■ USGS Bryce Canyon and Bryce Point, UT; Trails Illustrated #219

GEOLOGIC MAP ■ 20

KEY REFERENCES ■ 30, 31

PRECAUTIONS ■ The loose rocks along the trail are very crumbly and slippery— please stay on the trail and watch your step.

FOR INFORMATION ■ Bryce Canyon National Park

About the Landscape: Bryce Canyon is a natural spectacle beyond imagination. Its lofty pink cliffs are situated along the southeastern rim of the Paunsaugunt Plateau, one of the High Plateaus that define the Colorado Plateau's western margin. But despite its name, Bryce Canyon is not really a canyon at all.

Bryce Canyon is actually a series of rock amphitheaters artistically sculpted along the retreating edge of the Paunsaugunt Plateau. Perhaps better described as the "Bryce Cliffs," this fairyland of standing stone is part of a long escarpment formed by headward erosion of the Paria River along the Paunsaugunt Fault. Here, erosion has carved ancient river sediments and lakebeds of the Tertiary Claron Formation into an unbelievable variety of unusual landforms called hoodoos.

Trail Guide: Starting at Sunset Point in Bryce Canyon National Park, this hike follows a counterclockwise loop down the Navajo Loop Trail, connecting with the Queen's Garden Trail up to Sunrise Point, then returning back to Sunset Point along the Rim Trail.

To reach the Navajo Loop Trailhead at Sunset Point, turn south off Utah State Route 12 onto SR 63 and drive 4 miles to the entrance to Bryce Canyon National Park. From the visitor center, drive about 1.2 miles and turn left at the sign for Sunset Point. The trailhead is located at the Sunset Point Overlook, just a short walk from the parking area.

The view from Sunset Point looks down on the Bryce Amphitheater, where the highest concentration of hoodoos is found. This amazing collection of ornate landforms is known as the Silent City.

The endless variety of columns, pillars, and jagged fins of rock along the Bryce Cliffs are carved from sedimentary layers in the Claron Formation. This kaleidoscope of soft rock was deposited by streams and within a large, shallow freshwater lake that covered much of south-central Utah about 55 million years ago during the Eocene time. As the level of the lake fluctuated, sluggish meandering streams flowed across mudflats and deltas around the lake basin, depositing a tremendous amount of mud and silt. Local conglomerate layers represent gravel deposited in stream channels. Weathering and soil processes disturbed and oxidized the sediments, which set the stage for the colorful hues that we see today. The color spectrum is caused by minute amounts of oxide minerals dispersed throughout the rock. Like rust, different oxide ratios of iron produce red, yellow, and brown colors. Other oxides, like manganese, impart more pastel hues of lavender and purple.

The Claron Formation is divided into two members, each with a different environment of deposition. The most well developed hoodoos are carved in the lower "Pink Member" of the Claron Formation, which represents predominantly river sediments. The upper "White Member," which represents primarily lake deposits, occupies the higher elevations along the Bryce Cliffs and is well exposed on the Table Cliffs Plateau.

The infinite variety in the shapes and sizes of hoodoos is the product of several factors. First, the rock layers that make up the hoodoos do not erode at the same rate—a process called differential erosion. This is because the ancient stream and lake sediments in the Claron Formation are composed of alternating layers of limestone, siltstone, and mudstone. Limestone, which tends to be lighter or gray in color, is harder and more resistant to erosion here in the arid Southwest. The siltstone and mudstone layers are much softer and more easily eroded. The result is that resistant limestone layers tend to form protective caps on top of the softer siltstone and mudstone layers.

A second important factor for the formation of hoodoos is the presence of a pervasive fracture or joint pattern that slices up the Claron Formation. The joint pattern at Bryce Canyon essentially forms a grid-like pattern of cracks oriented northwest and northeast. A result of the uplift and faulting that has shaken the High Plateaus, the joints provide ready-made zones of weakness where water can infiltrate, accelerating the rates of weathering and erosion.

As you begin to descend below Sunset Point, scan the tops of the hoodoos and try to pick out the resistant limestone layers that cap them. A perfect example is Thors Hammer, a rock pillar below the trail on the left.

Only 50 yards below the rim, a T-junction marks the beginning of the Navajo Loop Trail. Take the right fork. Steep switchbacks descend 521 feet, winding back and forth across a *talus* slope. This steep pile of weathered rock dislodged from the surrounding cliffs is continually slumping down-hill and sometimes washes out the trail completely.

The sculpting of the Bryce Cliffs takes place by both mechanical and chemical processes. Water is the master physical sculptor here, using abrasive action during runoff and also frost wedging as ice forms in joints and fractures, forcing rocks apart. Look closely at the rocks along the trail to see how they have been fractured and broken by mechanical weathering.

Hoodoos rising into the fog below the rim on the Navajo Loop Trail

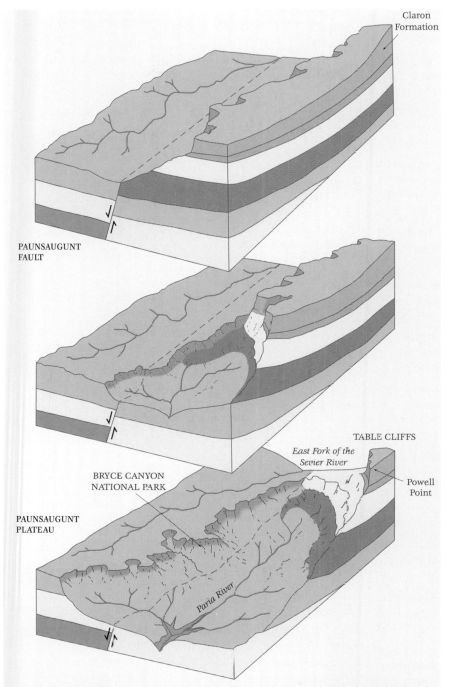

Claron
Formation

PAUNSAUGUNT
FAULT

TABLE CLIFFS

*East Fork of the
Sevier River*

Powell
Point

BRYCE CANYON
NATIONAL PARK

PAUNSAUGUNT
PLATEAU

Paria River

*Headward erosion along the Paria River carves Bryce Canyon on the
down-thrown side of the Paunsaugunt Fault*

Chemical weathering, on the other hand, involves dissolving the rock itself or the cement that holds the rock together. Water, in the form of rain or snowmelt, acts as a weak acid that dissolves and weakens the rock. Since the Claron Formation is rich in limestone—specifically the mineral calcite—which is pH basic, it is prone to chemical weathering. The work of chemical weathering is evident everywhere, from small pockets in the rock to the larger grottos seen high along the cliffs.

At the base of the switchbacks, the trail enters the narrow canyon known as "Wall Street." The overhang in the canyon walls developed as a layer of mudstone eroded more rapidly than the limestone above. The deep gully to the right of the trail has been scoured out by flash floods that periodically surge through this narrow canyon.

Emerging from Wall Street, the trail swings to the left and parallels the upper reaches of Bryce Creek. At the 0.7-mile point, the trail passes the junction with the Peek-a-boo Trail on the right, then immediately meets the junction with the trail to the Queens Garden. Instead of continuing on the Navajo Loop Trail to the left (which leads back up to the rim), go straight and follow this trail through the canyon bottom for about 0.75 mile to where it meets the Queens Garden Trail.

From the junction with the Queens Garden Trail, follow the short spur trail left to where it dead-ends among the colorful pinnacles in the Queens Garden. "Queen Victoria" is sculpted from a light-colored band of limestone. Back on the main trail, the 0.8-mile hike ascends 320 feet up to Sunrise Point on the Queens Garden Trail, winding through artistically sculpted spires and pinnacles. At each twist and turn along the trail there are great views of the Bryce Amphitheater.

Back on top at Sunrise Point, take in the view to the east toward the Table Cliffs Plateau, the last step in the Grand Staircase. "The Sinking Ship" is the name for the tilted layers in the foreground along the Paunsaugunt Fault, the easternmost fault that slices this western margin of the Colorado Plateau. Although it seems somewhat counterintuitive, Bryce Canyon is on the west, down-dropped side of this normal fault, while the Table Cliffs Plateau is on the east or high side of the fault. Movement along the Paunsaugunt Fault has dropped the eastern edge of the Paunsaugunt Plateau, while elevating the Table Cliffs Plateau to the east. Erosion along the fault has stripped away the more resistant Claron cliffs, exposing the softer, gray Cretaceous layers below. Over time, the softer Cretaceous rocks have washed away more rapidly, leaving the more resistant pink cliffs of the Bryce escarpment standing high above the Paria River valley.

Once you have studied the scene from Sunrise Point, follow the Rim Trail for 0.5 mile back to Sunset Point where this hike began.

TABLE CLIFFS PLATEAU

Hike 34

ATOP THE GRAND STAIRCASE

Hike to Powell Point for a view from the top of the Colorado Plateau's "geologic layercake."

DISTANCE ■ **2 miles round trip**

ELEVATION ■ **10,240 to 10,188 feet**

DIFFICULTY ■ **Easy**

TOPOGRAPHIC MAP ■ **USGS Pine Lake, UT**

GEOLOGIC MAP ■ **12**

KEY REFERENCES ■ **31, 32**

PRECAUTIONS ■ **Avoid this hike during afternoon thunderstorms. Because of the high elevation, the road to the trailhead may be impassable until all snow has melted, typically by mid- to late June.**

FOR INFORMATION ■ **Escalante Interagency Center**

About the Landscape: The Table Cliffs Plateau forms the top step of the Colorado Plateau's famed Grand Staircase. This high plateau is rimmed by the scenic pink cliffs of the Tertiary Claron Formation, the same sedimentary layers that color the cliffs of nearby Bryce Canyon National Park.

At Powell Point, you are standing on the uppermost layer of the Colorado Plateau's "geologic layercake." On his pioneering survey in 1879-80 of Utah's High Plateaus, Clarence Dutton named this promontory for Major John Wesley Powell. Along with the rest of the region, this great stack of sedimentary rock has been pushed skyward over the past 25 million years. Now perched above 10,000 feet in elevation, its sweeping view provides an excellent overview of southern Utah's geologic landforms.

Trail Guide: To reach the Powell Point trailhead, turn off Utah State Route 12 at the Bryce Canyon intersection, and drive 10.3 miles north on the Johns Valley Road. At the sign for Pine Lake, turn right onto the wide, gravel Forest Road 132. After 5 miles, bear left at the Pine Lake Campground and continue for another 6.1 miles to the junction with a two-track dirt road on the right (signed for Powell Point trailhead). Turn right and drive 3.5 miles to the trailhead at the end of the road.

The Powell Point trailhead is signed "Scenic Overlook, 3000 feet." From the parking area, an open view to the east looks out over the forested tableland of the Kaiparowits Plateau to rounded Navajo Mountain, one of the Colorado Plateau's many laccoliths on the far skyline. The blue-gray badlands in the foreground, known locally as "the blues," are stream-deposited mudstone and sandstone layers in the Cretaceous Kaiparowits Formation.

Ancient lakebeds of the Eocene Claron Formation eroding along the Table Cliffs Plateau

For the first 0.5 mile, the trail winds down a gentle forested slope to a saddle, then climbs an even grade another 0.5 mile out to Powell Point. Along the way there are several excellent views of the white and pink cliffs of the Claron Formation. These colorful limestone layers were deposited in a vast system of shallow lakes and streams that covered much of southern Utah during the Paleocene and Eocene around 55 million years ago. Similar to Bryce Canyon, erosion has artistically etched the plateau into a series of ornate spires and hoodoos.

The view from Powell Point, with the southern Utah landscape unfolding before you, rivals that of any in nearby Bryce Canyon. To the south, the Paria River drainage carves its way through the broad and gentle dome of the Kaibab Uplift. The prominent cliffs on the skyline are the "white cliffs" of the Navajo Sandstone.

The Table Cliffs Plateau is situated on the east or high side of the Paunsaugunt Fault, a long, north–south trending normal fault. In contrast, the pink cliffs of Bryce Canyon are on the west or down-dropped side of the fault, and lie 3000 feet below Powell Point. Where Utah Highway 12 crosses the fault in the distance, a sharp eye can pick out the trace of the fault where gray Cretaceous rocks are juxtaposed right up against the pink Tertiary Claron rocks.

The Paunsaugunt Fault is the easternmost of the three major Basin and Range faults that slice the western margin of the Colorado Plateau. It is speculated that motion along the Paunsaugunt Fault began around 15 million years ago when the land slowly started stretching apart. The fault was probably most active between 5 and 10 million years ago, and it continues to be intermittently active today. The other two faults, the Sevier and

Hurricane Faults, bound the Paunsaugunt and Markagunt High Plateaus to the west and have a similar history.

Like the other High Plateaus, the Table Cliffs Plateau was once capped by resistant layers of basalt, which protected the Claron sedimentary layers from rapid erosion and has helped keep the Table Cliffs standing high and mighty. Indeed, Barney Top, the highest point of the Table Cliffs Plateau to the north, still retains part of its basalt cap.

Millions of years ago, the pink cliffs of the Table Cliffs Plateau extended much farther south along the Paunsaugunt Fault where Bryce Canyon is located today. The steady headward erosion by the Paria River and its tributaries along the fault has excavated the cliffs of Bryce and caused the northward retreat of the Table Cliffs Plateau to where it stands today. The rate of cliff retreat is estimated at about 4 feet per 100 years, which translates into about 7 miles in one million years. This is a very rapid rate of erosion in the grand scheme of geologic processes. Had you been here a million years ago, you would have had to walk another 7 miles to reach Powell Point at the edge of the Table Cliffs Plateau.

Once you have marveled at the view, return to the trailhead by the route you came.

CEDAR BREAKS

The Colorado Plateau's Faulted Western Rim

Hike along the rim of the Cedar Breaks Amphitheater and view faults slicing the colorful and ancient lakebeds of the Claron Formation.

DISTANCE ■ **2 miles round trip**

ELEVATION ■ **10,400 to 10,000 feet**

DIFFICULTY ■ Moderate

TOPOGRAPHIC MAP ■ USGS Cedar Breaks, UT

GEOLOGIC MAP ■ See map in key reference.

KEY REFERENCE ■ 33

PRECAUTIONS ■ This hike follows close to a loose and crumbly rim—please stay on the trail and watch every step. Avoid this hike during afternoon thunderstorms.

FOR INFORMATION ■ Cedar Breaks National Monument

About the Landscape: Cedar Breaks is a natural rock amphitheater of staggering proportions. Here erosion has taken a huge bite out of the

Markagunt Plateau, the westernmost of Utah's High Plateaus. The western edge of the volcanic-capped Markagunt Plateau marks the boundary between the Colorado Plateau and the Basin and Range. Today, the plateau is still being sliced and diced by the Hurricane Fault, as the extensional forces of the Basin and Range continue to tug at its western margin.

Cedar Breaks is a wide gap more than 3 miles across and over 2000 feet deep where brilliantly colored pinnacles and hoodoos are being carved from sedimentary rocks in the Claron Formation. These are the same rocks, from Eocene freshwater lakes and streams, that paint the edges of the Paunsaugunt Plateau to the east, where Bryce Canyon is found, and also that fringe the Table Cliffs Plateau.

Because of the dramatic color contrast in the rock layers, numerous faults are easily visible in the cliffs of Cedar Breaks. This hike along the rim on the Spectra Point Trail is great for witnessing the magical glow of the rocks at sunset.

Trail Guide: The Spectra Point Trail is located within Cedar Breaks National Monument. To reach the trailhead from the north, turn off Utah State Route 143 onto SR 148 and drive south 3.9 miles, then turn right into the visitor center parking area. From the south, turn off SR 14 onto SR 148 and drive north 3.4 miles, then turn left into the visitor center parking area. The marked trailhead is located south (left) of the restrooms.

From the parking area, it is only a few steps up the Ramparts Trail to the rim. A jaw-dropping view greets you at the edge of the sheer main cliff or *escarpment* of the Cedar Breaks Amphitheater.

The colorful rocks of Cedar Breaks are composed of limestone, sandstone, and mudstone layers in the Claron Formation. These rocks were deposited during the Eocene about 55 million years ago in a system of freshwater lakes and streams.

From where it meets the edge, the Ramparts Trail winds south along the rim to Spectra Point, which is the promontory that pokes out below the main cliff. As you start down the first incline, notice how the white limestone layer where Spectra Point is located appears much lower than the white limestone ledge along the main cliff where you are walking. This is because the white limestone cliff is broken by a fault that has dropped Spectra Point down nearly 100 feet. The trace of the fault cuts through the steep ravine on the far side of the highpoint where the water tanks are located.

As you follow the trail downhill beyond the water tanks, you cross the fault along the way without knowing it. But after the trail turns to the west, look back up at the cliff below the water tanks to see where the white limestone is broken several times and seems to step down in a series of closely spaced faults.

The faults you see here are a microcosm of the Hurricane Fault, the major north–south trending fault that defines the western edge of the Markagunt Plateau. The Hurricane Fault is also not a simple fault defined by a single major break, but rather a wide zone of stair-stepping, down-to-the-west normal faults. The western edge of the Markagunt Plateau is sliced along a series of faults that have broken and fractured the rock, making it easier for erosion to work its magic in sculpting the amazing Cedar Breaks Amphitheater. The Hurricane Fault also marks the boundary between the Colorado Plateau and the Basin and Range. The fault continues to be active today and presents a serious threat for future earthquakes.

Beyond the fault, the trail winds down a steep, forested slope, then levels out along a cliff-edged section lined with a number of granddaddy bristlecone pine trees at about the 1-mile point. Here the trail meets a junction where a sign points left to the Wasatch Ramparts. Although you can follow this trail for another mile along the rim, continue straight ahead to Spectra Point only a few yards away.

The view from Spectra Point is breathtaking. Before you lies an amazing variety of ornate rock walls and hoodoos that seem to march up the cliffs. Headward erosion by Ashdown Creek and its tributaries has slowly eaten away at the rocks. Marked by offsets in the prominent white limestone layer, numerous faults are visible along the wide extent of the amphitheater. To the north, notice how a section of the white cliff has dropped down below Point Supreme, the fenced viewpoint just north of the trailhead.

As sunset approaches, the colors of the rock layers become increasingly

Hiking above cliffs of the Claron Formation at Cedar Breaks

more intense. The unusually colorful hues in the rocks are the result of small amounts of oxide minerals trapped in the rock. Oxides are formed when elements like iron and manganese combine with oxygen. In general, iron oxides tend to stain the rock varying shades of red and yellow, while manganese oxides add pastels like purple and lavender.

The prominent dark peak to the north is Brian Head. Like much of the Markagunt Plateau, Brian Head is capped by basalt lava that has protected the underlying Claron Formation from rapid erosion. Notice how faulting has tilted Brian Head's volcanic cap.

To the west, you are looking across the Hurricane Fault zone into the Basin and Range where tectonic forces are still actively stretching and extending the landscape, tugging at the margin of the Colorado Plateau and, in the process, creating the dramatic scenery before you. The Basin and Range is a vast tectonic province that continues west across Utah into Nevada and California, and south into Arizona and Mexico.

Once you have taken in the view and experienced the sunset, retrace your steps back to the trailhead.

Hike 36

ZION CANYON

THE SUBWAY ALONG THE LEFT FORK OF NORTH CREEK

Hike from a basalt-capped terrace past dinosaur tracks, waterfalls, and into a deep slot canyon called "the Subway."

DISTANCE ■ **9 miles round trip**

ELEVATION ■ **5200 to 4740 feet**

DIFFICULTY ■ **Strenuous**

TOPOGRAPHIC MAPS ■ **USGS The Guardian Angels; Trails Illustrated #214**

GEOLOGIC MAP ■ **See map in key reference.**

KEY REFERENCE ■ **34**

PRECAUTIONS ■ **This hike does not follow a maintained trail and requires a good deal of routefinding ability and stream crossings—bring a topo map and be prepared to get your feet wet! Flash floods are a real danger. Use extreme caution and be sure to check the local weather forecast before attempting this hike. A hiking permit is required for this day-use-only area; apply for the lottery well in advance of your trip.**

FOR INFORMATION ■ **Zion National Park**

About the Landscape: The canyons of Zion National Park are testimony to the power of erosion along the faulted and uplifted edge of Utah's High

Plateaus. In Zion Canyon, sheer walls of sandstone tower 2000 feet above the canyon floor. Several times over the last million years lava flows have spilled over the edge of the plateaus, demonstrating that the canyons of Zion National Park are very "recent" features of the landscape.

The Jurassic Navajo Sandstone is perhaps the most celebrated of all the rock layers of the Colorado Plateau. It is a strange quirk of geologic fate that the Virgin River and its tributaries have carved deep canyons where the Navajo Sandstone attains its maximum thickness. This 175-million-year-old, wind-blown layer of sand blankets the entire Colorado Plateau, but nowhere else does it reach over 2000 feet in thickness.

Here in Zion National Park, erosion has dissected an intricate network of deep canyons, exposing the large, sweeping cross-beds that make the Navajo Sandstone famous.

Trail Guide: To reach the Left Fork trailhead, drive west from the Zion National Park Visitor Center in Springdale, Utah, 14.5 miles on State Route 9 and turn right in the small town of Virgin onto Kolob Road (signed for "Kolob Reservoir"). Drive north 8.5 miles into Zion National Park to reach the marked trailhead and parking area on the right.

From the trailhead, the trail winds across a forested terrace capped by basalt lava and mantled with recent wind-blown sand. The black boulders and ledges of basalt are from the flows along Grapevine Wash which spilled from cinder cones along the rim of the Kolob Terrace about 270,000 years ago. These hot rivers of magma flowed down from the rim toward the Virgin River, filling canyons between sandstone cliffs on the way. Notice that many of the boulders are chock-full of tiny holes called vesicles, where gas bubbles were trapped in the once-molten lava.

After about 0.5 mile, the trail reaches the edge of the terrace and begins its abrupt descent into Great West Canyon, where the Left Fork of North Creek is located. This section of the trail is very steep and treacherous—use extreme caution.

There is a great view looking upcanyon from the rim. On the opposite (east) side of the canyon, notice the faulted wall face. The sheer cliff of Navajo Sandstone steps down to the right several hundred feet. The Navajo Sandstone represents stacks of large-scale, wind-blown dunes of a 175-million-year-old Jurassic desert. The red slopes and ledges below the Navajo cliffs are in the underlying Kayenta Formation, which represent river systems, small lakes, and sand dunes blowing across the floodplain.

As you carefully make your way down into the canyon, note the layers of basalt exposed in the cliffs to the right (west) of the trail. These are the Grapevine Wash flows. Because these lava flows erupted in a geologic "instant," they provide a snapshot of the landscape at the time they erupted.

Their position high above the canyons we see today indicates that a great deal of erosion and canyon-cutting has occurred in the last 270,000 years.

About 1 mile from the trailhead, the trail reaches the bottom of the canyon and the Left Fork of North Creek. A sign for the "Left Fork Trailhead" marks the junction with the inner canyon trail. Note the topography in this area so you don't miss this turn on your way back. Turn left here and begin hiking upcanyon. The trail quickly makes its first crossing to the right side of the creek

Note: There is no maintained trail through the canyon. Multiple trails cross the creek many times, skirt waterfalls, and climb around boulder jams. Try your best to follow the most traveled route. If you find yourself stuck, simply retrace your steps and choose another route. These routes are not technical and do not require ropes.

As the "trail" winds upstream through the wide canyon bottom, look for more black layers of basalt filling a wide notch in the canyon wall high above the creek to the left. These layers are part of the Lava Point flows and are much older than the Grapevine Wash flows. They fill an ancient valley eroded along the fault that cuts across the canyon, and mark the depth of the canyon about 1 million years ago when the lava flowed as glowing rivers of magma.

From the position of the Lava Point flows high above today's canyon floor, geologists have estimated the rate of canyon-cutting in the Zion Canyon region at about 1300 feet per million years (or 1.3 feet per thousand years). Thus, just 1 million years ago, the main canyon through Zion National Park was about half as deep as it is today and the famous "Narrows" in the upper canyon had not yet formed. Since the Navajo Sandstone is over 2000 feet thick, this means the canyons of Zion that we see today were carved in "only" the last 2 million years.

At about the 2-mile point from the trailhead, there is a large house-size boulder along the right side of the creek. On the opposite side of the creek from the huge boulder, there are two large tilted slabs of gray sandstone covered with dinosaur tracks. These three-toed tracks were left in the soft unconsolidated sand along an ancient river by large reptiles called theropods about 200 million years ago. *Theropods* were bipedal creatures and included many different species of dinosaurs that vanished from the earth at the end of the Cretaceous.

Beyond the dinosaur tracks, the canyon begins to narrow and the "trail," such as it is, becomes more difficult to follow. The route repeatedly crosses the creek and, in an attempt to avoid boulder jams and small waterfalls, some simple climbing and boulder hopping is necessary. Although you

Hidden waterfall along the Left Fork of North Creek, Zion National Park, Utah

will begin to wonder if the Subway really exists, there is little doubt once you finally get there.

The final approach to the Subway is marked by a series of waterfalls spilling over red rock steps. For about the last 0.25 mile, it is best to simply walk in the creekbed and, if you haven't already, succumb to getting your feet wet.

Once at the Subway, the canyon narrows rapidly; its walls are wider and rounded at the creek level with overhanging ledges above. Numerous deep "potholes" have been gouged into the creekbed by swirling boulders. In places, the water in the creek flows through narrow flutes eroded along joints in the rocks. In fact, the sharp bend in the canyon where it enters the Subway occurs along a prominent joint that breaks the rock apart, making it easier to erode.

You can easily hike as far as the first sharp bend in the dark, narrow slot canyon, but soon the potholes become waist-deep. Beware—this is not a good place to be in a flash flood!

Once your feet have become chilled and you yearn for the sun again, retrace your route (as best you can) back to the trailhead.

CORAL PINK SAND DUNES

Hike 37

RECYCLED JURASSIC SAND

Explore shifting dunes of colorful sand eroded from ancient wind-blown dunes of the Navajo Sandstone.

DISTANCE ■ 0.5-mile loop (or as far as you want to go!)

ELEVATION ■ 5900 to 5880 feet

DIFFICULTY ■ Easy

TOPOGRAPHIC MAP ■ USGS Yellow Jacket Canyon, UT

GEOLOGIC MAP ■ 21

KEY REFERENCE ■ 35

PRECAUTIONS ■ The sand on the dunes gets very hot in summer and can burn your feet. If you venture out onto the tallest active dunes where visibility is poor, be on the lookout for ATVs, which could come bearing down on you. If possible, plan your visit for weekdays, when ATVs on the dunes are less likely.

FOR INFORMATION ■ Coral Pink Sand Dunes State Park

About the Landscape: The colorful sands of Coral Pink Sand Dunes have been sand dunes before. These amazingly colorful dunes are made of sand recycled from the Navajo Sandstone, a formation of sand blown into giant dunes by ancient winds during the Jurassic about 175 million years ago. Since that time, the sand grains have been buried and trapped in sandstone. Liberated by weathering and erosion along the Vermilion Cliffs, modern-day winds have again whipped the sand back into active dunes.

Coral Pink Sand Dunes State Park is located along the Sevier Fault, one of the major normal faults that slice the High Plateaus region of the western Colorado Plateau. A short nature trail, complete with interpretive signs, winds through a vegetated area in the dunes that is off limits to ATVs (all-terrain vehicles). To really see geology in action, kick off your shoes and climb to the top of the tallest dunes.

Trail Guide: To reach the trailhead for this hike, drive 7.3 miles north from Kanab on U.S. Highway 89. At the sign for Coral Pink Sand Dunes, turn left and drive 9.8 miles to a T-intersection. Turn left again and drive 5.8 miles to the park entrance on the left. From Mt. Carmel Junction, drive 3.5 miles south on Highway 89 and turn right at the sign for Coral Pink Sand Dunes. Drive 10.2 miles to the park entrance on the left. The parking area for the trailhead is located at the day-use picnic area 0.25 mile from the park entrance station.

From the parking area, the first part of the trail follows a well-constructed boardwalk to a viewpoint overlooking the dunes. This is a good place to study the lay of the land. Be sure to look at the interpretive display that shows a geologic cross-section of the area.

The Coral Pink Sand Dunes have gathered here in a valley along the Sevier Fault, a major normal fault that extends south from central Utah to the Grand Canyon. Movement along the Sevier Fault dates back to the initiation of Basin and Range extension, when faulting began to break apart the western edge of the Colorado Plateau about 15 million years ago. The fault was probably most active between 5 and 10 million years ago, and it continues to be intermittently active today. Down to the west, movement along the Sevier Fault sliced off a segment of the Vermilion Cliffs, exposing red and maroon layers of the Moenave Sandstone in the steep cliffs of the Moquith Mountains across the dunes to the east.

The sand dunes here are the result of prevailing winds blowing from the southwest. The Navajo Sandstone is the most likely source of the sand, and is widely exposed across the Moccasin Terrace on the down-dropped side of the Sevier Fault southwest of the park. The dunes are formed as the wind approaches the valley along the cliffs. As the wind loses speed, it can no longer carry the sand. Once the sand is trapped in the valley, swirling winds, perhaps shifting directions with the seasons, continue to pile the sand and shape the dunes we see in the valley today.

From the end of the boardwalk the interpretive trail heads out across the rolling dune-scape, making a loop that will return to the boardwalk. Interpretive signs lead across the hummocks where the sand is anchored by vegetation, and also through swales or *blowouts*. Blowouts are low areas between the dunes where the wind has swept the sand away down to a surface of damp sand and small rocks that cannot be moved by the wind. In places, intricate sets of wind ripples decorate the surface of the dunes.

Sand from the Jurassic is recycled into dunes along the Sevier Fault, Coral Pink Sand Dunes State Park

Ripples form where the sand grains have been rolled and bounced into place by the driving force of the wind.

At about the halfway point, the trail meets the fence that separates the vegetated dune area from the more "active" dunes, which are open to ATVs. This is a good place to deviate from the trail and climb to the top of the tallest dunes. As you climb in the soft sand, note the impact that the ATVs have on the dunes. The vehicle tracks and shifting sand damages the vegetation and can keep new growth from gaining a foothold. Also, there is an endemic beetle that uses the dunes for home and travel. So please watch your step and tread lightly to limit your impact.

The shape of sand dunes is influenced by a number of factors including sand supply, strength and consistency of wind direction, and presence of topographic obstacles. The tallest dune directly east is an excellent example of a star dune. *Star dunes,* which commonly have a high central peak and three or four curving arms, form where winds from more than two directions build a dune. The large dunes to the south are *barchan dunes,* characterized by a concentric shape, a steep, concave slipface, and "horns" extending downwind from the central mass of the dune. Barchans generally form in areas where the wind direction varies less than 15 degrees and where the sand supply is limited.

As you make your way back to the trailhead, take a moment to pick up a handful of sand and examine it closely with your hand lens. Up close, the individual sand grains are clear grains of even-sized quartz. The color of the dunes results from reddish iron-oxide stains on the surface of each grain. Although the stain appears as only a trace on each individual grain, when the grains are piled high, the stain is enough to color these dunes pink—especially when highlighted by the last rays at sunset.

Each of the sand grains in your hand is on a journey through time. Geologists speculate that the sand in the Navajo Sandstone was originally weathered from metamorphic rocks somewhere near present-day Montana, and were then first transported by Jurassic rivers to the coast of the ancient North American continent. Ocean currents, waves, and tidal action then swept the grains along a sandy coastline where the wind picked them up and piled them into large dunes in a Sahara-like desert. As the dunes were buried by younger sediments, groundwater between the grains precipitated cement that hardened them into stone. The sandstone remained buried for millions of years until uplift of the Colorado Plateau set the stage for weathering and erosion that would liberate the grains once again. Now, perhaps almost 175 million years later, the sand grains have been recycled and are once again piled into dunes here as the Coral Pink Sand Dunes.

BULLION CANYON

WATERFALLS AND A GLACIATED HANGING VALLEY

Hike to Bullion Falls and a scenic hanging valley, carved by Ice Age glaciers into a volcano in the Tushar Mountains.

DISTANCE ■ **4 miles round trip**

ELEVATION ■ **7850 to 8900 feet**

DIFFICULTY ■ **Strenuous**

TOPOGRAPHIC MAP ■ **USGS Mount Brigham, UT**

GEOLOGIC MAP ■ **22**

KEY REFERENCE ■ **36**

PRECAUTIONS ■ **Use caution when climbing down to Bullion Falls. Old mines are dangerous—do not enter.**

FOR INFORMATION ■ **Beaver Ranger District**

About the Landscape: This hike up Bullion Canyon in the Tushar Mountains offers something completely different on Utah's High Plateaus. Surprisingly, here you'll find Rocky Mountain–like scenery complete with waterfalls, a glaciated valley, and snow-capped peaks. There is also a colorful mining history and ghosts from a town that once boasted a population of more than 1650 souls.

The Tushar Mountains are the tallest mountains between Colorado's Rockies and California's Sierra Nevada, with three peaks over 12,000 feet above sea level. These rounded summits were once the center for explosive volcanoes that smothered the western edge of the Colorado Plateau. In the process, the wind-blown Navajo Sandstone was baked into quartzite, a metamorphic rock.

The fireworks took place during the Oligocene and Miocene, between about 30 and 19 million years ago. A cluster of tall composite or stratovolcanoes spewed tremendous volumes of lava, ash, and breccia across a landscape of sedimentary rock. Although greatly modified by faulting and erosion, at least four calderas have been identified in and around the area we know as the Tushar Mountain Volcanic Field.

Trail Guide: To reach the Bullion Canyon Trailhead, turn west off U.S. Highway 89 onto Center Street in the town of Marysvale, Utah. Drive 1.4 miles west and turn left just past the LDS (Mormon) Church onto the Bullion Canyon Road. Follow this road (which turns to gravel) 4.1 miles to a bridge across Pine Creek. Park after crossing the bridge. Signs mark the trailhead, found at the old road just before the bridge on the right.

The Bullion Canyon Trail starts out following an old mining road alongside Pine Creek. The road passes several old structures, reminders of a bygone era when this "canyon of gold" was a center of activity.

Bullion Canyon sprang to life in 1865 when placer gold was discovered in the sand and gravel along Pine Creek. Prospectors soon discovered traces of gold, silver, and lead along veins in the canyon walls. By 1869 the first canyon road was completed so that the ore could be hauled out by wagon before the first mill was built. The main camp, called Bullion City, sprang up in the area above where the bridge is today. By 1881 the population had swelled to 1651, but ten years later less than 300 remained. The boom and bust cycles continued until the last mill closed in 1938 when gold was $35 per ounce. Today, only enough work is done to keep the mining claims legal.

Leaving the road behind at about the 0.5-mile point, a trail worn by all-terrain-vehicles (ATVs) switchbacks steeply up a forested slope, passing an entrance to an old mining tunnel on the right. The trail crosses a steep talus slope where Cascade Falls comes into view on the opposite side of the canyon. Although there are no solid outcrops, the rocks here are quartzite, a type of metamorphic rock. *Quartzite* forms when sandstone is heated to high temperatures, fusing the individual sand grains together. In this case, igneous intrusions and volcanic activity in the Tushar Mountains caused the heat.

Beyond the talus slope, the loose rocks along the trail are volcanic rocks of mostly greenish-gray andesite and reddish-purple rhyolite. Notice the light-colored feldspar crystals encased in a fine-grained matrix. The scattered white rocks are chunks of quartz from fractures in the volcanic rocks.

At the point where the ATV trail ends and the trail becomes a footpath, there is another old mining structure and a sign that reads "Bullion Falls, 200 yards." Soon the roar of Bullion Falls beckons.

At the 1-mile point, a steep spur trail leads down to the left to the plunge pool at the base of the falls—watch your step. The outcrop to the right of the trail at the junction is quartzite. This hard, resistant rock also forms Bullion Falls, which is only one step along a series of cascades through the narrow quartzite canyon.

Bullion Falls—sparks fly in the Tushar Mountains

Once you have enjoyed the coolness of the impressive falls, continue following the Bullion Canyon Trail as it switchbacks steeply up the north side of the canyon.

Although outcrops are rare, one section of the trail is blasted through solid igneous rock coated with blue-black and yellow stains of iron and manganese oxide. This outcrop is also riddled with thin veins of quartz. The staining on the rock beside the trail, and the rusted and weathered look of the cliffs along the hillside above, suggest that *hydrothermal* fluids have altered these rocks. This is common where upwelling magma works its way toward the surface. Underground, the hot, mineral-rich fluids percolate through the rocks and sometimes move into the surrounding rock, leaving behind economically valuable minerals—in this case gold and other precious metals in the quartzite of Bullion Canyon.

Nearing the top of the ridge, the trail levels out in the forest. As it reaches a stand of aspen trees, look for an old mine-digging left of the trail. This is a good place to climb onto the rounded rock outcrop for a jaw-dropping scenic view of the high volcanic peaks to the west and the faulted Sevier Valley to the east.

Once you have found a suitable lofty perch, notice that the outcrop you are standing on is more of the quartzite you have been passing on the trail. Bullion Falls is located near the base of a deep notch carved into this quartzite ridge by Pine Creek. Notice also the original layering in the rock, and the slanted patterns or cross-bedding. Amazingly, this rock is the Jurassic Navajo Sandstone, the same formation found in Zion Canyon and all across Utah's canyon country. Here, its wind-blown sand grains were fused by heat and buried within the base of the Tushar Mountain volcano.

Notice also that the Navajo quartzite has been worn smooth and polished by the action of Ice Age glaciers, which scoured the landscape during the last 1.8 million years. The Tushar Mountains were one of the few areas on the Colorado Plateau where enough snow and ice accumulated to form glaciers during the Pleistocene. In places you can find scratches or *striations* where rocks trapped in the moving ice scraped gouges in the hard bedrock surface. The bowl-like basins or *cirques* between the two high peaks on the western skyline were gouged near the head of the glaciers. The U-shape of the alpine valley also suggests that glaciers helped scour the landscape. Because the glaciers could not wear down this hard ridge of quartzite, Upper Bullion Canyon is a *hanging valley* above the main canyon below.

Although it is possible to continue hiking up the alpine valley for miles, this is the turnaround point for this hike. Once you have admired the view, carefully retrace your steps back to the trailhead.

Black Canyon of the Gunnison

Part 3
COLORADO'S PLATEAU HIKES

Chapter 7
THE WESTERN SLOPE

It may come as a surprise that Colorado is more than just mountains. Although Colorado is deservedly called the Rocky Mountain State, west of the Rockies the incredible canyons, cliffs, and mesas of the Colorado Plateau continue uninterrupted. Here, in a region known as Colorado's "Western Slope," the Colorado Plateau's sedimentary layers lap against the vaulted skyline of the Rocky Mountains. This is where you will find the cliff ruins of Mesa Verde, the red rock canyons of the Dolores River, the sandstone spires of Colorado National Monument, and the canyonlands of Dinosaur National Monument.

Distant views of the mountains from the canyon country are a constant reminder that if not for the Rocky Mountains next door, the Colorado Plateau would appear much different than it does today. The headwaters of the mighty Colorado River are not found in the canyons or on the mesas of the Colorado Plateau. They are found high in Colorado's Rocky Mountains. In the past, it was meltwater from the Ice Age glaciers that provided torrents of water that helped carve the canyon country of the Four Corners region. Today it is the melting snow from the Rockies' lofty peaks that feeds the Colorado River and its tributaries—including the Gunnison, Dolores, and San Juan Rivers—providing the power that continues to dissect Colorado's Western Slope, creating an intricate network of layered sandstone canyons.

The distant views of the mountains from the canyon country are also a reminder of the profound differences in their geologic history. While the Rockies were repeatedly uplifted and eroded, faulted and folded, seared by intrusions, and buried by explosive volcanic eruptions, the Colorado Plateau was an island of relative geologic calm. Throughout these major events, which upset and removed the sedimentary layers that once covered much of Colorado, the layers still remain intact across the Western Slope.

There are exceptions, of course. One major interruption in the calm is the Uncompahgre Plateau, where 300 million years ago the western range of the Ancestral Rocky Mountains pushed up along the eastern edge of the Colorado Plateau. Erosion of these ancient mountains stripped away overlying sedimentary layers and exposed the basement rock core. The sediment that washed from the mountains helped fill the Paradox Basin, a deep, fault-bounded trough that developed along the southwestern flank

208

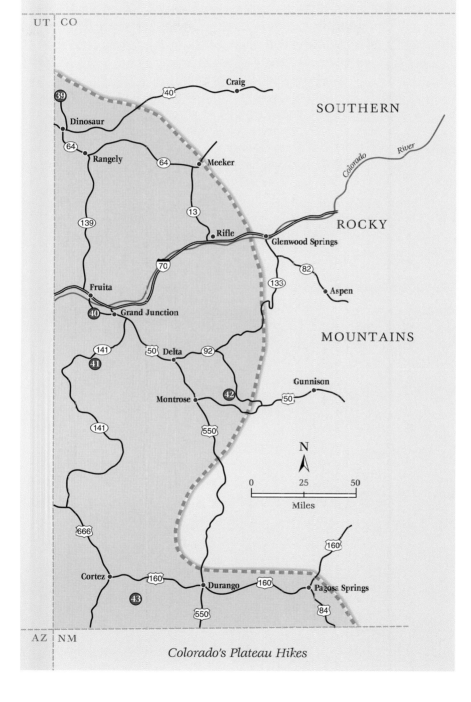

UT | CO

Craig

39

Dinosaur

SOUTHERN

64

Rangely 64 Meeker

Colorado River

13

139

Rifle

ROCKY

Glenwood Springs

70

82

Fruita

133 Aspen

40 Grand Junction

MOUNTAINS

141

50 Delta 92

41

Gunnison

Montrose 42

50

550

N

0   25   50

Miles

141

666

160

Cortez 160 Durango 160 Pagosa Springs

43

84

550

AZ | NM

Colorado's Plateau Hikes

of the mountains. During Mesozoic time, the eroded roots of this old highland were crossed by Triassic rivers, buried by Jurassic wind-blown dunes, and then submerged beneath the Cretaceous seaway. Later, about 65 million years ago during the Laramide orogeny, uplift reactivated deep-seated faults and pushed the basement rocks skyward once again.

The Colorado Plateau's basement rocks are revealed now along the flanks of the Uncompahgre Plateau near Grand Junction and where the Gunnison River has cut its way down in Black Canyon. Their juxtaposition directly beneath the Mesozoic red sedimentary rocks that covered them creates the Great Unconformity where over 1 billion years of layers, including all the Paleozoic, are missing from the record. These missing Paleozoic layers are still present elsewhere on the Colorado Plateau, and are best exposed in the walls of the Grand Canyon.

Although uplift of the Rocky Mountains ruffled the plateau's eastern edge, the landscape quickly transitions into deeply incised canyons and mesas carved into the colorful sedimentary layers for which the Colorado Plateau is famous.

Cliffs of Wingate Sandstone at Colorado National Monument

Hike 39

HARPERS CORNER

BIRD'S-EYE VIEW OF FAULTS AND FOLDS

The ripple effects of the Uinta Mountain Uplift are revealed in the canyons of the Yampa and Green Rivers in Dinosaur National Monument.

DISTANCE ■ 2 miles round trip

ELEVATION ■ 7600 to 7510 feet

DIFFICULTY ■ Easy

TOPOGRAPHIC MAPS ■ USGS Jones Hole; Trails Illustrated #220

GEOLOGIC MAP ■ 23

KEY REFERENCE ■ 37

PRECAUTIONS ■ Please remain on the trail and use extreme caution at the precipitous overlook. Avoid the overlook during approaching thunderstorms.

FOR INFORMATION ■ Dinosaur National Monument

About the Landscape: If you have ever dreamed of a bird's-eye view of geologic features, this trail is for you. The Harpers Corner Trail leads to a spectacular viewpoint rising more than 2000 feet above Echo Park, where the Green and Yampa Rivers meet. From this high vantage point, three canyons are in view—Lodore and Yampa Canyons upstream and Whirlpool Canyon downstream. The Laramide Uinta Mountain Uplift ruffled the once flat-lying sedimentary layers in the canyons, dramatically upturning them along the Mitten Park Fault and monocline.

Although Dinosaur National Monument is best known for its prolific dinosaur quarry in the Jurassic Morrison Formation, its landscape along the northern edge of the Colorado Plateau, dominated by these bent and broken rock layers in the twisting maze of canyons, is not to be missed. This is one of the best places to view the geological transition of landforms where the Colorado Plateau meets the Rocky Mountains.

Trail Guide: To reach the Harpers Corner trailhead, drive 1.5 miles east from Dinosaur on U.S. Highway 40 to the sign for Dinosaur National Monument. Turn left (north) and follow the Harpers Corner Scenic Drive 32.5 miles to the parking area at the end of the road.

The Harpers Corner Trail traverses a narrow, forested ridge to a rock promontory high above Whirlpool Canyon and Echo Park. The trail starts out by making a couple of switchbacks down a gentle grade, then follows a well-worn trail all the way to the viewpoint. The boulders along the trail are from the Bishop Conglomerate, composed of rocks eroded from the crest of the Uinta Uplift. This widespread layer blanketed much of the area before canyon-cutting began.

As the trail climbs a gentle incline to the viewpoint, the rocks beneath your feet are beds of solid gray limestone. Look closely to find fossils of clam-like shells of brachiopods, disc-shaped segments of crinoid stems, and tiny, twig-like fossils called bryozoans. You are walking on an ancient sea floor from the Morgan Formation of Pennsylvanian age.

From the viewpoint, the Green River in Whirlpool Canyon lies to the west (left) and Echo Park to the east (right). The confluence between the Green and Yampa at Echo Park is obscured by Steamboat Rock, a long ridge of light-colored sandstone. This light-colored strata is the Weber Sandstone, a thick layer of wind-blown sand that accumulated in this area about 275 to 300 million years ago during late Pennsylvanian to early Permian time. Although not exposed at river level, the Morgan Formation that you stand on is also the rock layer that lies just below the white sands of the Weber Sandstone.

But how can you be standing on these limestone layers so high, when the Weber Sandstone forms the walls of the canyons far below?

The answer involves the disruption of the rock layers along the Mitten Park fault and monocline. The fault is visible across the river on the right side (east) of the viewpoint. At river level, the rock layers that extend to the left from Steamboat Rock are bent sharply upwards at the fault zone against horizontal layers on the left. This fault shifted older rocks, left of the fault, upward relative to the younger rocks on the right of the fault. The dark red Precambrian sandstones raised to river level left of the fault are 1-billion-year-old Uinta Mountain Group, sedimentary basement rocks.

Motion along the fault caused the layers on top to be folded into a steep monocline, although the top step in the monocline has eroded away. Look far to the right (south) of the river to see where the white Weber Sandstone steps upward twice more along monoclines draped over the Yampa Fault zone.

This bending and breaking of rocks took place as the Uinta Mountains pushed skyward during the Laramide orogeny about 65 million years ago. The motion warped these sedimentary layers along the northern edge of the Colorado Plateau. Renewed uplift over the past 25 million years further disrupted these once flat-lying strata.

A curious feature of the scene before you is that the rivers cut directly across the faults and folds, rather than taking the easy way around. This is because the rivers established their courses when the faults and folds in the rocks were buried beneath a younger veneer of sediments eroded from the nearby mountains (including the Bishop Conglomerate). The

Upturned sedimentary layers along the Mitten Park fault and monocline

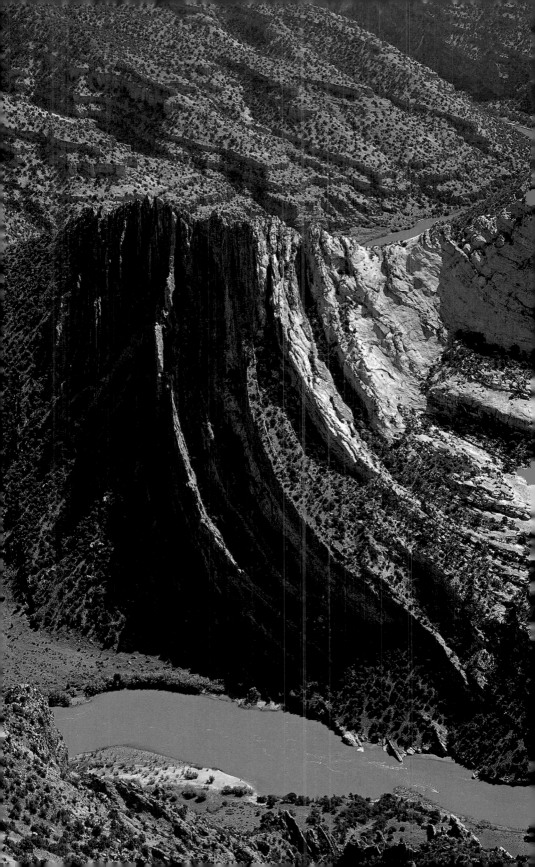

rivers first established themselves as they carved a lazy, sinuous course through the flat-lying layers. With renewed uplift of the region, the rivers entrenched themselves in their own meanders. As they eroded more deeply, they eventually reached the older, folded and faulted layers. By this time, however, they were set in their ways and continued to follow these courses despite the faults, folds, and resistant rock layers they encountered.

After taking in this spectacular view of the geologic landscapes before you, simply retrace your steps back to the trailhead.

MONUMENT CANYON

SANDSTONE MONUMENTS AND THE GREAT UNCONFORMITY

The Wingate Sandstone is eroded into a number of free-standing fins and spires along the Redlands Monocline of the Uncompahgre Plateau.

DISTANCE ■ **6 miles round trip**

ELEVATION ■ **6260 to 5350 feet**

DIFFICULTY ■ **Moderate**

TOPOGRAPHIC MAPS ■ **USGS Colorado National Monument; Trails Illustrated #208**

GEOLOGIC MAP ■ **24**

KEY REFERENCE ■ **38**

PRECAUTIONS ■ **Carry plenty of water, wear a hat, and avoid the extreme midday heat in summer.**

FOR INFORMATION ■ **Colorado National Monument**

About the Landscape: Colorado National Monument is an area of colorful Triassic and Jurassic sedimentary rocks that were bent, faulted, and fractured as the Uncompahgre Plateau uplifted during the Laramide orogeny. This hike follows a massive red rock cliff of Wingate Sandstone that has eroded into spectacular free-standing fins and spires along the Redlands Monocline, which defines the northern edge of the Uncompahgre Plateau. The trail also leads into the heart of the sandstone canyons along the northeastern edge of the plateau, and traverses the Great Unconformity where over 1 billion years' worth of rock layers are missing.

Trail Guide: To reach the Monument Canyon trailhead from Grand Junction, enter the park at its east entrance and follow the Rim Rock Road to the Monument Canyon Trail parking area (just after Artists Point). From the west entrance at Fruita, follow Rim Rock Drive past the visitor center to the trailhead.

The Monument Canyon Trail winds down to the base of the red rock cliffs and follows a side canyon that eventually leads to the head of Monument Canyon. After a few switchbacks, the trail follows a ledge in a salmon-colored cliff of Entrada Sandstone. Cross-bedding patterns in the rock formed as the faces of advancing sand dunes were buried by Jurassic winds about 160 million years ago.

After passing the junction with the Coke Ovens Trail on the right, you come to the trail register. At this point, the trail steps down through stream-deposited sandstone and conglomerate of the Kayenta Formation. Look for ripple marks and medium-scale, curved cross-beds produced by currents in Jurassic stream channels.

Below the Kayenta ledge, a series of tight switchbacks follow a talus slope down to the base of the towering Wingate cliff. Large, sweeping cross-beds are evident along the cliff face. The Wingate is a pile of wind-blown sand that accumulated earlier in the Jurassic.

The Jurassic Wingate Sandstone forms rock spires in Monument Canyon.

The character of the landscape changes as the trail meets the canyon bottom and winds its way over rounded, deeply weathered outcrops of Precambrian basement rock. These metamorphic rocks are banded gneiss and schist that were formed by heat and pressure at great depth during mountain-building events about 1.7 billion years ago. Then about 1.4 billion years ago, magma squeezed into cracks in the rock and cooled to form pegmatite dikes and irregular granitic bodies. Chunks of granite-like rock that contain large crystals of quartz and feldspar, and flakes of mica have weathered from the pegmatite dikes.

You have now reached the Great Unconformity, a gap in the rock record that spans more than a billion years. Thousands of feet of Precambrian and Paleozoic rocks, present in other areas of the Colorado Plateau, are missing between the brick red Chinle Formation, deposited by streams during the Triassic about 225 million years ago, and the underlying basement core of the Uncompahgre Plateau. These missing rocks were stripped off by erosion during uplift and demise of the ancestral Uncompahgre Highland, the western arm of the Ancestral Rocky Mountains that vaulted skyward about 300 million years ago in roughly the same place where the present Uncompahgre Plateau is located.

As the trail swings around to the north, the canyon opens up and the first of many free-standing stone towers comes into view. From this vantage point, the vertical fractures that give the tower its shape are clearly evident.

As the trail winds along the base of the cliff, heading west, more sandstone pillars appear, including the beloved Kissing Couple (you'll know it when you see it!). The trail eventually leads to the sandstone fin named Independence Monument, where a short spur trail takes you up a saddle in the Chinle Formation to the base of the 450-foot-high fin of Wingate Sandstone. From here, it's easy to imagine a continuous rock wall joining the cliffs on either end of this monument as well as the other fins and spires. The orientation of the sandstone fin is determined by vertical fractures that cut through the rock. Erosion was more rapid along the fractures and, over time, has removed the surrounding rock on either side. Today, only a small, resistant cap of Kayenta sandstone protects the top of the monument. Once that cap rock erodes away, Independence Monument will wither. This type of weathering is called *differential erosion*. The Kayenta sandstone is cemented with quartz, making it more durable and resistant to erosion. The Wingate Sandstone is held together by calcite, which is softer and tends to dissolve when wet.

Although the Monument Canyon Trail continues for another 3 miles where it emerges to meet Colorado State Route 340, this is the turnaround point for this hike. Return to the trailhead by reversing your route.

UNAWEEP CANYON

Ancient River Channel and the Great Unconformity

The mysterious carving of Unaweep Canyon through 1000 feet of solid basement rock took the force of a river far mightier than the two small streams that occupy it today.

Hike 41

DISTANCE ■ 1 mile round trip

ELEVATION ■ 6780 to 6840 feet

DIFFICULTY ■ Easy

TOPOGRAPHIC MAP ■ USGS Jacks Canyon

GEOLOGIC MAP ■ 24

KEY REFERENCE ■ 39

PRECAUTIONS ■ This hike does not follow a designated or maintained trail; walk on rock outcrops as much as possible to avoid crushing the cryptobiotic soil.

FOR INFORMATION ■ Grand Junction Resource Area

About the Landscape: In the Ute language 'Unaweep" means "canyon with two mouths," and the origin of this unusual canyon still puzzles geologists. The canyon slices across the midsection of the Uncompahgre Plateau, a 100-mile-long uplift located southwest of Grand Junction, Colorado. Today, only two small streams flowing in opposite directions (East and West Creeks) occupy the canyon. But it must have taken the erosive power of a much larger river over an extended time period to cut 1000 feet into the resistant Precambrian igneous and metamorphic basement rocks of the uplifted Uncompahgre Plateau. Where is that river today?

Imagine a river flowing through the canyon, swollen with snowmelt, carving the canyon deeper and deeper. Though the evidence is only circumstantial, geologists speculate that the Gunnison River, now located east of the Uncompahgre Plateau, may once have flowed westward through Unaweep Canyon. Gravels of similar composition are found along the present-day Gunnison and toward the west end of Unaweep Canyon near Gateway, Colorado. It is possible that an ancestral channel of the Gunnison River slowly carved Unaweep Canyon over millions of years as the Uncompahgre Plateau uplifted.

At some point, uplift may have outpaced the river and the Gunnison may have begun to flow northward, joining with the Colorado River and abandoning its channel through the canyon. Or, the Colorado River "captured" the flow of the Gunnison, forcing it to abandon its route through the canyon. This process, called *stream piracy*, occurs when a river cuts a

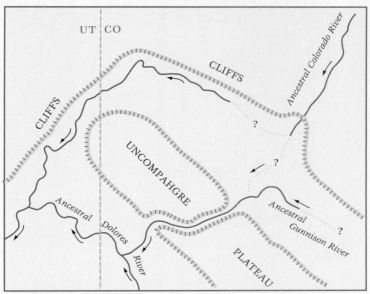

A. Before abandonment of Unaweep Canyon

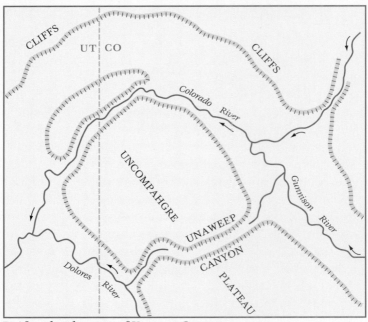

B. After abandonment of Unaweep Canyon

Possible cutting of Unaweep Canyon by ancestral channels of the Gunnison and Colorado Rivers

channel through soft rocks until it ultimately erodes headward into the course of another river nearby, thereby capturing its flow.

The competing theory of the canyon's origin is that both the Colorado and Gunnison may have once carved the canyon together. Then the Colorado River was pirated away by a nearby stream and ultimately pirated the Gunnison away from the ancestral course.

Trail Guide: To reach the start of this hike, drive to Divide Road, located 15 miles west of Whitewater or 20 miles east of Gateway on Colorado State Route 141. Turn onto Divide Road, a well-maintained gravel road, and drive 0.5 mile to the first switchback. Park facing the red rock cliff, on the short spur to the left.

This hike does not follow a designated or maintained trail, but routes are easy to find and there is never any danger of cliffs. Start out from the parking area by finding your way through fallen boulders of red Wingate Sandstone. After about 50 yards, the route traverses over outcrops of dark Precambrian basement rock.

Traverse upslope over the basement outcrops until you reach a bench at the base of the red rock slope. You are now standing at about the level of the Great Unconformity. Below your feet is the Precambrian basement, and above is a slope of the Triassic Chinle Formation red rock, capped by a red rock cliff of the Jurassic Wingate Sandstone.

Missing between the Chinle Formation and the ancient basement of the Uncompahgre Plateau are thousands of feet of Precambrian and Paleozoic rocks that are present in other areas of the Colorado Plateau. This unconformity was formed nearly 300 million years ago during Pennsylvanian-Permian time when basement rocks pushed upward to form the western segment of the Ancestral Rocky Mountains, called the Uncompahgre Highland. Overlying sedimentary layers were stripped away by streams flowing off the mountains, beveling the uplift down to a nearly level plain. Later, during the Triassic, Chinle streams meandered across the region, depositing sand and mud along their courses. Great Jurassic dunes of wind-blown sand engulfed the area, leaving behind a sand pile that would later become the Wingate Sandstone. Together, the eroded basement rocks and the sedimentary layers covering them would later rise to become the Uncompahgre Plateau.

Today, the unconformity forms a bench all along the rim of Unaweep Canyon. Try to follow a route that contours along this bench and circumnavigate the Wingate Sandstone cliff that rises above you. Look carefully for an outcrop of conglomerate that forms a 3-foot ledge in the Chinle slope with a shallow overhang underneath. You have found the actual surface of the Great Unconformity! The conglomerate at eye level was left behind more than 200 million years ago by the Chinle Formation streams. Under your feet are crystalline rocks more than 1.4 billion years old, a staggering gap in the rocks of over 1 billion years!

Continue downslope over basement outcrops until you reach a rock promontory with an excellent view to the west up Unaweep Canyon. Above you a Wingate cliff forms a narrow sandstone fin. This landform was possibly carved by a meander in the ancestral river when it flowed through Unaweep Canyon eons ago.

The origin of Unaweep Canyon still puzzles geologists.

After taking in the views of Unaweep Canyon and puzzling over its origin, return to your vehicle by retracing your steps.

STREAM PIRACY ON THE COLORADO PLATEAU

Geologists grapple with a paradox when considering how the great rivers of the Colorado Plateau came to be. Instead of flowing around uplifted features, many rivers cut directly across the crests of the region's major uplifts, showing little or no regard for the path of least resistance.

The examples are numerous. The Colorado River slices through the Kaibab Plateau to create the Grand Canyon; the goosenecks of the San Juan River cross the midsection of the Monument Uplift; and the Green River cuts through Split Mountain. The Paradox Basin, in fact, got its name because the Dolores River cuts directly across the upturned limbs of several anticlines rather than flowing around them.

Since John Wesley Powell's first explorations 100 years ago, geologists have debated this paradox of the Colorado Plateau's river courses. Powell proposed that the rivers had already established their courses long before uplift began. He envisioned that meandering rivers simply deepened their channels as uplift occurred, effectively entrenching themselves into the landscape over time. Other geologists consider the rivers younger than the geologic structures they cross. In this scenario, rivers establish themselves in the upper sedimentary layers. As the landscape is slowly uplifted, the rivers cut down through the sedimentary layers and eventually encountered older buried geologic structures. As uplift continued the rivers superimposed their courses across the uplifts with little or no regard for the once buried structures.

A third possible explanation is known as *stream piracy*. In this case, a river extends its length by *headward erosion* toward its source. As it cuts deeper and deeper into the higher regions of its drainage basin, a more aggressive river, or a river cutting through softer rock layers, might work its way headward until it "captures" the flow of a nearby river. Thus, the flow of one river diverts into the channel of another, and may then flow over an uplifted region.

All three explanations may ultimately be correct because, as it turns out, each river has its own story.

NORTH VISTA TRAIL

BLACK CANYON OF THE GUNNISON

Stand 2000 feet above the Gunnison River for a dramatic view at Exclamation Point.

DISTANCE ■ 3 miles round trip

ELEVATION ■ 7650 to 7702 feet

DIFFICULTY ■ Easy

TOPOGRAPHIC MAPS ■ USGS Grizzly Ridge; Trails Illustrated #245

GEOLOGIC MAP ■ 25

KEY REFERENCE ■ 40

PRECAUTIONS ■ Use extreme caution when exploring along the canyon rim. Avoid exposed areas during summer thunderstorms.

FOR INFORMATION ■ Black Canyon of the Gunnison National Park

About the Landscape: Few canyons in the world rival the Black Canyon of the Gunnison for its dramatically sheer depths.

The Black Canyon region was caught in both the Ancestral Rocky Mountain and Laramide orogeny uplifts and was also the battleground for violent volcanic eruptions that built the West Elk and San Juan Mountains. But despite all this action, a river was born and established itself with a mind of its own, carving a deep chasm down the length of a Laramide-age uplift, called the Gunnison Uplift, cored by Colorado's 1.7-billion-year-old basement rocks.

The Black Canyon of the Gunnison River spans two worlds. Along its lower reaches, the tilted layers of colorful Mesozoic strata flanking the river belong in the realm of the Colorado Plateau. Upriver, remnants of once widespread volcanic rocks overlay the dark, Precambrian basement rocks of the canyon's inner gorge. Clearly, the Black Canyon lies at a crossroads between the Colorado Plateau and the Rocky Mountains.

Trail Guide: To reach the North Vista trailhead on Black Canyon's North Rim, drive 21 miles east from Delta on Colorado State Route 92 to Hotchkiss, where the highway makes a jog to the south toward Crawford. About 3.3 miles past Crawford, turn right onto Black Canyon Road (just past Crawford Lake) and follow the signs 12 miles to Black Canyon of the Gunnison National Park. The trailhead is located at the North Rim Ranger Station.

From the ranger station, this easy trail follows the forested North Rim of Black Canyon to Exclamation Point.

About 0.5 mile down the trail, a sign marks an overlook on the left. Here at the end of a short spur trail is the first good view into Black Canyon. The famous Painted Wall forms the steep cliff to the right (west). Rising almost 2300 feet above the river, the Painted Wall is the tallest escarpment in Colorado. Under your feet at the edge of the overlook is the pink- to salmon-colored Entrada Sandstone. This colorful layer sits directly on top of the nearly 2 billion-year-old metamorphic basement rocks.

Metamorphic basement rocks exposed in the depths of Black Canyon

The Entrada dunes were deposited by Jurassic winds along what was left of the eroded western arm of the Ancestral Rocky Mountains called the Uncompahgre Highland. Paleozoic sedimentary layers were stripped from the crest of the uplift, setting the stage for the Great Unconformity. During the early part of the Mesozoic period, Triassic and Jurassic sediments were deposited up to, but not over, the beveled highland. About 165 million years ago, the Jurassic Entrada sands swept across the surface, creating a gap in the record that spans more that 1.5 billion years. Across the canyon, the Entrada has eroded, and the planed-off highland now serves as the bench at rim level.

The trail continues through the forest until it forks about 1.25 miles from the trailhead. A sign marks a trail to the left that leads to Exclamation Point. Follow this trail until you can walk no more—you have reached the edge of the abyss! From this vantage point, there is a clear view upstream (east) into the narrows of the inner canyon. Downstream, the Painted Wall towers above the river.

The Gunnison River has carved this deep chasm into the Gunnison Uplift, a Laramide-age uplift that pushed upward about 65 million years ago along faults that date back to the Ancestral Rockies. The rim and walls of the canyon are carved from igneous and metamorphic basement rocks with prominent veins of pegmatite. How did the Gunnison River entrench itself in some of the hardest rock in Colorado?

Long before dams were built upstream holding back floods of water and gritty sediment, the Gunnison River raged as a powerful torrent that entrained rocks and boulders like a great tumbler. Initially, the river flowed across a landscape of West Elk and San Juan volcanic rocks that smothered the Gunnison Uplift and the older sedimentary layers covering it. As the volcanic piles grew, the area slowly warped downward into a syncline and the west-flowing drainage became channeled between the volcanic centers directly above the Gunnison Uplift.

Slowly, the river scoured deeper into its channel. Once entrenched, the river continued to follow its established course with complete disregard for the hard basement rocks that lay hidden below. As the area uplifted with the rest of Colorado, the river cut deeper and deeper over the last 10 million years, ultimately superimposing itself on the basement core.

The river has carved most of its path through the resistant basement rock over only the last 2 million years, supercharged by floods of water and grit from melting Ice Age glaciers—just yesterday in geological terms!

After taking in the view (but not stepping too close to the edge!) follow the trail back to the ranger station.

MESA VERDE

Sandstones of the Cretaceous Seaway

Explore geologic clues that reveal the marine environment where the mesa's defining sandstone cliffs formed.

DISTANCE ■ 2 miles round trip

ELEVATION ■ 7820 to 7860

DIFFICULTY ■ Easy

TOPOGRAPHIC MAP ■ USGS Point Lookout

GEOLOGIC MAP ■ 26

KEY REFERENCE ■ 41

PRECAUTIONS ■ Watch for rock falls and stay away from crumbling ledges.

FOR INFORMATION ■ Mesa Verde National Park

About the Landscape: This hike proves that a trail does not have to be long or difficult to be rewarding. A short walk over level terrain provides classic views of the rocks that form Mesa Verde's precipitous North Rim, a massive sandstone cliff or *escarpment*. Along the way, clues in the rocks hint that the North Rim was once a sandy shore.

Mesa Verde is a deeply dissected plateau of Cretaceous sedimentary rock that dominates the landscape in the Four Corners region of southwestern Colorado. It is a relict of a past landscape connected to the lower reaches of the La Plata and San Juan Mountains. Erosion along its north rim separated Mesa Verde from the mountains. Isolated now, it stands more than 2000 feet above Montezuma Valley to the north.

This plateau is most famous for housing the largest Ancestral Puebloan cliff dwellings in the southwest. Apart from these spectacular cliff dwellings, the most prominent feature of Mesa Verde is the resistant, massive sandstone cliff that forms the northern edge of the plateau. This imposing cliff is made of the Cretaceous Mesaverde Group, a sedimentary sequence that records the retreat and advance of a vast inland sea which extended from Texas and Mexico north to the Arctic Ocean. Between 100 and 70 million years ago, the Cretaceous seaway repeatedly submerged the Colorado Plateau.

Trail Guide: To reach the Knife Edge trailhead, drive 10 miles east from Cortez, or 8 miles west from Mancos, on U.S. Highway 160 to the Mesa Verde National Park entrance. Follow the winding park road 4 miles to the Morefield Campground. The trailhead is located off the parking area at the extreme north end of the campground.

Follow the trail north through a meadow to the head of Morefield

Canyon. A short distance after passing the junction with the Prater Ridge Trail, the Knife Edge Trail turns left (west) where it meets an old road. Here, only 0.3 mile from the trailhead, is one of Mesa Verde's classic views.

The massive cliffs of the North Rim stretch from east to west. The cliffs are composed of the Point Lookout Sandstone, an 80-million-year-old marine deposit made of barrier beaches and sandbars near the shoreline of the retreating Cretaceous seaway. Point Lookout, for which the sandstone formation is named, is the farthest promontory to the east. At the base of the cliff, the Mancos Shale Formation stretches out in barren slopes. The Mancos Shale is largely a deposit of mud and silt that settled in deep offshore water. As the Cretaceous seaway retreated (and thus got smaller), its shoreline receded across the shale, juxtaposing barrier beaches and sand bars on top of the earlier, deep-water shale deposits.

From here, the trail follows the old "Knife Edge" road, which continues west below the cliff that forms Prater Ridge. A number of yellow, refrigerator-size Point Lookout Sandstone boulders have fallen from the cliff above and scattered along the trail. Where the trail passes between two knee-high boulders, take a close look at the upper surface of the larger boulder on the left. Notice the network of marks that stand out in slight relief.

These features are the trackways and burrows of shrimp-like crustaceans that inhabited the Cretaceous seafloor not far from shore. Called trace fossils—since they reveal only the traces of organisms and not their hard body parts—they indicate that the Point Lookout Sandstone was deposited in a marine environment. The traces are preserved along a bedding plane, a surface that once formed the bottom of the sea and remained undisturbed as the next layer of sand was deposited on top.

Continue on to an area where Volkswagen-size Point Lookout Sandstone boulders are strewn along the trail. Ripple marks are exposed on top of one of the boulders closest to the edge of the trail. These ripples were formed by currents washing back and forth across the sandy bottom of the Cretaceous seaway. Some of the boulders display cross-beds. These thin, slanted lines in the rock are cross-sections of areas where many layers of sediment were deposited on the undulating surfaces of the seafloor.

At the end of the maintained trail, a sign reads, "Do not go beyond this point." Return to the trailhead by the same route, keeping an eye out for additional evidence of the ancient Cretaceous shorelines.

Cliffs of Cretaceous sandstone at Mesa Verde

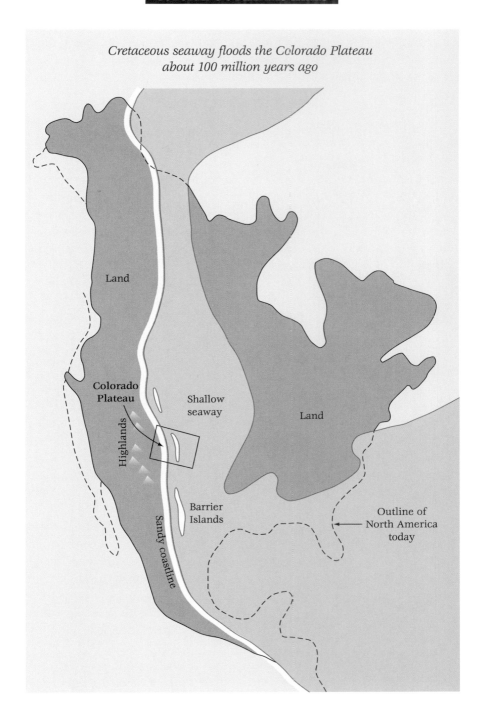

Cretaceous seaway floods the Colorado Plateau about 100 million years ago

Land

Colorado Plateau

Shallow seaway

Highlands

Land

Barrier Islands

Sandy coastline

Outline of North America today

Ship Rock reigns supreme in the Four Corners region of New Mexico.

Part 4

NEW MEXICO'S PLATEAU HIKES

Chapter 8
THE SOUTHEASTERN PLATEAU

Some of New Mexico's most enchanted landscapes sweep across the wide open spaces of the southeastern Colorado Plateau. Bounded by pastoral valleys of the Rio Grand Rift on the east, and by desert lands of the Basin and Range to the south beyond the Mogollon Rim, this is wild country, even today. And it is of cultural interest as well. A large part of the Navajo Nation—America's largest Indian reservation—and numerous pueblos,

Looking into the Rio Grande Rift from Tent Rocks in the Jemez Mountains

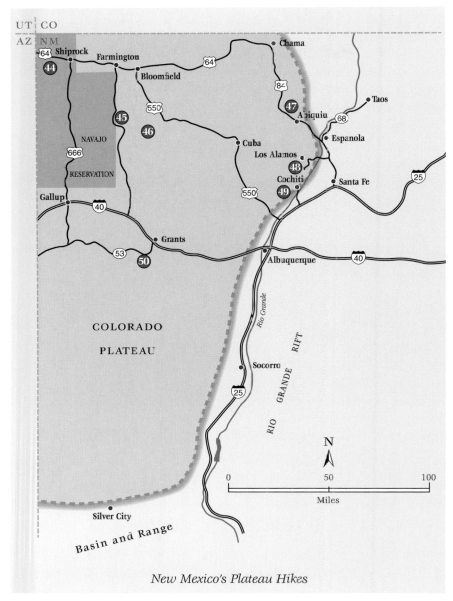

New Mexico's Plateau Hikes

including the Zuni, Acoma, and Laguna, are all located here in northwestern New Mexico.

For millions of years, this region of broad plateaus, cliff-edged mesas, and shallow canyons has been the center of a slowly subsiding basin where over 14,000 feet of sedimentary rock accumulated, called the San Juan Basin. Uplift and erosion have sculpted the Colorado Plateau's sedimentary layers here into vast tablelands that reach beyond the horizon.

Breaking the skyline is Ship Rock, a volcanic neck or *diatreme* that reigns supreme over the Four Corners region, the only place in the U.S. where four states meet. Elsewhere, the red rocks of Ghost Ranch, the Ancestral Puebloan ruins of Chaco Canyon, the bizarre landforms in the Bisti Badlands, the Jemez Mountain caldera, and the volcanic moonscape of El Malpais all make New Mexico an important part of the Southwest's geologic landscape.

THE RIO GRANDE RIFT

Beginning about 30 million years ago during the Oligocene, the land east of the Colorado Plateau began to pull apart as though caught in a tug-of-war. As the landscape along its border slowly stretched and thinned, a network of deep, down-faulted valleys developed called the *Rio Grande Rift*. The rift slices the eastern edge of the Colorado Plateau from Colorado south through New Mexico along the Rio Grande River.

This rifting most likely originated from a change in tectonic forces—from subduction to strike-slip—along the western margin of North America following the Laramide orogeny. This caused huge reverberations inland as a zone of spreading developed along the rift and magma began to well up from below. As the magma pushed higher, the tremendous heat from the molten rock caused swelling and expansion at the surface, further uplifting and stretching the landscape. Geologists still debate whether stretching along the rift began because there was upwelling from below, or upwelling from below began because the land was stretching.

As the edge of the Colorado Plateau was caught in this tug-of-war along the rift, it slowly rotated a few degrees in a clockwise direction, reactivating old faults and also developing new ones. During this movement, which intensified about 10 million years ago and continues today, the land adjusted to the tension in the rocks. Some mountain-size blocks lowered, or subsided, forming grabens along the Rio Grande Valley. Others tilted and uplifted, creating steep fault-block mountains, or *horsts,* such as the Sangre de Cristo Range and Sandia Mountains.

Coincident with this action, a phase of volcanic activity spread across the eastern and southeastern edges of the Colorado Plateau, as magma pushed to the surface through the faults and fractures in the rocks. Although not all of the volcanic activity of the period was

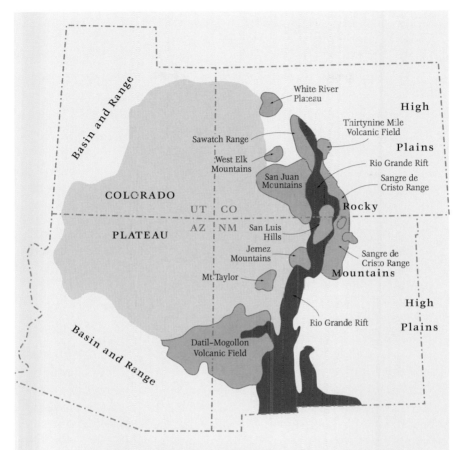

The location of the Rio Grande Rift along the eastern edge of the Colorado Plateau

directly related to the Rio Grande Rift, the rift was a major fault zone that was and still is affected by these volcanics. Even today, numerous hot springs bubble to the surface from faults along the margins of the Rio Grande Rift.

The Rio Grande is a relative latecomer to the rift. Only within the last 5 million years did rivers flow off the mountains and down the rift to become the Rio Grande. In contrast to other rivers of the Colorado Plateau that are downcutting in response to uplift of the land, the rift itself controls the course of the Rio Grande. In New Mexico, the major canyons and gorges along the Rio Grande are the result of the river having to carve through volcanic rocks that have blocked or altered its flow.

SHIP ROCK

Hike 44

ROCKS FROM THE DEEP

Ship Rock is an eroded diatreme, the neck of an explosive volcano.

DISTANCE ■ 1 mile round trip

ELEVATION ■ 5600 to 5740 feet

DIFFICULTY ■ Easy

TOPOGRAPHIC MAP ■ USGS Ship Rock, NM

GEOLOGIC MAP ■ 27

KEY REFERENCE ■ 42

PRECAUTIONS ■ Ship Rock is located on the Navajo Indian Reservation. Please respect the privacy of the people who make this their home. A backcountry permit should be obtained from the Navajo Parks and Recreation Department. The dirt access road can become muddy and impassable when wet. Use caution hiking along the dike as the rock is crumbly in places. Climbing Ship Rock itself is extremely dangerous and is prohibited.

FOR INFORMATION ■ Navajo Parks and Recreation Department

About the Landscape: Like an imaginary giant sailboat disappearing over the distant horizon, Ship Rock is a prominent landmark in extreme northwestern New Mexico. Ship Rock is the remains of an explosive volcanic vent or *diatreme*, and it is the most spectacular of the many diatremes that punctuate the Navajo Volcanic Field in the Four Corners region. These freestanding pinnacles are eroded pipes or conduits—also called *volcanic necks*—formed during explosive volcanic eruptions that rocked the Colorado Plateau during the Oligocene between about 30 and 19 million years ago. Other well-known examples of diatremes include Church Rock, east of Kayenta, Arizona, and Agathla Peak, south of Monument Valley.

Ship Rock has deep roots. The material that fed the Ship Rock diatreme made its way through more than 10,000 feet of older sedimentary layers and below that through thousands of feet of igneous and metamorphic basement rock. In fact, some of the rock that makes up Ship Rock came from the Earth's mantle, perhaps as deep as 20 miles or more! Although the exact timing and mechanism remains poorly understood, this material was emplaced as a chaotic slurry during a violent gas-driven eruption—called a *mantle blowout.* Presumably this action was caused by the release of deep, pressurized gases and perhaps aided by the interaction of hot magma with underground water.

A short hike provides easy access to the base of Ship Rock, and returns along one of the major dikes that radiates from its base.

Trail Guide: To reach the start of this hike, drive 6.5 miles south from the town of Shiprock on U.S. Highway 666. Turn right onto Navajo Road 13 (also called the Red Rock Highway) and travel west for about 8 miles. Just before a prominent dark wall of rock (an igneous dike) meets the highway, turn right again and follow a well-traveled dirt road north toward the Ship Rock pinnacle. Bear left at the first major **Y**-intersection 2.1 miles from the highway, and continue about 1 mile to where the road climbs a small hill. Here the going gets rough and multiple roads split off in several directions. Continue the best you can and park at any suitable spot just over the top of the hill.

The hill near where you parked offers a spectacular overview of Ship Rock. Towering 1700 feet above the surrounding landscape, this gigantic mass of volcanic rock was the conduit for a violent explosion that rocketed upward about 20 million years ago to form a volcanic crater thousands of feet wide. Under your feet, the soft earth is the Mancos Shale, which represents mud and silt that settled on the floor of the Cretaceous seaway, an ancient ocean that flooded the Four Corners region about 100 million years ago. Much of this surrounding sedimentary rock has long since been removed by erosion, leaving the harder, more resistant volcanic core of the diatreme standing tall.

After taking in the view, follow the well-traveled dirt road north toward the base of Ship Rock. About 0.25 mile from where you parked, the road

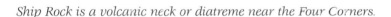

Ship Rock is a volcanic neck or diatreme near the Four Corners.

crosses three consecutive dirt roads trending roughly east–west. Cross these roads and continue straight ahead, following the road uphill until it fades out near the large boulders at the base of Ship Rock. Once at the boulders, take some time to see what they are made of.

Notice that the first large boulders are composed of an assortment of smaller rocks and pebbles of a variety of colors stuck together. This mixture of material is a composite rock type called tuff-breccia, which is a chaotic assemblage of ash and rock fragments welded together. It is this rock, mostly tan to reddish brown in color, that makes up the core of the Ship Rock diatreme.

The exact processes and events that formed the Ship Rock diatreme are still debated by geologists. Although the process is poorly understood, somehow gas-rich magma forced its way upward from deep in the earth, perhaps initially rising along deep cracks or faults in the basement rock. On its way up, the hot slurry entrained bits and pieces of the surrounding basement rock and overlying sedimentary layers. Nearing the surface, it may have encountered groundwater, which only added to the volatile mixture. Ultimately, the fast-moving froth of gas and magma exploded, blasting out a huge crater at the surface. This violent eruption spread ash and rock debris far and wide across the ancient landscape. It is this chaotic mixture that solidified within the crater to form the tuff-breccia that cores the Ship Rock diatreme.

Just beyond the first large boulder of tuff-breccia there is another large boulder that is much darker in color. This rock is dark brown to black, and very hard and dense much like basalt; but because of its unique mineral content (it lacks plagioclase) the rock is a special variety called *minette*. The fact that there are no small gas holes or *vesicles* within the rock suggests that the magma was gas-poor and cooled underground. Take a close look at this dark boulder to see if you can find chunks of lighter-colored rock encased within it. This granitic rock, probably Precambrian in age and over 1 billion years old, was carried up from the basement as this dark magma worked its way upward some 20 million years ago.

A careful look up at the broken and fractured south face of Ship Rock reveals large patches of the darker minette rock cutting through the lighter-colored tuff-breccia. The minette was injected as dikes sometime after the major violent eruption of the Ship Rock diatreme. The minette also makes up the long dikes that radiate from the base of Ship Rock, and cores the smaller subsidiary vents along Ship Rock's east side.

Thus, the complete story of Ship Rock involves an initial violent gas-rich eruption, recorded by the tuff-breccia, followed by a more quiescent upwelling of darker, gas-poor magma, represented by the basalt-like dark minette rock. Eons of weathering and erosion followed, stripping away the surrounding sedimentary layers and leaving the core of the Ship Rock diatreme standing tall above the Four Corners landscape.

After studying the boulders, continue walking westward toward the dike. Once you intersect the dike, follow it to the south, scrambling up on top of the dike for good views wherever possible. The dike is 10 to 15 feet wide and is also filled with dark minette. Although you can't see its end, it extends southward for more than 5 miles. In places the dike is discontinuous and appears to be offset and segmented, as if along small faults. Notice how the light-colored sedimentary rock that encases the dike is caked onto the dike's vertical faces, and in places is incorporated within the dike rock. A close look at the dark dike rock with a hand lens reveals flecks of biotite mica and glassy crystals of olivine and augite.

After following the dike for about 0.25 mile, you'll meet a dirt road that cuts through a major break in the dike. To return to your vehicle, turn left and follow the road downhill. At the first junction, turn right and follow the road up to the small hill where you are parked.

BISTI BADLANDS

Hike 45

FANTASY IN STONE

Explore artistically sculpted badlands in the San Juan Basin.

DISTANCE ■ 3 miles round trip (or as far as you want to go)

ELEVATION ■ 5750 to 5800 feet

DIFFICULTY ■ Easy

TOPOGRAPHIC MAP ■ USGS Alamo Mesa West, NM

GEOLOGIC MAP ■ 28

KEY REFERENCE ■ 43

PRECAUTIONS ■ There are no established trails within the Bisti/De-na-zin Wilderness, which is closed to all mechanized travel including dirt bikes. Although the wide-open landscape is easy for cross-country travel, some routefinding skills are required. Please take care to minimize impact on the fragile rock formations and remember that collecting is prohibited. Avoid this hike during the heat of summer.

FOR INFORMATION ■ Farmington Field Office, Bisti/De-na-zin Wilderness

About the Landscape: The fanciful landscape of the Bisti/De-na-zin Wilderness is near the center of New Mexico's San Juan Basin, located on the southeastern Colorado Plateau where over 14,000 feet of sedimentary strata accumulated. The name Bisti (pronounced "BIS-tie") is the Navajo word for badlands. Here, the artistic forces of erosion have sculpted an amazing variety of landforms in sedimentary rocks of the Cretaceous

Fruitland Formation. Petrified wood litters the ground—the remains of ancient trees swept downstream in rivers over 65 million years ago. Dark layers of shale and coal are the remains of organic material that accumulated within swampy areas in the ancient river valleys.

This easy hike provides the freedom to explore a wide-open landscape with no marked or established trails. Over the eons, differential erosion has created a variety of landforms where resistant sandstone layers alternate with soft, easily eroded shale layers. Balanced rocks, hoodoos, and mushroom formations challenge the imagination.

Trail Guide: To reach the Bisti/De-na-zin Wilderness trailhead, turn off New Mexico State Route 371 at the sign for the Bisti Wilderness Area (between mile markers 70 and 71) and drive 2 miles east on San Juan County Road 7297. Bear left at the T-intersection, and then drive another 1.2 miles to the trailhead parking area on the right.

From the trail register, pass through the gate and begin hiking east following the faint traces of an old road. About 50 yards from the trailhead, the dark sedimentary layers on the left are organic-rich shales and thin coal seams. Coal represents the accumulation of dead trees and plants in swampy areas. Over time, these deposits of organic carbon are buried beneath other sediments and are slowly converted by pressure into coal.

Continue following along the base of the hills on the north side of the valley. After about 0.25 mile, cross over the wash and continue heading east paralleling the wash, which is now on your left. The pinkish-red rocks

Balanced Rock in the Bisti/De-na-zin Wilderness

capping some of the hills formed when coal fires once burned at the surface or underground. Called *clinker*, these rocks formed as the sandstone and shale surrounding the coal was oxidized or "cooked" by the burning coal. The burning is a natural process sparked by lightning when coal beds are at or near the surface. Erosion has now exposed the clinker beds.

At about the 1-mile point, light-colored layers of sandstone on the south side of the valley begin to emerge within the soft layers of shale. The sandstone layers, along with the petrified wood that litters the ground in places, mark the channels of ancient streambeds. At the time when these sediments were deposited, dinosaurs roamed the swamps and riverbeds. The sandstone layers, harder and more resistant, form protective caps protecting the softer shale layers underneath. Over time, the artistic forces of erosion have sculpted a fanciful landscape of balanced rocks and mushroom formations, and also exposed dinosaur tracks and bones (of tridactyls) discovered in these same rocks not far from the Bisti/De-na-zin Wilderness.

From this point, let your imagination be your guide as you explore the many nooks and crannies carved by erosion. Once you have had your fill of this intricate landscape—and perhaps have gotten "lost" once or twice—continue exploring the valley farther east, or return to the trailhead by the route you came.

Hike 46

CHACO CANYON

ANCIENT VOICES AND ANCIENT SHORELINES

Hike the Pueblo Alto Trail over sandstone cliffs with clues in the rock of an ancient shoreline and an excellent view of Pueblo Bonito.

DISTANCE ■ 3.2 miles round trip (or 5.4-mile loop)

ELEVATION ■ 6200 to 6440 feet

DIFFICULTY ■ Moderate

TOPOGRAPHIC MAP ■ USGS Pueblo Bonito, NM

GEOLOGIC MAP ■ 29

KEY REFERENCE ■ 44

PRECAUTIONS ■ This hike requires a free backcountry permit available at the visitor center. Take care hiking along the cliff-edged mesa. This is sacred ground—please do not disturb the archeological sites. Watch out for summer storms and lightning.

FOR INFORMATION ■ Chaco Culture National Historical Park

About the Landscape: Chaco Canyon is legendary for its numerous Ancestral Puebloan dwellings occupied between about 900 and 1150 A.D.

239

Located near the center of the San Juan Basin, Chaco Canyon is a wide, shallow canyon carved from sandstone layers within the Cretaceous Mesaverde Group. Coincidentally, these are the very same rock layers found at Colorado's Mesa Verde National Park, which is also known for its abundant Puebloan cliff dwellings. But unlike the cliff dwellings at Mesa Verde, the dwellings at Chaco Canyon were built at the base of cliffs along the valley floor and on top of the mesas.

Sandstone layers of the Mesaverde Group record the fluctuation of ancient shorelines along a vast inland sea that extended from Texas and Mexico north to the Arctic Ocean. Between about 100 and 70 million years ago, the Cretaceous seaway repeatedly submerged the Colorado Plateau region. During this time, the Chaco Canyon area was part of a migrating sandy coastline.

The Pueblo Alto Trail climbs up through the Cliff House Sandstone, then traverses along the cliff-edged mesa above Pueblo Bonito before continuing to the top of the mesa where Pueblo Alto is located. Along the way, look for clues in the rock that reveal its origin along an ancient shoreline.

Trail Guide: To reach the Pueblo Alto Trail in Chaco Culture National Historical Park (NHP), drive 40 miles south from Bloomfield or 50 miles north from Cuba on U.S. Highway 550 to the sign for Chaco Culture NHP (at mile 112.5). Turn and follow this paved road (CR 7900) 4.5 miles to the next sign for Chaco Culture NHP and turn right onto San Juan County Road 7950. Follow this graded dirt road 16.3 miles to the paved park road. At the

Fossil clam shells in the Cliff House Sandstone, Pueblo Alto Trail

intersection just beyond the visitor center, stay right and follow the loop road 4 miles to the trailhead, which is located at the end of a short spur road off the main loop road, at the Chacoan site Pueblo del Arroyo.

This hike begins by following the gated service road beyond Pueblo del Arroyo to Kin Kletso. After 0.25 mile, the Pueblo Alto Trail starts out behind Kin Kletso and immediately begins climbing through fallen boulders along the base of the cliff. Just before the first switchback, look for fossils on a waist-high gray boulder. Look for more fossils in the cliff face to the left where the trail enters the narrows that climb up and through the cliff. These are fossil bivalves (like clams) that were broken apart, transported, and deposited by currents along a sandy shoreline during the Cretaceous.

The trail through the cliff follows a natural crack or *fracture* in the lower part of the Cliff House Sandstone. Imagine the ancient Pueblo peoples using this same route as they returned home to Pueblo Alto from visits to Pueblo Bonito and other sites.

Emerging from the crack, the trail follows a route marked by rock cairns along a bench at the top of the cliff. Underfoot, look for iron-stained nodules, long cylinders like rusty metal rebar, in the rock. These features are the burrows of shrimp-like crustaceans that inhabited the Cretaceous seafloor not far from shore. Called trace fossils since they reveal only the traces of organisms and not their hard parts, they indicate that the Cliff House Sandstone was deposited in a marine environment.

As the trail continues to follow the bench along the cliff, look for horizontal layering in the sandstone. Unlike the steep cross-beds preserved in wind-blown sandstone, flat or horizontal layers suggest deposition along shorelines where swift currents wash back and forth.

After about 0.5 mile, where the trail reaches the junction with the Pueblo Alto Trail, cairns mark a short spur trail to the cliff-edge overlooking Pueblo Bonito. Looking down on this amazing structure, note the large rockfall that destroyed a portion of the site on the left. One huge boulder came to rest in the middle of an excavated kiva. These rocks are what is left of Threatening Rock, a large detached segment of the cliff named by archeologists. It was also known to be a threat by the Pueblo peoples when they lived here because they attempted to support the rock by placing rocks beneath it; they also placed prayer sticks along the cliff nearby. The rock came crashing down in 1941 following a year of heavy rains, almost 900 years after Pueblo Bonito was abandoned.

Back at the trail junction, the trail to Pueblo Alto begins climbing over ledges to a broad sandy bench that leads to higher cliffs in the Cliff House Sandstone. After about 0.25 mile, the trail reaches a series of ledges with remnants of stone steps built by the Puebloan peoples. Climbing higher, the cairns lead to another ledge where a sign points to a roped-off area where stones were cleared by long-ago residents to form a Chacoan "road" along this well-traveled route. Above this ledge, the trail crosses a broad bench that leads to Pueblo Alto at the top of the mesa.

From the top, there is a sweeping view looking out from the sites across the San Juan Basin. Be sure to take time to explore Pueblo Alto and ponder what life here must have been like centuries ago.

From this point you have a choice, either to return by the route you came, or follow the loop trail that traverses the mesa 3.2 miles back to the trailhead.

GHOST RANCH

New Mexico's Red Rock Country

Hike the Chimney Rock Trail and discover ancient sand dunes, a vanished sea, and colorful sedimentary layers where some of the world's earliest known dinosaurs once roamed.

DISTANCE ■ 2.5 miles round trip

ELEVATION ■ 6450 to 7040 feet

DIFFICULTY ■ Moderate

TOPOGRAPHIC MAP ■ USGS Ghost Ranch, NM

GEOLOGIC MAP ■ 30

KEY REFERENCE ■ 45, 46

PRECAUTIONS ■ Watch for loose rocks and avoid getting too close to the cliff edge at the top of the mesa. This trail can become muddy and slick after recent rain or snow. Signs indicate that this is a potential plague area— stay away from any live, sick, or dead rodents. Please stay on the trail.

FOR INFORMATION ■ Ruth Hall Museum of Paleontology

About the Landscape: The rugged cliffs of Ghost Ranch seem out of place in New Mexico. This multicolored landscape immortalized in the paintings of Georgia O'Keeffe looks more like Utah's canyon country, or perhaps Arizona's Painted Desert.

By a quirk of geologic fate this area somehow escaped the upheavals that affected the surrounding region. Miraculously, the colorful rocks at Ghost Ranch, located along the Colorado Plateau's extreme eastern edge, managed to avoid major uplift during the Laramide orogeny and subsequent removal by the intense erosion that followed. This area has also escaped being torn apart by faulting along the Rio Grande Rift, which lies to the east. Over time, erosion has simply worked its magic on this remote and isolated slice of the Colorado Plateau's geologic layercake, creating a wonderland of cliffs, canyons, and mesas.

The dramatic landscape of Ghost Ranch is hewn from a stack of Mesozoic sedimentary rocks. Here in the shadow of the Jemez Mountains, which shook the area with explosive volcanic eruptions just over 1 million years ago, dinosaur fossils were discovered in badlands of the Triassic Chinle Formation.

The dinosaur quarry at Ghost Ranch (which is located on the Kitchen Mesa Trail and is currently covered to prevent erosion) has yielded one of the richest concentrations of dinosaur fossils in the world. The discoveries made here include one of the oldest and most complete dinosaur skeletons in the world of the theropod dinosaur Coelophysis (pronounced "seal-o-FI-sis"), which is New Mexico's state fossil.

This hike begins at the Ruth Hall Museum of Paleontology, where you can view ongoing fossil discoveries being unearthed from an 8-ton block of rock around which the museum was constructed Currently, museum paleontologists are working on a yet-to-be-named crocodile-like species preserved within this treasure trove of fossils. Once you are out the museum's back door, the trail to Chimney Rock offers outstanding views of Ghost Ranch and surrounding landscapes.

Trail Guide: Ghost Ranch is located about 65 miles northwest of Santa Fe. To reach the Chimney Rock trailhead, drive north from Santa Fe on U.S. Highway 84/State Route 285 to Espanola and turn left onto Highway 84. Drive about 40 miles west, through Abiquiu, to Ghost Ranch. A sign marks the right turn off the highway (between mileposts 224 and 225). Then drive 1 mile on the graded ranch road to the Ruth Hall Museum of Paleontology on the left. The marked trailhead is located at the old gate directly behind the museum. Be sure to get a trail guide keyed to markers along the trail.

The Chimney Rock Trail begins by winding uphill through layers of purple and gray shale in the Chinle Formation, mostly covered by a slide here. After about 0.25 mile the trail levels out as it crosses a broad terrace overlooking the main Ghost Ranch compound. Beyond the terrace, the trail continues uphill past boulders of sandstone and conglomerate from the Dakota Formation. At about the 0.75-mile point, an unmarked spur trail on the left leads to excellent viewpoints of Chimney Rock. This is the perfect vantage point to study the sedimentary layers that make up the dramatic cliffs of Ghost Ranch.

The multihued slopes and badlands that stretch out below the cliffs are in the Triassic Chinle Formation, the same rock layers that define northern Arizona's Petrified Forest and Painted Desert region. About 225 million

Chimney Rock is capped by the Todilto Formation, Ghost Ranch.

years ago, the Ghost Ranch area was located along a broad coastal plain crossed by sluggish, meandering rivers that deposited mostly fine mud and silt that would become colorful shale and siltstone. Thin lenses of sandstone and conglomerate represent river channel or flood deposits. To the southwest, a chain of volcanoes created by subduction along the western edge of the continent spewed great amounts of volcanic ash across the region, ash that would later weather into clay. At that time, the Colorado Plateau region was much closer to the equator, and the climate was warmer and wetter than today. The mottled and varied hues of maroon, purple, lavender, and yellow are thought to indicate ancient soil horizons, or *paleosols,* that developed on the floodplains as the water table fluctuated in response to seasonal rains.

The swampy lowlands where the Chinle sediments accumulated teemed with life, including the theropod dinosaurs Coelophysis, whose fossilized remains would be discovered millions of years later at Ghost Ranch. These primitive reptiles, which were small, bipedal creatures reaching just over 6 feet in length, thrived in a swampy, coastal plain environment. Significantly, fossil remains of Coelophysis are not unique to North America. Discoveries on other continents, including Africa and Europe, provide important clues that North America was still connected to the supercontinent Pangea when these unique reptiles plied the Chinle swamps.

Above the Chinle, the knife-edged cliffs of sandstone are in the Entrada Sandstone of Jurassic age. These cliffs of tan, gray, and yellow sandstone form a spectacular wall of rock extending for miles across the Ghost Ranch landscape. The Entrada represents ancient wind-blown sands that were piled into dunes that blanketed much of the Four Corners region about 150 million years ago.

Capping the Entrada cliffs is a band of white to gray gypsum and limestone layers in the Todilto Formation. Follow these layers along the top of the cliff with your eyes and notice how they pinch and swell across the area. The Todilto rocks represent the remains of a salty lake or shallow seaway that covered parts of New Mexico during the Jurassic. Similar to Utah's Great Salt Lake today, intense evaporation created supersaline conditions that caused salt minerals, mostly gypsum, to crystallize on the floor of the lake. Limestone also formed in the lake, perhaps associated with algae that precipitated calcium carbonate minerals (calcite and dolomite). Over time, the gypsum and limestone accumulated into layers that in some places are more than 100 feet thick.

Chimney Rock is hewn from the Entrada Sandstone and capped by Todilto gypsum and limestone beds. Thus, the impressive spire is made from both ancient desert sands and the remains of a vanished sea.

Above the Entrada-Todilto cliffs are receding slopes and ledges in the Jurassic Morrison Formation. The pastel-colored layers of sandstone, siltstone, and shale in the Morrison represent river and mudflat deposits where large dinosaurs once roamed. Above, layers of sandstone and conglomerate in the Cretaceous Dakota Sandstone cap the skyline at Ghost Ranch. The resistant Dakota layers mark the advance of the Cretaceous seaway across the Colorado Plateau region more than 100 million years ago.

Back on the main trail, the route climbs steadily as it winds its way to the base of the Entrada cliff, where it then begins to climb steeply to the top of the cliffs. Note the large, sweeping cross-beds in the Entrada Sandstone, which are indicative of its wind-blown origins. Where the trail crosses an old fence line (trail marker 17), the contact between the Entrada and overlying Todilto Formations is on the left. A close look reveals thin-bedded limestone-dolomite layers of the Todilto sitting directly on top of sandstone of the Entrada.

As the trail approaches the top of the ridge it makes an abrupt switchback to the left, then emerges on flat ground on top of the Todilto. Ripple marks along the trail here are in sandstone in the Summerville Formation, which lies above the Todilto and below the Morrison Formation. For the best overlook, follow the well-worn trail to the left toward Chimney Rock. The trail ends abruptly at eye level with the top of Chimney Rock. From here, sweeping views look west along the cliffs toward Echo Ampitheater, south toward the Chama River and the Jemez Mountains, and east toward impressive red rock mesas. Visible below Chimney Rock are the pastel-hued badlands in the Chinle Formation.

Once you have soaked in this landscape that has inspired countless artists, return to the trailhead by the route you came.

FRIJOLES CANYON

Waterfalls and Volcanoes at Bandelier

Two generations of volcanic activity are exposed along Frijoles Canyon.

DISTANCE ■ 5 miles round trip

ELEVATION ■ 6066 to 5520 feet

DIFFICULTY ■ Moderate

TOPOGRAPHIC MAPS ■ USGS Frijoles, NM; Trails Illustrated #209

GEOLOGIC MAP ■ 31

KEY REFERENCES ■ 47, 48, 49

PRECAUTIONS ■ The trail is narrow and uneven in places with steep drop-offs—watch your step. Also watch for falling rocks. This is a hot hike in summer—carry ample water.

FOR INFORMATION ■ Bandelier National Monument

About the Landscape: The Jemez (pronounced "hay-mez") Mountains straddle the Colorado Plateau's eastern boundary along the Rio Grande Rift. The forested summits and sloping plateaus of the Jemez Mountains are the eroded remnants of a large composite or stratovolcano. Part of the expansive Jemez Volcanic Field, this area has a long and fiery history dating back over 10 million years, with the last series of eruptions occurring less than 100,000 years ago.

Bandelier National Monument includes a series of canyons carved into the eastern slope of the Jemez Mountains. Frijoles (Spanish for "beans") Canyon, one of the longest canyons, provides a window into the explosive volcanic history of the area. This hike follows the Frijoles River all the way to its confluence with the Rio Grande (Spanish for "large river"). Along the way, the trail passes two waterfalls and winds between towering cliffs of volcanic rock formed during two different generations of volcanic activity.

Trail Guide: To reach the Falls trailhead, drive north from Santa Fe on U.S. Highway 84/State Route 285 for about 12 miles. Follow the signs for Los Alamos and exit onto New Mexico Highway 502 at Pojoaque Pueblo. Drive about 8 miles and bear right onto New Mexico Highway 4 to White Rock. About 10 miles past White Rock, turn left at the entrance to Bandelier National Monument. Follow the park road to the visitor center. Pick up a trail guide for the Falls Trail at the visitor center then continue on to the Falls trailhead in the backcountry parking area, which is located across the river and to the left at the end of the road.

From the trailhead, the trail follows a wide and well-worn path through the forest. Keep right at the first junction with a short spur trail leading down to the river on the left. After about 0.25 mile, a small pull-out on the left provides an overlook of Frijoles Creek, a perennial stream with its headwaters high in the Jemez Mountains.

The trail continues winding downstream passing large boulders of rhyolite tuff that have tumbled down from the cliffs on the right. This is a good place to take a close look at these rocks that make up the walls of Frijoles Canyon and much of Bandelier National Monument. Note the fine, powdery texture; glassy quartz crystals; and small fragments of pumice. The rock is porous and relatively soft and, therefore, easily eroded. This is the rock into which the Ancestral Puebloan people carved their cliff dwellings in Bandelier and surrounding areas.

These tan and pinkish-colored rocks of tuff formed during a series of violent eruptions that spewed tremendous volumes of ash and rock debris across the New Mexico landscape around 1.4 million years ago, and again about 1.1 million years ago. Known today simply as the Bandelier Tuff, the tuff was deposited by hot, glowing clouds of ash, rock, and gas— called *ash flows*—that swept down the flanks of the Jemez Mountain volcano with hurricane force. It is estimated that, taken together, these eruptions were 600 times more powerful than the 1980 eruption of Mount St. Helens, and spread ash downwind as far away as Iowa. In places, the ash was up to 1000 feet deep where it filled ancient canyons carved into older volcanic rocks below. So much material was ejected from the volcano that it collapsed in on itself, forming a large circular crater or *caldera* 14 miles in diameter.

About 0.5 miles from the trailhead (trail marker 5) the trail passes rock formations popularly called *tent rocks*. The name is somewhat of a misnomer, since they look more like cone-shaped teepees. Tent rocks are eroded remnants of the Bandelier Tuff that form in a number of ways. One way is by escaped gases from an eruption moving vertically up through the ash layers, causing some particles to weld together more firmly with cooling. These areas are more resistant to erosion when exposed to the elements. A more common, or at least more obvious, way tent rocks form is when boulders within the tuff act as a cap rock, protecting the softer ash underneath from rapid erosion. Once the caprock boulders fall off their pedestals, the tent rocks below wither away relatively quickly.

Beyond the tent rocks, the trail starts down through layers of dark basalt to the right of the trail. This dark volcanic rock represents an older generation of volcanic activity dated at about 2.8 million years ago. Prior to the eruptions of the Bandelier Tuff, basalt flows spread across the area, periodically damming the Rio Grande. The source of this activity was to the east of the Jemez Mountains in the Cerros del Rio (Spanish for "mountains of the river") Volcanic Field. Here in Frijoles Canyon, the creek has cut down through to the base of the Bandelier Tuff exposing these older volcanic rocks. Note the small holes called vesicles that formed where gas was trapped in the once molten lava as it cooled.

At about the 0.75-mile point the trail reaches the bottom of the canyon along Frijoles Creek and passes more tent rock formations left of the trail. Just before the first bridge across the river there is a sheer wall of Bandelier Tuff right of the trail. After crossing the bridge, you'll see more dark basalt at left (trail marker 9). A geologic puzzle is developing. While the entire cliff left of the trail is made of basalt, on the opposite side of the canyon there is no basalt at all. There, the cliffs are composed entirely of the Bandelier Tuff. What is going on here? The answer to the puzzle will present itself farther down the trail.

An autumn day in Frijoles Canyon, Jemez Mountains

At about 1 mile, the trail reaches the second bridge. Here, a key relationship is revealed in the canyon wall left (north) of the trail. Notice how the dark cliff of basalt ends abruptly against the light cliff of Bandelier Tuff. The explanation for this relationship is that the tuff filled an ancient canyon carved down into the basalt. The vertical wall of basalt represents the rim of the ancient canyon. Today, Frijoles Canyon has exhumed a portion of this ancient canyon.

Beyond the second bridge the trail begins to climb, then contours along a steep hillside as the canyon narrows. The hill at right is all basalt. Left of the trail, the river has carved a deep, narrow canyon through the basalt. The opposite side of the canyon reveals a large amphitheater complete with tent rock formations carved from the Bandelier Tuff filling the ancestral canyon between ancient basalt cliffs. After another bend or two in the trail there are fantastic views looking down the canyon toward White Rock Canyon along the Rio Grande. Soon the roar of the Upper Falls echoes off the canyon walls.

The trail switchbacks down to an overlook where the Upper Falls comes into view (trail marker 15). Upper Falls drops about 80 feet over resistant layers of basalt.

From this viewpoint, the rocks in the opposite wall of the canyon display an abrupt and amazing change. The upper part of the canyon wall is composed of thick lava flows. In contrast, the lower part of the canyon wall appears as thin sedimentary-looking layers with lone boulders and pockets of boulders weathering out of the cliff. The boundary between the different layers forms an angle which slopes away in opposite directions and the basalt layers thicken rapidly from right to left forming a wedge-shaped appearance in cross-section.

Geologists suspect that you are standing along the rim of an ancient volcano that was buried underneath the Bandelier Tuff. It is a special type of volcano, called a *maar volcano,* that erupted when lava came in contact with water, either underground water or perhaps a stream or lake. Violent maar eruptions spread shattered fragments of rock and lava in thin layers sloping away from a central vent. These layers are composed of particles that look similar to sedimentary rocks like sandstone and conglomerate, but were deposited during a volcanic eruption when the material was blasted out laterally at great speeds (called a *base surge*). Larger boulders fell through the air as volcanic bombs and in places warped the layers upon impact. This maar volcano is estimated to be about 2 miles wide and 100 feet high. The wedge-shaped layers of basalt in the cliff face represent lava that pooled and hardened with the central crater. The resistant basalt ledge that forms the Upper Falls is believed to be the hardened vent or throat of the volcano.

From the viewpoint, the trail continues to switchback down to the river where it crosses a bridge. The canyon bottom directly downstream of the Upper Falls is closed to access because of the danger of falling rocks. The trail continues for another mile, winding down through the canyon to the banks of the Rio Grande. Along the way, it passes an overlook (trail marker 19) where you can see the Lower Falls, which drops about 45 feet over another ledge of resistant basalt. There are also several close looks at the maar volcanic deposits in the canyon wall complete with volcanic bombs (large boulders).

Once in the canyon bottom, the trail narrows and crosses the creek several times on stepping stones to finally reach the Rio Grande. The river has had to work hard over the ages, continually recarving its canyon as volcanoes spilled lava and ash that repeatedly blocked and altered its course. After you have enjoyed the views looking up- and downstream, carefully retrace your steps back to the trailhead.

TENT ROCKS

Hike 49

Volcanic Landscape in the Jemez Mountains

Hike a slot canyon through layers of volcanic tuff to an overlook in Kasha-Katuwe Tent Rocks National Monument.

DISTANCE ■ **2.6 miles round trip**

ELEVATION ■ **5750 to 6300 feet**

DIFFICULTY ■ **Moderate**

TOPOGRAPHIC MAP ■ **USGS Canada, NM**

GEOLOGIC MAP ■ **31**

KEY REFERENCES ■ **47, 49, 50**

PRECAUTIONS ■ **Rocks along the trail are soft and friable so watch your step. Please avoid the private property bordering the monument by staying on the marked trails. The canyon is prone to flash floods. Do not attempt this hike if thunderstorms are predicted.**

FOR INFORMATION ■ **Albuquerque Field Office, Kasha-Katuwe Tent Rocks National Monument**

About the Landscape: Tent Rocks describes unique rock formations along the southeastern flank of the Jemez Mountains. Along the Tent Rocks Canyon Trail, erosion has sculpted a bizarre landscape in light-colored layers of rhyolite tuff. These soft and easily eroded layers of ash and rock, called the Peralta Tuff, were ejected during a series of eruptions from nearby volcanoes between 6 and 7 million years ago. The Peralta Tuff is older than the 1.4- to 1.1-million-year-old Bandelier Tuff that blankets much of the Jemez Mountains region.

This hike explores Tent Rock Canyon, a series of narrow slot canyons carved in the Peralta Tuff along the Parajito Fault, a major fault along the Colorado Plateau's eastern boundary with the Rio Grand Rift. Along the way, the trail passes artistically eroded, balanced rocks and tent rock landforms, and ultimately emerges above the canyon for a grand overlook of the Jemez Mountains and Rio Grande Valley. This fragile area was protected recently within the Kasha-Katuwe Tent Rocks National Monument (designated in 2001).

Trail Guide: To reach Kasha-Katuwe Tent Rocks National Monument, take exit 264 off Interstate 25 and drive 8.6 miles west on New Mexico Highway 16 to the T-intersection with New Mexico Highway 22. Turn right and drive 2.8 miles, then turn left at the sign for the national monument. Continue following Highway 22 to Cochiti Pueblo and turn right after 1.8 miles (another sign for the national monument) onto Forest Road 266 (Tribal Route 92). After about 0.4 mile the pavement ends. Continue another 4.5 miles on this graded dirt road to the monument parking area on the right. An interpretive display and trail register mark the trailhead. There is a fee of $5 per vehicle.

The Tent Rocks Canyon Trail begins by following a wide, sandy path north from the trailhead. After about 50 yards, stay right at the junction with the Cave Trail to get the first good view of the tent rocks that adorn the cliff-edged ridge left of the trail.

As you can see, the name "tent rocks" is actually somewhat of a misnomer, since the landforms look more like cone-shaped teepees. These eroded remnants of tuff can form in a number of ways. Escaping gases following an eruption can move vertically up through the ash layers causing some particles to weld together firmly as the ash cools. These welded areas within the tuff are more resistant to erosion when later exposed to the elements. Over time, erosion sculpts the welded ash layers into tent rocks.

Another way that tent rocks form is when boulders encased within the tuff act as cap rocks protecting the softer ash underneath from rapid erosion. Differential erosion by water and wind then works its magic, removing the softer tuff layers below the cap rock, and creating the conical "tents." Once the caprock boulders fall off their pedestals, the softer ash layers of the tent rocks melt away quickly. From this trail vantage point, you can see boulder-capped pedestals high on the skyline as well as tent rocks along the base of the cliff that have lost their protective "hard hats."

Continue following the Canyon Trail along a wide wash starting at about the 0.25-mile point. The trail follows this wash for another 0.25 mile to the entrance to Tent Rocks Canyon. The Cave Trail meets the wash on the left just before entering the canyon.

Balanced cap rocks are important in the formation of tent rocks.

As you enter the cool, shady canyon, you can see the layered nature of the Peralta Tuff in the canyon walls. Notice the balanced rocks perched on pedestals in the cliff on the left. These textbook examples demonstrate the initial stages in the formation of tent rocks. Over time, erosion by water and wind will continue to sculpt the soft ashy tuff below the cap rocks and enlarge the pedestal.

The soft, easily eroded tuff layers in the canyon walls are an amalgam-ation of pyroclastic particles and rock debris within the Peralta Tuff of the Bearhead Rhyolite. A close look reveals an assortment of rock types in-cluding porous fragments of pumice, red and maroon pebbles and cobbles of rhyolite, and occasional gray cobbles and small boulders of andesite. Some of the more conglomerate-looking layers or *lenses* were created as streams reworked the ash deposits between volcanic events.

The layers in and around Tent Rocks Canyon provide a record of erup-tions from at least twenty volcanic vents. Some of the layers represent pumice and ash falling from the sky from more distant sources, including Bearhead Peak about 5 miles to the northwest. Other layers represent flows and base surges from vents within only a mile or two of the present-day canyon. It is estimated that as many as thirty-five explosive episodes spread rock and ash across the landscape and, in the process, constructed a number of rhyolite domes in the southern Jemez Mountains. All this activity took place in less than 200,000 years, between about 6 and 7 million years ago.

The trail follows the canyon floor, which becomes extremely narrow in places. The canyon is strewn with boulders transported during flash floods that periodically carve and deepen the canyon. About 50 yards into the canyon a large ponderosa pine tree on the right has had its roots exposed by a recent phase of down-cutting and erosion.

As you emerge from the first narrows, there is a break in the canyon wall on the right where the rocks appear to be broken and offset. Down-to-the-east movement places thin layers of tuff directly against a massive tuff layer. Note also that the layers in the canyon walls are tilted. This is because Tent Rocks Canyon is being carved along a fault zone. This fault and other small faults are part of the Parajito Fault, one of the major bound-ing faults along the west side of the Rio Grand Rift.

After a sharp bend in the canyon there is another narrows. This second slot canyon is longer than the first and requires passing beneath a large boul-der to continue upstream (easily done). The narrows end abruptly where the canyon widens. Here there are tent rock formations on either side of the trail and twin balanced rocks that rise from the canyon floor right of the trail. The canyon then turns to the west and begins to climb more steeply.

At about the 1-mile point, a sign with an arrow on a fallen boulder points to the right where the trail steepens and leaves the canyon bottom. As the trail climbs a series of tight switchbacks up a steep hillside, there are great views of classic tent rock formations against the skyline. At one point it is necessary to climb up a low ledge using steps chipped into the rock (easily done).

Once on top, the trail levels out and winds along the ridge for about 0.25 mile to a viewpoint above Tent Rock Canyon. Looking down into the canyon from this vantage point, the faults that slice the canyon are clearly seen as breaks in the cliff where the white tuff layers are broken and down-dropped to the east. There are also sweeping views to the northwest, where cliffs of pinkish Bandelier Tuff edge the Jemez Mountains and Parajito Plateau, and to the east, where the Rio Grande flows down valleys along large fault-blocks that have dropped down along the Rio Grande Rift.

Once you have admired the view and absorbed this amazing volcanic landscape, carefully retrace your steps back to the trailhead.

EL MALPAIS

LAVA TUBES OF THE BANDERA FLOW

Peek into the hidden world of North America's longest network of lava tubes.

DISTANCE ■ **2 miles round trip**

ELEVATION ■ **7600 to 7640 feet**

DIFFICULTY ■ **Strenuous**

TOPOGRAPHIC MAP ■ **USGS Ice Caves, NM**

GEOLOGIC MAP ■ **32**

KEY REFERENCES ■ **51, 52**

PRECAUTIONS ■ **Although a high-clearance vehicle is recommended to reach the trailhead, passenger cars can usually negotiate the few rough spots. Be aware that the road becomes impassable when wet, however, for any vehicle, so check at the park information center for current conditions. The trail traverses loose volcanic rock—watch every step and follow the cairns carefully. Sturdy hiking boots are essential. Use extreme caution scrambling into the lava tubes. To explore the darkness beyond the entrance, hard hats, three sources of light per person, and protective clothing are required. Do not explore the caves alone.**

FOR INFORMATION ■ **El Malpais National Monument**

About the Landscape: The volcanic moonscape of El Malpais (pronounced "el-mal-pie-EES") is a relative newcomer to the Colorado Plateau scene. Located in the shadow of Mount Taylor near the southeastern edge of the Plateau, this wilderness of dark volcanic rock was born during a "recent" episode of fluid Hawaiian-like eruptions. Although few trails (or roads!) penetrate the formidable volcanic landscape, cairns mark the way to the Big Tubes area where it is possible to peek inside the Bandera flow and experience the cool darkness that lies hidden underground.

It was only "yesterday" that great rivers of molten lava flowed for tens of miles, lapping up against the cliffs of colorful sedimentary layers that ring the Zuni Mountains. When the last lava flow cooled just 3000 years ago, it completed a vast expanse of broken and jagged basalt rock that the Spanish explorers called El Malpais "the bad country." Locked here within the hardened layers is a record of at least fifteen major lava flows that scorched the landscape repeatedly over the past 750,000 years.

Now protected within the El Malpais National Monument and Conservation Area, the products of this fiery tempest created what is today called the Zuni-Bandera Volcanic Field. The Bandera flow is one of the youngest of the lava flows in the volcanic field. Charcoal encased within the lava has been radiocarbon-dated at about 11,000 years. From its source at Bandera Crater in the northwestern part of the volcanic field, fluid basalt lava breached the south wall of the crater and flowed as a glowing river of red-hot magma for 22 miles. The Bandera flow is known for its amazing network of lava tubes. To date, 17 miles of tubes have been discovered and explored—making this the longest known system of lava tubes in North America.

Trail Guide: To reach the Big Tubes trailhead, take exit 81 off Interstate 40 west of Grants and turn left (south) onto New Mexico Highway 53. Drive south for 26 miles toward El Malpais and El Morro National Monuments and turn left onto County Road 42. The turn is about 1 mile past Bandera Crater and Ice Caves (privately owned but worth the stop). Follow this dirt road (also called Chain of Craters Backcountry Byway) 4.5 miles to the sign for the Big Tubes area. Turn left again and drive 3.2 miles to the trailhead.

From the parking area, the trail immediately steps up onto a forested landscape of uneven and loose dark gray to black volcanic rock. Be sure to spot the next cairn before moving ahead—it is easy to lose the trail!

The dark rock underfoot is basalt of the Bandera lava flow. Look closely to see tiny holes in the rock called vesicles, caused by gas bubbles trapped in the lava when it cooled. You will see that some of the vesicles appear to be elongated or stretched, an indication that the lava was still flowing as it cooled. The jumbled and broken nature of the basalt is a type of lava called *a'a* (a Hawaiian word pronounced "ah-ah"). A'a lava forms when thick, viscous lava cools rapidly and breaks into a shifting pile of rubble covering a core of still red-hot lava moving underneath.

Well-placed cairns lead across this treacherous expanse of a'a lava, crossing a series of elongate mounds and shallow depressions. These features formed as the hardened crust responded to changes in the moving lava below, buckling up along pressure ridges, or *squeeze-ups,* and sagging downward into collapse pits.

In places the lava surface is much smoother, appearing almost corrugated or ribbed. This ropy texture is characteristic of a second type of lava called *pahoehoe* (another Hawaiian word, pronounced "pa-hoy-hoy"). In contrast to the blocky a'a lava, pahoehoe lava forms from the slower cooling of more fluid lava. The pahoehoe formed where red-hot lava squeezed up through fractures in the broken a'a surface. Pahoehoe lava is also common in the lava tubes where the molten lava was insulated from rapid cooling.

At about the 0.5-mile point, the trail reaches a junction marked by a sign pointing right to Seven Bridges Collapse and Four Windows Cave, and left to Big Skylight Cave and Caterpillar Collapse. The plan for this hike is to go left, making about a 1-mile loop that returns to this point after passing all the major volcanic features of the Big Tubes area.

Follow the cairns to the left up to the entrance to the Big Skylight Cave only 100 yards from the sign. The sharp-walled trench before you is a collapsed section of North America's most extensive lava tube system. The entrance to the 600-foot-long Big Skylight Cave is the dark opening to the

Window to the sky—lava tube on the Big Tubes Trail

right. To the left, a section of the original lava tube roof forms a natural bridge that spans the width of the trench.

Although it is a bit of a scramble down to the cave's entrance, Big Skylight Cave is one of the most accessible lava tubes found anywhere. *Lava tubes* are long caves that form where channels of red-hot lava roof over with a chilled outer crust. Openings to the tube are created where catastrophic roof failure takes place, which usually occurs during the latter stages of tube formation or immediately after cooling. The large blocks of lava that fell when the roof collapsed make walking in Big Skylight Cave a challenge.

As you make your way down into the cave, the coolness of the air is refreshing. The light streaming into the cave through the Big Skylight—a round hole in the cave's roof—makes it possible to explore the entrance area without a flashlight. The obvious horizontal bands on the walls of the tube represent the changing levels of red-hot lava that flowed through the tube. The beautiful, streamlined *dripstone* textures seen on the walls and ceiling formed as the intense heat within the tube remelted the encasing rock. Please avoid walking on the delicate, moss-covered boulders directly underneath the opening. If you have the required equipment, and are not alone, exploring the eerie darkness beyond the skylight is an unforgettable experience. Return to the rim by the route you came.

Back out in the daylight, follow the cairns along the rim of the trench, then traverse through the forest to the Caterpillar Collapse only about 0.25-mile away. Caterpillar Collapse is the strikingly sinuous trench of a once-covered lava tube. In places the roof sagged inward into the tube, but in other areas it collapsed completely. Step over the collapse feature near the sign and then follow the cairns to the right along the opposite rim. The cairns ultimately strike off through the forest, leading to the entrance of Four Windows Cave, a mere 0.25 mile away.

Four Windows Cave is an impressive lava tube more than 1200 feet long. Entering the cave requires climbing down over large blocks of lava from the collapsed roof. Only a short distance inside you can look up through the four windows to the sky. The Park Service has roped off a portion of the cave to protect the moss gardens below the openings. Most of the treasures of Four Windows Cave lie hidden in the darkness. Explore further only if you are properly equipped.

The cairns beyond the Four Windows Cave lead through the forest another 0.25 mile to the Seven Bridges Collapse, named for the seven natural bridges that span the chasm. Turn to the right and follow the cairns along the rim, passing two of the natural bridges along the way.

Ultimately, the cairns head back to the sign at the trail junction where the loop began. From this point, follow the cairns back to the parking area.

Glossary

a'a—Hawaiian term for a type of basaltic lava whose upper surface consists of jagged, tumbled pieces of lava

alluvial fan—large fan-shaped accumulation of sediment deposited by streams where they emerge at the front of a mountain range

Ancestral Rocky Mountains—ancient basement-cored mountains (the Uncompahgre Highland) and uplifts (Defiance Uplift) that rose 300 million years ago, warping overlying sedimentary layers

andesite—fine-grained, typically medium-gray volcanic rock; intermediate in composition between rhyolite and basalt

angular unconformity—see *unconformity*

anticline—upward fold in rock layers; arched or dome-like uplift of sedimentary layers

arkose sandstone—sandstone that contains more than 25 percent feldspar

ash—fine particulate material ejected by a volcanic eruption

badlands—intricate or fluted topography and landforms carved by erosion into soft rocks (like shale and mudstone)

basalt—dark-colored fine-grained volcanic rock rich in iron-bearing minerals

base surge—laterally directed volcanic eruption that moves radially outward at high velocity to form thin-bedded tuff and breccia

basement rock—general term for the oldest rocks of Precambrian age; generally gneiss, schist, and granitic rocks

Basin and Range—The geologic province in the southwestern U.S. characterized by fault-block mountains separated by down-dropped basins. Borders the Colorado Plateau on the south and west.

bomb—a large spindle- or lens-shape volcanic rock ejected from a volcano; its shape forms while cooling in the air while still molten

brachiopod—clam-like organism; common fossil in Paleozoic limestones

breccia—rock formed from large pieces of rock; usually bound within volcanic ash

breccia pipe—a cylindrical or pipelike feature formed underground and filled with broken rock fragments (breccia); usually hydrothermally altered and a host for mineral ore

bryozoans—marine colonial organism common in ancient limestones, and ranging in age from Ordovician to recent times

cairn—small rock pile commonly used to mark trail routes

caldera—large circular-shaped depression formed by explosion or collapse of a volcano

calcite—light-colored mineral with the formula $CaCO_3$ (calcium carbonate) that often fills veins in igneous rocks and forms the sedimentary rock limestone

cement—general term for the minerals, commonly quartz or calcite, that bind sediments together to form solid rock

chert—a finely crystalline variety of the mineral quartz; common in sedimentary rocks especially limestone, and particularly abundant in the Permian Kaibab Formation where the silica for the quartz was derived from siliceous sponges

cinder cone—a small volcano constructed of loose rock fragments (cinders) ejected from a central vent and commonly marked by a crater at its summit

cinders—general term for vesicular volcanic particles approximately the size of sand; also called scoria

cirque—bowl-like depression carved in rock by ice at the head of a glacier

clinker—sedimentary rock baked, altered, and oxidized by the heat of coal burning underground

coal—sedimentary rock rich in carbon formed from layers of buried plant material

Colorado Plateau—The geologic province in the Four Corners region of the southwestern U.S. characterized by uplifted, flat-lying sedimentary layers dissected by the Colorado River and its tributaries.

composite volcano—a large volcano built from alternating layers of pyroclastics (ash and rock debris) and rock solidified from lava flows; also called stratovolcano

conglomerate—coarse-grained sedimentary rock composed of rounded pebbles and gravel cemented together, usually found with sandstone

contact—describes the surface or boundary between different rock types or formations

continental accretion—growth or increase in size of a continent by collision of plates that then become part of the continental mass; the process often results in mountain building and intense metamorphism

Cretaceous seaway—shallow inland sea that stretched from the Arctic to the Gulf of Mexico and flooded the Colorado Plateau about 100 million years ago

crinoid—small, disk-like fossil from the segmented stem of a marine animal; common in Paleozoic limestones

cross-bed—pattern of slanting or angled parallel lines common in sedimentary rocks (typically sandstone) that marks the advancing crests of wind-blown or water-transported sediment

crust—outermost layer of the Earth ranging in thickness from about 5 to 30 miles and composed of more brittle, less dense material than the underlying mantle

cryptobiotic soil—delicate, black, crusty soil composed of lichens, mosses, blue-green algae, and fungi; helps stabilize sand and retards erosion throughout the Southwest (also called cryptogamic)

dacite—a medium to dark gray volcanic rock of intermediate composition between rhyolite and andesite

desert varnish—general term to describe the vertical streaks of mineral stain or patina that coats canyon walls in the Southwest

diatreme—cylindrical or funnel-shaped breccia pipe formed by an explosive, gas-rich eruption; when eroded, it forms a topographic feature called a volcanic neck

differential erosion—varying rates of weathering, most common in sedimentary rocks, where some areas or layers of rock are more resistant than others

dike—narrow igneous intrusion along vertical fractures cut through surrounding rock

diorite—a medium to dark gray igneous rock of intermediate composition between granite and gabbro

dolomite—a common carbonate mineral similar to calcite (calcium carbonate) but which contains magnesium; also a general term for a limestone-like rock that contains greater than 50 percent dolomite

erosion—the physical breakup or removal of rock by an agent such as running water, glacial ice, or wind

escarpment—cliff or step-slope edging higher land

extrusive igneous rock—molten rock that cools at the Earth's surface (volcanic)

fault—break in rocks where movement has occurred

fault-block—uplifted section of rock bounded on either side by faults

feldspar—group of light-colored minerals; the most common rock-forming mineral

fissure—a long crack or fracture; also a volcanic term to describe where magma erupts not from a central vent, e.g. fissure eruption

fold—curve or bend in rock strata

formation—a body of rock or group of rock layers that has recognizable characteristics or similarity making it distinguishable from adjacent rock units; a convenient unit for mapping, describing, or interpreting the geology of a region

fracture—crack or break in rocks along which no movement has occurred; also called joint

fumerole—a vent that emits gas and water vapor; a type of hot spring

gneiss—metamorphic rock that displays distinct banding of light and dark mineral layers (pronounced "nice")

glacier—mass of ice moving under the influence of gravity and which forms by compaction and recrystallization of old snow; also called ice sheet or ice cap

graben—down-dropped block of rock bounded on either side by faults

Grand Staircase—popular term that describes the retreating cliffs or escarpments of resistant sedimentary layers along the southern Colorado Plateau

granite—light-colored, coarse-grained igneous rock with quartz and feldspar as dominant minerals and typically peppered with mica and hornblende

granitic—general term for light-colored, granite-like igneous rocks

Great Unconformity—erosion surface separating younger sedimentary layers from much older basement rocks below; originally named by John Wesley Powell in 1875

group—two or more adjacent formations that are considered a stratigraphic unit based on similar age, character, or geologic history

gypsum—see *salt*

hanging valley—valley whose floor is high above a main valley; usually formed where a small glacier once met a large glacier

hand lens—small magnifying glass used to examine rocks up close

headward erosion—a weathering process that lengthens a valley in an uphill or upstream direction

hoodoo—popular term for a rock pillar or pinnacle; sometimes called goblin

hornblende—common dark mineral in igneous and metamorphic rocks

horst—see *fault-block*

hydrothermal—describes rocks and minerals formed or altered by hot water generated deep underground; associated with mineral deposits and hot springs

261

Ice Age—general term for glacial episodes during the Pleistocene (1.8 million to 8,000 years ago)

igneous rock—rock that forms from the solidification of molten rock or magma

intrusive igneous rock—molten rock emplaced within preexisting rock that hardens before it reaches the surface

Kaibab Uplift—a broad anticline that arched upward during the Laramide orogeny; defined by the Kaibab Plateau today (North Rim of the Grand Canyon)

laccolith—igneous intrusion that squeezes between sedimentary layers and domes up the overlying layers

Laramide orogeny—major uplift and mountain-building event between 65 and 50 million years ago when huge blocks of basement rocks pushed up from below warping overlying sedimentary layers into steep monoclines and broad anticlines

lava—fluid, molten rock erupted on the Earth's surface

lava dome—steep, dome-shaped volcano built from viscous rhyolite or dacite lava flows

lava tube—a cave within a lava flow formed by partial or complete withdrawal of molten lava after a crust cooled on top

limestone—sedimentary rock composed mostly of the mineral calcite

magma—molten or fluid rock material from which igneous rock is derived

mantle—a thick zone that separates the Earth's crust above from the Earth's core below. Reaching 1800 miles below the surface, the mantle is composed of relatively high-density iron and magnesium silicate rock.

member—a subdivision of a formation differentiated by a separate or distinct composition

metamorphic rock—a rock produced by the transformation of preexisting rock in response to changes in temperature and pressure conditions, such as deep burial or igneous intrusion

mica—group of minerals that form thin, platy flakes, typically with shiny surfaces

Mogollon Highlands—an ancient mountain range that existed south of the Colorado Plateau and shed a tremendous amount of sediment to the north; presumably uplifted about 300 million years ago with the Ancestral Rocky Mountains and again in the Mesozoic

Mogollon Rim—topographic feature defined by a series of cliffs or escarpments which represent the southern edge of the Colorado Plateau.

monocline—bend in rock layers where all strata are inclined in the same direction; step-like fold in rock

moraine—sediment piled by the action of glaciers

mudstone—general term for fine-grained sedimentary rock formed from hardened clay and silt (mud) which lacks the thin layers that characterize shale

normal fault—fault caused by extension in which the block above the fault plane has moved down relative to the other block

Pangea—ancient supercontinent that broke apart 200 million years ago to form present-day continents

pahoehoe—Hawaiian term for a type of basaltic lava whose upper surface is smooth or ropy, not fractured or broken

pegmatite—extremely coarse-grained intrusive igneous rock of granitic composition, which typically fills fractures to form veins and is common in Colorado's basement rocks

petrified wood—fossil trees preserved by replacement of the original organic wood by minerals carried in groundwater

pictograph—rock art of the Ancestral Puebloan peoples painted onto rock surfaces; differs from petroglyph which is etched into the rock surface

plate—large, mobile slab of crustal rock making up large sections of the Earth's surface; also tectonic plate

plate tectonics—theory that the Earth's surface is divided into huge slabs of rock (tectonic plates) that move relative to one other causing earthquakes, mountain building, and other geologic events such as volcanic activity

pluton—igneous body that cools deep underground, e.g. batholith

pumice—light-colored, frothy rock composed of volcanic glass and rhyolite

pyroclastic—rock fragments produced by explosive volcanic eruptions

pyroxene—mineral group of mostly dark minerals, e.g. augite

outcrop—describes a rock surface that is exposed, or at least not covered by soil or vegetation

quartz—very hard, light-colored mineral composed of silica (SiO_2)

quartzite—metamorphosed sandstone composed of sand-sized quartz grains fused together

reverse fault—a fault caused by compression in which the block above the fault plane has moved up relative to the other block

rifting—process whereby the Earth's crust is stretched and thinned; usually where two plates or sections of plates are pulling apart

Rio Grande Rift—a network of deep, down-faulted valleys or grabens that extend along the Rio Grande, from central Colorado south through New Mexico into Texas

rock—naturally formed, consolidated material composed of grains of one or more minerals

rhyolite—light-colored, volcanic igneous rock which is the extrusive equivalent of granite

ripple marks—small ridges on sediment surfaces formed by moving wind or water

salt—general term for sediment formed by evaporation of sea water; includes the minerals halite (table salt) and gypsum (calcium sulfate)

salt anticline—arching of sedimentary layers associated with the movement or collapse of salt underground

salt tectonics—bending, fracturing, and faulting of sedimentary layers associated with the movement or collapse of salt underground

sandstone—sedimentary rock composed of sand-size grains cemented together

schist—metamorphic rock composed of mica minerals aligned in the same direction

scoria—see *cinders*

sediment—collection of loose, solid particles derived (weathered) from preexisting rocks; also crystallized from water (e.g., salt), or secreted by organisms (e.g., coral)

sedimentary rock—rock resulting from a consolidation of loose sediment, remains of organisms, and/or crystals that form directly from water

sedimentary structures—features found within sedimentary rocks, usually formed during or shortly after deposition and before hardening by cement

shale—fine-grained sedimentary rock formed from hardened clay and silt, which generally fragments into thin layers

siltstone—fine-grained sedimentary rock formed from hardened silt, though not as fine-grained as shale or mudstone

slickenside—describes the grooved, smooth, or polished surface along a fault zone, formed by movement and friction along the fault surface

slickrock—bare rock surfaces of exposed sandstone worn smooth by erosion

soft sediment deformation—process that disturbs or deforms the original layering in sediment before it is hardened into rock; associated with movement of groundwater or sediment slumping on sand dunes

spatter cone—a small, steep-sided volcano built from lava spattering from a central vent

strata—distinct layers of rock; stratified rocks

stratigraphy—the science and study of how rock layers or strata fit together; includes distribution of rock type, regional correlation, character and sedimentary structures, age relations, and fossil content

stratovolcano—see *composite volcano*

stream piracy—the natural diversion or capture of the headwaters of one stream by the channel of another

striation—scratch or groove in rocks caused by rocks grinding beneath glacial ice

strike—describes the orientation of rock layers defined by the trend of a horizontal line projected on the surface of a layer or bedding plane

strike-slip fault—fault where rocks slide horizontally past one another

subduction—the process where one tectonic plate descends beneath another

syncline—trough-like downward sag or fold in rock layers

talus—accumulation of broken rocks or boulders at the base of a cliff; e.g., talus slope

tectonics—study of the global-scale forces generated within the Earth that result in uplift, movement, or deformation of the Earth's crust

thrust fault—special kind of reverse fault where older rock layers are pushed up and over younger rock layers; movement takes place along a low angle (less than 45 degrees) or almost horizontal surface

trilobite—group of extinct marine arthropods, ranging in age from Cambrian to Permian

tuff—igneous rock formed from hardened volcanic ash

unconformity—surface that represents a break or gap in the geologic record where rock layers were eroded or never deposited, resulting in younger layers lying directly atop much older rocks; described as an angular unconformity when the rock layers of different ages meet at an angle

weathering—group of processes, both chemical and physical, that change rock at the Earth's surface

vesicles—tiny holes in volcanic rock caused by gas bubbles trapped in lava as it cooled

volcanic rock—rock that forms from the solidification of molten rock or magma at the Earth's surface (extrusive igneous rock)

volcano—a hill or mountain constructed by the extrusion from a vent of lava or rock

Appendix A
Recommended Reading

Beyond the Hundredth Meridian: John Wesley Powell and the Second Opening of the West. W. Stegner. Lincoln: University of Nebraska Press, 1982.

Centennial Field Guide: The Rocky Mountain Region. S. S. Beus (ed.). Geologic Society of America, Rocky Mountain Section, v. 2, 1987.

Colorado, The. F. Waters. Athens, Ohio: Ohio University Press, 1946.

Colorado Plateau, The: A Geologic History. D. L. Baars. Albuquerque, New Mexico: University of New Mexico Press, 2000.

Desert Solitaire: A Season in the Wilderness. E. Abbey. New York: Simon and Schuster, 1968.

Exploration of the Colorado River and its Canyons, The. J. W. Powell. New York: Dover Publications, 1961. (First published 1895)

Field Guide to Geology, The. D. Lambert. New York: Facts on File, 1988.

Four Corners: History, Land, and People of the Desert Southwest. K. A. Brown. New York: Harper Collins Publishers, 1995.

Geologic Evolution of Arizona. J. P. Jenny and S. J. Reynolds (eds.). Tucson, Arizona: Arizona Geologic Society Digest 17, 1989.

Geologic Highway Map of Arizona. M. E. Cooley (ed.). Arizona Geological Society, 1967. 1:1,000,000.

Geologic Highway Map of Colorado. R. D. Christiansen. Colorado Geological Survey, 1991. 1:1,000,000.

Geologic Highway Map of New Mexico. R. W. Kelly (ed.), New Mexico Geological Society, 1982. 1:1,000,000.

Geologic Highway Map of Utah. L. F. Hintze. Brigham Young University Geology Studies, Special Publication 3, 1997.

Geologic History of Utah. L. F. Hintze. Provo, Utah: Brigham Young University Geology Studies, Special Publication 7, 1988.

Geology of Arizona. D. Nations and E. Stump. Dubuque, Iowa: Kendall/ Hunt Publishing, 1981.

Geology of the Colorado Plateau. F. Peterson and C. Turner-Peterson. Washington, DC: American Geophysical Union, 28th International Field Conference, 1989.

Geology of the Parks, Monuments, and Wildlands of Southern Utah, The. R. Filmore. Salt Lake City, Utah: The University of Utah Press, 2000.

Geology of Utah's Parks and Monuments. D. A. Sprinkel, T. C. Chidsey Jr., and P. B. Anderson (eds.). Salt Lake City, Utah: Geological Association Publication 28, 2000.

Grand Canyon Geology, S. S. Bues and M. Morales (eds.). Flagstaff, Arizona: Museum of Northern Arizona Press, Flagstaff, 1980.

Hiking Arizona's Geology. I. Lucchita. Seattle: The Mountaineers Books, 2001.

Hiking Colorado's Geology. R. L. Hopkins and L. B. Hopkins. Seattle: The Mountaineers Books, 2000.

Historical Atlas of the Earth, The. R. Osborne and D. Tarling. New York: Henry Holt and Company, 1996.

Introduction to Grand Canyon Geology, An. L. G. Price. Grand Canyon, Arizona: Grand Canyon Association, 1999.

Navajo Country: A Geology and Natural History of the Four Corners Region. D. L. Baars. Albuquerque, New Mexico: University of New Mexico Press, 1995.

Monkey Wrench Gang, The. E. Abbey. New York: Avon Books, 1975.

Pages of Stone: Geology of Western National Parks and Monuments. Number 4: Grand Canyon and the Plateau Country. H. Chronic. Seattle: The Mountaineers Books, 1988.

Physical Geology. C. C. Plummer and D. McGeary. Dubuque, Iowa: Wm. C. Brown, 1996.

Roadside Geology of Arizona. H. Chronic. Missoula, Montana: Mountain Press Publishing Company, 1983.

Roadside Geology of Colorado. H. Chronic. Missoula, Montana: Mountain Press Publishing Company, 1980.

Roadside Geology of New Mexico. H. Chronic. Missoula, Montana: Mountain Press Publishing Company, 1987.

Roadside Geology of Utah. H. Chronic. Missoula, Montana: Mountain Press Publishing Company, 1990.

Sedona Through Time: Geology of the Red Rocks. W. Ranney. Flagstaff, Arizona: Zia Interpretive Services, 2001.

Shadows of Time: The Geology of Bryce Canyon National Park. F. DeCourten. Bryce Canyon, Utah: Bryce Canyon Natural History Association, 1994.

Structural Geology of the Colorado Plateau Region of Southern Utah. G. H. Davis. Boulder, Colorado: Geological Society of America Special Paper 342, 1999.

Traveler's Guide to the Geology of the Colorado Plateau, A. D. L. Baars. Salt Lake City: The University of Utah Press, 2002. *Volcanoes of Northern Arizona: Sleeping Giants of the Grand Canyon Region.* W. A. Duffield. Grand Canyon, Arizona: Grand Canyon Association, 1997.

Wind in the Rock: The Canyonlands of Southeastern Utah. A. Zwinger. Tucson, Arizona: University of Arizona Press, 1978.

Appendix B
Key References

PART 1: ARIZONA'S PLATEAU HIKES

1. Geomorphology and Structure of the Colorado Plateau/Basin and Range Transition Zone, Arizona. R. A. Young, R. W. Peirce, and J. E. Faulds. In: G. H. Davis and E. M. Vander Dolder. *Geologic Diversity of Arizona and its Margins: Excursions to Choice Areas.* Arizona Bureau of Geology and Mineral Technology, Geological Survey Branch Special Paper 5, 1987, p. 182-196.
2. An Oligocene (?) Colorado Plateau Edge in Arizona. H. W. Peirce, M. Shafiquallah, and P. E. Damon. *Tectoniphysics,* v. 61, 1984, p. 1-24.
3. Regional significance of recurrent faulting and intracanyon volcanism at Oak Creek Canyon, southern Colorado Plateau, Arizona. R. F. Holm and R. A. Cloud. *Geology,* v. 18, p. 1014-1017.
4. San Francisco Mountain: A late Cenozoic composite volcano in northern Arizona. R. F. Holm. In: S. S. Beus (ed.). *Centennial Field Guide.* Geological Society of America, Rocky Mountain Section, v. 2, 1987, p. 389-392.
5. Holocene scoria cone and lava flows at Sunset Crater, northern Arizona. R. F. Holm and R. B. Moore. In: S. S. Beus (ed.). *Centennial Field Guide.* Geologic Society of America, Rocky Mountain Section, v. 2, 1987, p. 393-397.
6. *Volcanoes of Northern Arizona: Sleeping Giants of the Grand Canyon Region.* W. A. Duffield. Grand Canyon, Arizona: Grand Canyon Association, 1997.
7. *Grand Canyon Geology,* S. S. Beus and M. Morales (eds.). New York: Oxford University Press, 1990.
8. Petrified Forest National Park. S. R. Ash. In: S. S. Beus (ed.). *Centennial Field Guide.* Geologic Society of America, Rocky Mountain Section, v. 2, 1987, p. 405-410.
9. Pennsylvanian and Permian Geology of Arizona. R. C. Blakey. In: J. P. Jenny and S. J. Reynolds (eds.). *Geologic Evolution of Arizona.* Arizona Geological Society Digest 17, 1989, p. 313-347.
10. Triassic and Jurassic Geology of the Southern Colorado Plateau. R. C. Blakey. In: J. P. Jenny and S. J. Reynolds (eds.). *Geologic Evolution of Arizona.* Arizona Geological Society Digest 17, 1989, p. 369-396.
11. Monument Valley, Arizona and Utah. R. C. Blakey and D. L. Baars. In: S. S. Beus (ed.). *Centennial Field Guide.* Geological Society of America, Rocky Mountain Section, v. 2, 1987, p. 361-364.

12. Geology of Monument Valley Navajo Tribal Park, Utah–Arizona, W. L. Chenowith. In: D. A. Sprinkel, T. C. Chidsey Jr., and P. B. Anderson (eds.). *Geology of Utah's Parks and Monuments.* Utah Geological Association Publication 28, 2000, p. 529-533.

13. Cyclic Eolian Stratification on the Jurassic Navajo Sandstone, Zion National Park: Periodicities and Implications for Paleoclimate. M. A. Chan and A. W Archer. In: D. A. Sprinkel, T. C. Chidsey Jr., and P. B. Anderson (eds.). *Geology of Utah's Parks and Monuments.* Utah Geological Association Publication 28, 2000, p. 607-617.

PART 2: UTAH'S PLATEAU HIKES

14. Geology of Goosenecks State Park, Utah. G. M. Stevenson. In: D. A. Sprinkel, T. C. Chidsey Jr., and P. B. Anderson (eds.). *Geology of Utah's Parks and Monuments.* Utah Geological Association Publication 28, 2000, p. 433-447.

15. Paleogeography of the Late Cretaceous of the western interior of middle North America: Coal distribution and sediment accumulation. L. N. Roberts and M. A. Kirschbaum. *USGS Bulletin,* v. 561, 1995, 115 p.

16. Geology of Natural Bridges National Monument, Utah. J. E. Huntoon, J. E. Stanesco, R. F. Dubiel, J. Dougan. In: D. A. Sprinkel, T. C. Chidsey Jr., and P. B. Anderson (eds.). *Geology of Utah's Parks and Monuments.* Utah Geological Association Publication 28, 2000, p. 233-249.

17. Geology of Arches National Park, Utah. H. H. Doelling. In: D. A. Sprinkel, T. C. Chidsey Jr., and P. B. Anderson, P. B. (eds.). *Geology of Utah's Parks and Monuments.* Utah Geological Association Publication 28, 2000, p. 11-36.

18. Upheaval Dome, Canyonlands, Utah: Strain Indicators that Reveal an Impact Origin. P. W. Huntoon. In: D. A. Sprinkel, T. C. Chidsey Jr., and P. B. Anderson (eds.). *Geology of Utah's Parks and Monuments.* Utah Geological Association Publication 28, 2000, p. 619-628.

19. Geology of Canyonlands National Park, Utah. D. L. Baars. In: D. A. Sprinkel, T. C. Chidsey Jr., and P. B. Anderson (eds.). *Geology of Utah's Parks and Monuments.* Utah Geological Association Publication 28, 2000, p. 61-83.

20. *Structural Geology of the Colorado Plateau Region of Southern Utah.* G. H. Davis. Geological Society of America, Special Paper 342, 1999, p. 124-130.

21. Geology of Goblin Valley State Park, Utah. M. R. Mulligan. In: D. A. Sprinkel, T. C. Chidsey Jr., and P. B. Anderson (eds.). *Geology of Utah's Parks and Monuments.* Utah Geological Association Publication 28, 2000, p. 421-431.

22. *The Geology of Capitol Reef National Park.* M. Collier. Capitol Reef Natural History Association, 1987, 48 p.

23. Geology of Capitol Reef National Park, Utah. T. E. Morris et al., In: D. A. Sprinkel, T. C. Chidsey Jr., and Anderson, P. B. (eds.). *Geology of Utah's Parks and Monuments.* Utah Geological Association Publication 28, 2000, p. 85-105.

24. Report on the geology of the Henry Mountains. G. K. Gilbert. *U.S. Geographical and Geological Survey of the Rocky Mountain Region,* 1877, 160 p.

25. Geology and geography of the Henry Mountain region, Utah. C. B. Hunt, et al. *USGS Professional Paper 228,* 1953, 234 p.

26. The laccolith-stock controversy: New Results from the Henry Mountains. M. D. Jackson and D. D. Pollard. *Geological Society of America Bulletin,* v. 100, 1988, p. 117-139.

27. Geology of Grand Staircase–Escalante National Monument, Utah. H. H. Doelling et al., In: D. A. Sprinkel, T. C. Chidsey Jr., and Anderson, P. B. (eds.). *Geology of Utah's Parks and Monuments.* Utah Geological Association Publication 28, 2000, p. 198-231.

28. Geology of Kodachrome Basin State Park, Utah. J. L. Baer and R. H. Steed. In: D. A. Sprinkel, T. C. Chidsey Jr., and Anderson, P. B. (eds.). *Geology of Utah's Parks and Monuments.* Utah Geological Association Publication 28, 2000, p. 449-463.

29. The Cockscomb Segment of the East Kaibab Monocline: Taking the Structural Plunge. S. E. Tindall, In: D. A. Sprinkel, T. C. Chidsey Jr., and Anderson, P. B. (eds.). *Geology of Utah's Parks and Monuments.* Utah Geological Association Publication 28, 2000, p. 629-643.

30. *Shadows of Time: The Geology of Bryce Canyon National Park.* F. DeCourten. Bryce Canyon, Utah: Bryce Canyon Natural History Association, 1994, 128 p.

31. Geology of Bryce Canyon National Park, Utah. G. H. Davis and G. L. Pollack. In: Sprinkel, D.A., Chidsey, Jr., and Anderson, P. B. (eds.). *Geology of Utah's Parks and Monuments.* Utah Geological Association Publication 28, 2000, p. 37-60.

32. Tectonic development of Upper Cretaceous to Eocene strata of southwestern Utah. P. M. Goldstrand. *Geological Society of America Bulletin,* v. 106, 1994, p. 145-154.

33. Geology of Cedar Breaks National Monument, Utah. S. C. Hatfield, P. D. Rowley, E. G. Sable. D. J. Maxwell, B. V. Cox, M. D. McKell, D. E. Kiel. In: Sprinkel, D.A., Chidsey, T.C., and Anderson, T.C. (eds.). *Geology of Utah's Parks and Monuments.* Utah Geological Association Publication 28, 2000, p. 139-154.

34. Geology of Zion National Park, Utah. R. F. Biek et al. In: D.A. Sprinkel, T. C. Chidsey Jr., and Anderson, P. B. (eds.) *Geology of Utah's Parks and Monuments.* Utah Geological Association Publication 28, 2000, p. 107-135.

35. Geology of Coral Pink Sand Dunes State Park, Kane County, Utah. R. L. Ford and S. L. Gillman. In: Sprinkel, D.A., Chidsey, T. C. Jr., and Anderson, P. B. (eds.). *Geology of Utah's Parks and Monuments.* Utah Geological Association Publication 28, 2000, p. 365-389.

36. Calderas of the Marysvale volcanic field, west-central Utah. T. A. Steven et al.. *Journal of Geophysical Research,* v. 89, 1984, p. 8751-8764.

PART 3: COLORADO'S PLATEAU HIKES

37. Neogene tectonics and geomorphology of the eastern Uinta Mountains in Utah, Colorado, and Wyoming. W. R. Hansen. *USGS Professional Paper 1356,* 1986, 78 p.

38. The Geologic Story of Colorado National Monument. S. W. Lohman. *USGS Bulletin,* v. 1508, 1981, p. 137-143.

39. Ancient drainage changes in and south of Unaweep Canyon, southwestern Colorado: S. W. Lohman. In: R. C. Epis (ed.), *Western Slope Colorado.* New Mexico Geological Society, 32nd Field Conference Guidebook, 1981, p. 137-143.

40. *The Black Canyon of the Gunnison: In Depth.* W. R. Hansen, Southwest Parks and Monuments Association, 1987, 57 p.

41. Guide to the geology of Mesa Verde National Park. M. O. Griffitts, Mesa Verde Museum Association, 1990, 88 p.

PART 4: NEW MEXICO'S PLATEAU HIKES

42. Ship Rock, New Mexico: The vent of a violent volcanic eruption. P. T. Delaney. In: S. S. Beus (ed.). *Centennial Field Guide.* Geological Society of America, Rocky Mountain Section, v. 2, 1987, p. 411-415.

43. Stratigraphy, paleontology and age of the Fruitland and Kirtland Formations (Upper Cretaceous), San Juan Basin, New Mexico. A. P. Hunt and S. C. Lucas. New Mexico Geological Society Guidebook, 43rd Field Conference, San Juan Basin IV, 1992, p. 217-239.

44. Chaco Culture National Historical Park. H. Chronic. *Pages of Stone: Geology of Western Parks and Monuments, v. 4: Grand Canyon and the Plateau Country,* 1988, p. 75-78.

45. The Triassic dinosaur *Coelophysis.* E. H. Colbert. *Museum of Northern Arizona Bulletin 57,* 1989, 160 p.

46. The Little Dinosaurs of Ghost Ranch. E. H. Colbert. Columbia University Press, 1995, 247 p.

47. The Valles Caldera, Jemez Mountains, New Mexico. K. J. De Nault. In: S. S. Beus (ed.). *Centennial Field Guide.* Geologic Society of America, Rocky Mountain Section, v. 2, 1987, p. 425-429.

48. The Cerros Del Rio Volcanic Field. J. C. Aubele. In: R.V. Ingersoll (ed.), *Guidebook to Santa Fe Country*, New Mexico Geological Society, 1979, p. 243-252.

49. *The Jemez Mountains Region.* F. Goff et al. (eds.). New Mexico Geological Society, 47th Annual Field Conference, 1996, 484 p.

50. The Geology of Tent Rocks. G. A. Smith. In: F. Goff, B. S. Kues, M. A. Rogers, L. D. McFadden, and J. N. Gardner. (eds.). *The Jemez Mountains Region.* New Mexico Geological Society, 47th Annual Field Conference, 1996, p. 89-90.

51. *The Volcanic Eruptions of El Malpais—A Guide to the Volcanic History and Formations of El Malpais National Monument.* M. V. Mabery, R. Moore, and K Hon. Santa Fe, New Mexico, Ancient City Press, 1999.

52. In the basement—Lava-tube origins and morphology. B. W. Rogers and C. J. Mosch. In: Mabery, K. (ed.). *Natural History of El Malpais National Monument.* New Mexico Bureau of Mines & Mineral Resources, 1997, p. 61-68.

Appendix C
Geologic Maps

PART 1: ARIZONA'S PLATEAU HIKES

1. Geologic map of the Fossil Springs Roadless Area. G. W. Weir and L. S. Beard, *USGS Misc. Field Studies Map MF-1568-C*, 1984. 1:24,000.

2. Geologic map of the Sedona 30' X 60' quadrangle, Yavapai and Coconino Counties, Arizona. G. W. Weir et al., *USGS Misc. Investigations Series Map I-1896, 1989. 1:100,000.*

3. Geologic map of San Francisco Mountain, Elden Mountain, and Dry Lake Hills, Coconino County, Arizona. R. F. Holm, *USGS Misc. Investigations Map I-1663*, 1988. 1:24:000.

4. Geologic map of the east part of the San Francisco volcanic field, Arizona. E. W. Wolfe, et. al., *USGS Field Studies Map MF-1960*, 1987. 1976. 1:50,000.

5. Geologic map of the northwest part of the San Francisco Volcanic Field, north-central Arizona. E. W. Wolfe et al., *USGS Misc. Field Studies Map MF-1957*, 1987. 1:50,000.

6. Geologic map of the eastern part of Grand Canyon National Park, Arizona. P. W. Huntoon et al., Grand Canyon Association, 1996.1:62,500.

7. Geologic map of Vulcans Throne and vicinity, Western Grand Canyon, Arizona. G. H. Billingsley and P. W. Huntoon, Grand Canyon Natural History Association, 1983. 1:48,000.

8. Geologic map of Petrified Forest National Park, G. W. Billingsley (available for purchase at park visitor center).

9. Regional hydrogeology of the Navajo and Hopi Indian Reservations, Arizona, New Mexico, and Utah. M. E. Colley et al., *USGS Professional Paper 531-A*, 1969. 1:125,000.

10. Geologic map of the Vermilion Cliffs-Paria Canyon Instant Study Area and adjacent Wilderness Study Areas, Coconino County, Arizona, and Kane County, Utah. A. L. Bush. *USGS Misc. Field Studies Map MF-1475-A*, 1983. 1:62,500.

PART 2: UTAH'S PLATEAU HIKES

11. Geology, structure, and uranium deposits of the Cortez quadrangle, Colorado and Utah. D. D. Haynes et al., *USGS Misc. Investigations Map I-629*, 1972. 1:250,000.

12. Geology, structure, and uranium deposits of the Escalante quadrangle, Utah and Arizona. R. J. Hackman and D. G. Wyant, *USGS Misc. Investigations Map I-744*, 1973. 1:250,000.

13. Geology, structure, and uranium deposits of the Moab quadrangle, Colorado and Utah. P. L. Williams, *USGS Misc. Geol. Investigations Map I-360,* 1964. 1:250,000.
14. Geologic map of Arches National Park and vicinity, Grand Canyon, Utah. H. H. Doelling. Utah Geological and Mineral Survey, Map 74, 1985. 1:50,000.
15. Geologic map of Canyonlands National Park and vicinity, Utah. P. W. Huntoon, G. H. Billingsley, and W. J. Breed, Canyonlands Natural History Association, 1982. 1:62,500.
16. Geology of the Salina quadrangle, Utah. P. E. Williams and R. J. Hackman, *USGS Misc. Investigations Series Map I-591,* 1971. 1:250,000.
17. Geologic map of Capitol Reef National Park and vicinity, Utah. G. H. Billingsley et al., *Utah Geological and Mineral Survey Map 87,* 1986. 1:62,000.
18. Geologic map of the Little Rockies Wilderness Study Area and the Mount Hillers and Mount Pennell Study Areas and vicinity, Garfield County, Utah. M. J. Larson et al., *USGS Misc. Field Studies Map MF-1776-B,* 1985. 1:50,000.
19. Geologic map and coal sections of the Butler Valley quadrangle, Kane County, Utah. W. E. Bowers, *USGS Coal Investigations Series Map C-95,* 1983. 1:24,000.
20. Geologic map of Bryce Canyon National Park and vicinity, south-western Utah. W. E. Bowers, *USGS Map I-2108,* 1991. 1:24,000.
21. Geologic map of the Kanab quadrangle, Kane County, Utah, and Coconino County, Arizona. K. A. Sargent and B. C. Philpott, *USGS Map GQ-1603,* 1987. 1:62,500.
22. Geologic map of the Tushar Mountains and adjoining areas, Marysvale volcanic field, Utah. C. G. Cunningham et al., *USGS Misc. Geol. Investigations Map I-1430-A,* 1983. 1:50,000.

PART 3: COLORADO'S PLATEAU HIKES

23. Geologic map of Dinosaur National Monument and vicinity, Utah and Colorado. W. R. Hansen et al., *USGS Misc. Investigations Series Map I-1407,* 1983. 1:50,000.
24. Geology and structure of Grand Junction quadrangle, Colorado and Utah. P. L. Williams, *USGS Misc. Investigations Map I-736,* 1973. 1:250,000
25. Geologic Map of the Black Canyon of the Gunnison River and vicinity, western Colorado. W. R. Hansen, *USGS Misc. Geol. Investigations Map I-584,* 1971. 1:31,680.
26. Geologic map of the Mesa Verde area, Montezuma County, Colorado. A. A. Wanek. *USGS Oil and Gas Investigations Map OM-152,* 1954. 1:63,360.

PART 4: NEW MEXICO'S PLATEAU HIKES

27. Geology, structure, and uranium deposits of the Shiprock quadrangle, New Mexico and Arizona. R. B. O'Sullivan and H. M. Beikman (eds.), *USGS Misc. Investigations Series Map I-345*, 1963. 1:250,000.
28. Geologic and isopach maps of the Bisti, De-na-zin, and Ah-shi-sle-pah Wilderness Study Areas, San Juan County, New Mexico. J. L. Brown. *USGS Misc. Field Studies Map MF-1508-A*, 1983. 1:50,000.
29. Geologic map of the Chaco Culture National Historical Park, northwestern New Mexico. G. R. Scott et al., *USGS Misc. Investigations Series Map I-1571*, 1984. 1:50,000.
30. Geologic map of Rio Arriba County, New Mexico. E. C. Bingler (ed.), *New Mexico Bureau of Mines Bulletin 91, Plate 1b*, 1967.
31. Geologic map of the Jemez Mountains, New Mexico. R. L. Smith, R. A. Bailey, and C. S. Ross, *USGS Misc. Investigations Series Map I-571*, 1970. 1:125,00.
32. Geologic map of El Malpais lava field and surrounding area, Cibola County, New Mexico. C. H. Maxwell, *USGS Misc. Investigations Series Map I-1595*, 1986. 1:62,500.

Appendix D
Addresses and Contact Information

Albuquerque Field Office, Kasha-Katuwe Tent Rocks National Monument, Bureau of Land Management, 435 Montano Road N.E., Albuquerque, NM 87107; (505) 761-8700; *www.nm.blm.gov*

Arches National Park, P.O. Box 907, Moab, UT 84532-0907; (435) 719-2299; *www.nps.gov/arch*

Arizona Strip Land Office, Paria Canyon–Vermilion Cliffs Wilderness, Bureau of Land Management, 345 E. Riverside Drive, St. George, UT 84790; (435) 688-3200; *http://azwww.az.blm.gov/rec/pariaver.htm*

Bandelier National Monument, HCR 1, Box 15, Suite 5, Los Alamos, NM 87544; (505) 672-3861; *www.nps.gov/band*

Beaver Ranger District, Fishlake National Forest, 575 South Main Street, Beaver, UT 84713; (801) 438-2436; *www.fs.fed.us/r4/fishlake*

Black Canyon of the Gunnison National Park, 102 Elk Creek, Gunnison, CO 81230; (970) 641-2337; *www.nps.gov/blca*

Bryce Canyon National Park, P.O. Box 170001, Bryce Canyon, UT, 84717-0001; (435) 834-5322; *www.nps.gov/brca*

Cannonville Visitor Center, Grand Staircase–Escalante National Monument, 10 N. Main, Cannonville, UT 84718; (435) 679-8981; *www.ut.blm.gov/monument*

Canyon de Chelly National Monument, P.O. Box 588, Chinle, AZ 86503; (928) 674 5500; *www.nps.gov/cach*

Canyonlands National Park, 2282 S. West Resource Blvd., Moab, UT 84532; (435) 719-2313; *www.nps.gov/cany*

Capitol Reef National Park, HC 70, Box 15, Torrey, UT 84775-9602; (435) 425-3791; *www.nps.gov/care*

Cedar Breaks National Monument, 2390 West Highway 56, Suite 11, Cedar City, UT 84720-4151; (435) 586-9451; *www.nps.gov/cebr*

Chaco Culture National Historical Park, P.O. Box 220, Nageezi, NM 87037; (505) 786-7014; *www.nps.gov/chcu*

Colorado National Monument, Fruita, CO 81521-0001, (970) 858-3617; *www.nps.gov/colm*

Coral Pink Sand Dunes State Park, P.O. Box 95, Kanab, UT 84741-0095; (435) 648-2800; *http://parks.state.ut.us*

Dinosaur National Monument, 4545 East Highway 40, Dinosaur, CO 81610-9724, (970) 374-3000; *www.nps.gov/dino*

El Malpais National Monument, 123 East Roosevelt Avenue, Grants, NM 87020; (505) 783-4774; *www.nps.gov/elma*

Escalante Interagency Center, Dixie National Forest, P.O. Box 246, Escalante, UT 84726; (435) 826-5400; *www.fs.fed.us/dxnf/d4*

Farmington Field Office, Bureau of Land Management, 1235 La Plata Highway, Suite A, Farmington, NM 87401; (505) 599-8900; *www.nm.blm.gov/ffo*

Goblin Valley State Park, P.O. Box 637, Green River, UT 84525-0637; (435) 564-3633; *http://parks.state.ut.us*

Grand Canyon National Park, P.O. Box 129, Grand Canyon, AZ 86023-0129; (928) 638 7888; *www.nps.gov/grca*

Grand Junction Resource Area, Bureau of Land Management, 2815 H Road, Grand Junction, CO 81506; (970) 244-3000; *www.co.blm.gov/gjra*

Grand Staircase–Escalante Interagency Visitor Center, 755 West Main Street (Highway 12), Escalante, UT 84726; (435) 826-5499; *www.ut.blm.gov/monument*

Henry Mountain Field Station, Bureau of Land Management, P.O. Box 99, Hanksville, UT 84734; (435) 542-3461; *www.ut.blm.gov/richfield*

Hopi Tribal Offices, P.O. Box 123, Kykotsmovi, AZ 86039; (928) 734-2244; *www.hopi.nsn.us*

Hovenweep National Monument, McElmo Route, Cortez, CO 81321-8901; (970) 562-4282; *www.nps.gov/hove*

Kodachrome Basin State Park, P.O. Box 180069, Cannonville, UT 84718-0069; (435) 679-8562; *http://parks.state.ut.us*

Mesa Verde National Park, P.O. Box 8, Mesa Verde, CO 81330-0008; (970) 529-4465; *www.nps.gov/meve*

Moab District Office, Bureau of Land Management, 82 East Dogwood Avenue, Moab, Utah 84532; (435) 259-2100; *www.ut.blm.gov/moab*

Monument Valley Tribal Park, P.O. Box 360289, Monument Valley, UT 84536; (435) 727-3353 or 727-3287

Natural Bridges National Monument, Box 1, Lake Powell, UT 84533-0101; (435) 692-1234; *www.nps.gov/nabr*

Navajo Parks and Recreation Department, P.O. Box 2520, Window Rock, AZ 86515; (928) 871-6647; *www.navajonationparks.org*

Payson Ranger District, Tonto National Forest, 1009 East Highway 260, Payson, AZ 85541; (928) 474-7900; *www.fs.fed.us/r3/tonto*

Peaks Ranger District, Coconino National Forest, 5075 N. Highway 89, Flagstaff, AZ 86004; (928) 526-0866; *www.fs.fed.us/r3/coconino*

Petrified Forest National Park, P.O. Box 2217, Petrified Forest National Park, AZ 86028; (928) 524-6228; *www.nps.gov/pefo*

Ruth Hall Museum of Paleontology, Ghost Ranch Conference Center, HC 77 Box 11, Abiquiu, NM 87501-9601; (505) 685-4333; *www.ghostranch.org*

San Juan Resource Area, Bureau of Land Management, 435 N. Main, Monticello, UT 84535: (435) 587-1500; *www.ut.blm.gov/monticello*

San Rafael Resource Area, Bureau of Land Management, 125 South 600 West, Price, UT 84501; (435) 636-3600; *www.ut.blm.gov/price*

Red Rock District, Coconino National Forest, Red Rock–Secret Mountain Wilderness, P.O. Box 300, Sedona, AZ 86339-0330; (928) 282-4119; *www.fs.fed.us/r3/coconino*

Sunset Crater Volcano National Monument, Flagstaff Area National Monuments, 6400 N. Highway 89, Flagstaff, AZ 86004; (928) 526-1157; *www.nps.gov/sucr*

Zion National Park, SR 9, Springdale, UT 84767-1099; (435) 772-3256; park backcountry office (435) 772-0170; *www.nps.gov/zion*

Are you sure that dinosaurs are extinct?

Index

A

a'a lava 66, 256
Abbey, Edward 118
agate 142
Agathla Park 234
all-terrain vehicles (ATVs) 203
alluvial fan 138
Ancestral Rocky Mountains 33, 102, 104, 124, 137–138, 208, 216, 219, 222
andesite 28
angular unconformity 22
anticlines 38, 143–144
Araucarioxylon 100
Arches National Park 140–149
arkose 133, 138
ash 28
Ashdown Creek 195
augite 17, 28

B

badlands 96, 98, 99–100, 105, 237–239, 243–245
Ballerina Geyser 179
banded gneiss 30
Bandelier National Monument 246–250
Bandelier Tuff 247–249, 254
Bandera Flow 254–257
basalt 28, 44, 77, 196, 247–248
base surge 249
basement rocks 33, 35, 74, 208–209, 216
Basin and Range 14, 196
Bass Limestone 74
Bearhead Peak 253
Bearhead Rhyolite 253
bentonite 99–100
Big Skylight Cave 256–257
Bill Williams Mountain 58
biotite mica 28

Bishop Conglomerate 211–212
Bisti/De-na-Zin Badlands 237–239
Black Canyon 30, 33, 209, 222–224
blowouts 202, 234
Blue Mesa 98–101
bombs 57, 73, 249–250
Bonito Lava Flow 64–66
Boulder Mountain 163
brachan dunes 203
brachiopods 89, 125
breaks. *See* faults
breccia 28
breccia pipes 83
Brian Head 196
Bright Angel Shale 21
Bryce Canyon 184–190
bryozoans 212
Bullion Canyon 204–206
Burro Canyon Formation 130

C

Cache Creek Valley 141
calcite 17, 20, 25, 189, 216, 245
calderas 60–63
Calf Creek 174–176
Canyon De Chelly 35, 101–104
Canyonlands National Park 150–154
Cape Final 85–88
Capitol Reef National Park 162–167, 183
Cardenas Lavas 87
Carmel Formation 105, 158, 179, 182
Cascade Falls 205
Caterpillar Collapse 257
Cedar Breaks 184, 193–196
Cedar Mesa Sandstone 111, 131, 133
cement 17, 149, 203
Cerros del Rio Volcanic Field 247
Chaco Canyon 239–242

chemical weathering 189

chert 88, 89, 125

Chimney Rock Shale 127

Chinle Formation 21, 96, 98, 100, 102, 104, 111–112, 152, 154–156, 216, 219–220, 243–244

Chocolate Cliffs 185

Chuar Group 86–87

Church Rock 234

cinder cones 28, 57, 71–73

cinders (scoria) 66

Circle Cliffs Uplift 35

cirque 206

Claron Formation 184–190, 192–196

clay 25

Cliff House Sandstone 241

cliffs 97

clinkers 239

coal 106, 238

Coal Mine Canyon 105–108

Cockscomb, The 180–182

Coconino Sandstone 19, 24, 44, 54–55, 75–76, 81–82, 86, 89–90, 93

Coelophysis 244

Colorado National Monument 22

Colorado Plateau
Cretaceous seafloods on 228
described 13–14
effects of plate tectonics on formation of 31–39
effects of salt tectonics on 143–144
geologic history of 14–16
laccoliths in 121–123
preparing for hikes in 39–42
rocks of 16–31
stream piracy on 221
volcanic activity in 58–60

Colorado River 78, 87, 92, 93, 95, 137, 217–219, 221

composite volcanoes (stratovolcanoes) 28

conglomerate 19–20

continental accretion 31, 35

Coral Pink Sand Dunes State Park 200–203

Cottonwood Canyon Road 180

Cottonwood Creek Trail 83

Cow Springs Sandstone 105, 107–108

Coyote Buttes 112–116

Coyote Gulch 171–173

Crazy Jug Monocline 91

Cretaceous Ferron Sandstone 169

Cretaceous seaway 106, 128, 209, 225–228, 235, 240

crinoids 89, 125

cross-beds 24, 116, 125, 129–130, 227

crusts 26, 31–32

cryptobiotic soil 92, 165, 176, 217

Cutler Formation 111, 133, 137–140

D

dacite 28, 57

Dakota Sandstone 105–106, 108, 128, 130, 245

Datil-Mongollon Volcanic Field 44

De Chelly Sandstone 19, 24, 96, 101–104, 109, 111, 133

Defiance Plateau 33, 103–104

Defiance Uplift 35

Delicate Arch 140–143

desert varnish 25, 176

Devils Garden 145–149

Dewey Bridge Member 148

diatremes 234

differential erosion 97, 187, 216, 251

dikes 56, 64, 215, 234–237

Dinosaur National Monument 211

dinosaurs 244

diorite 26, 28, 123

dolomite 44, 245

Dolores River 144, 221

Double O Arch 148

Dox Formation 74

Dox Sandstone 86

Dry Fork 171–173

dunes 200–203

Dutton, Clarence 86, 183, 191

Dutton Point 91

E

earthquakes 195

East Kaibab Monocline 87, 113, 180–182

Echo Park 211

El Malpais 254–257

Elden Mountain 57–58

Entrada Sandstone 107–108, 118, 140–143, 145–146, 148, 160–161, 170, 176–179, 215, 223–224, 244–245
erosion 20, 24, 38, 47, 78, 84, 87, 97, 118–119, 142, 166–167, 169, 183–184, 225
Escalante River 171
escarpments 44, 47–48, 185, 186, 190, 194, 223, 225
Esplande Sandstone 82, 93
extrusive igneous rocks 28

F

fault-blocks (horsts) 232
faults (breaks) 36–39, 97, 184–185, 194–195, 211–214, 232–233
feldspar 17, 19, 30
Ferron Sandstone 169
Fisher Towers 137–140
fissures 262
Flagstaff 48
folds 36–39, 211–214
formations 21
Fossil Springs 48–51
fossils 88–89, 100, 125, 212, 227, 239, 243–244
Four Windows Cave 257
fractures 36–39, 97, 145, 232
Fred Flintstone Spire 177
Fremont River 162–164
Frijoles Canyon 246–250
Fruitland Formation 238
fumeroles 262

G

gabbro 26, 28
Galeros Formation 87
geologic maps 40–41
Ghost Ranch 242–245
Gilbert, G. K. 121–123, 167–168
glaciers 58, 62, 185
Glen Canyon 118
Glen Canyon Dam 95
gneiss 29–30, 33
Goblin Valley 160–161
grabens 262
Grand Canyon 14, 16, 18–22, 28–30, 33, 35, 74–95, 209, 221

Grand Canyon Supergroup 74, 85–88
Grand Falls 57, 67–70
Grand Staircase 14, 74, 185–193
Grand Staircase–Escalante National Monument 171–176, 180–182
Grandview Trail 79–83
granite 26, 28
granitic rock 236
granodiorite 26, 28
Grapevine Wash flows 197, 199
Gray Cliffs 185
Great Unconformity 74, 79, 86, 209, 216–221, 224
Green River 211–212, 221
groups 21
Gunnison River 209, 217–219, 222–224
Gunnison Uplift 222, 224
gypsum 19, 88, 144, 158, 245
Gypsum Valley 144

H

Hackberry Mountains 49, 51
halite 19
hand lenses 262
hanging valleys 262
Harpers Corner 211–214
headward erosion 78, 221
hematite 25
Henrieville Sandstone 179
Henry Mountains 121–123, 167–171
Hermit Shale 19–20, 93
Hickman Bridge 164
High Plateaus 183–206
Hillerman, Tony 108
Honaker Trail 123–127
hoodoos 105, 186–187
Hopi Indian Reservation 105–108
Horn, The 127
hornblende 17, 28–30
Horseshoe Mesa 79–84
horsts (fault-blocks) 232
House Mountain 48
Hovenweep National Monument 128–130
Humphreys Peak 62
Hurricane Fault 185, 193–195
hydrothermal rocks and minerals 206

I

Ice Age 16, 58, 208
igneous rocks 26, 28–29, 32, 123
Inner Basin 60–63
Inner Gorge 21, 79, 84
intrusive igneous rocks 26, 28
iron 25, 28, 100, 196, 203
Island in the Sky 150–154

J

jasper (red chert) 125
Jemez Mountains 16, 250–254
Jemez Volcanic Field 246–250
joints 145

K

Kachina Bridge 134
Kaibab Formation 19–20, 33, 35, 44–
46, 54–55, 67, 69, 80–81, 86, 88–89,
93, 104
Kaibab Plateau 78, 84, 88, 221
Kaibab Sea 76
Kaibab Uplift 33, 35, 84, 176, 180
Kaiparowits Plateau 106
Kayenta Formation 151, 156, 163–166,
185, 197, 215–216
Kodachrome Basin 176–179

L

La Plata Mountains 225
La Sal Mountains 142, 146, 154
laccoliths 119, 121–123, 142, 167–171
Lake Bidahochi 78
Lake Powell (Powell Reservoir) 118
Landscape Arch 146–147, 149
Laramide orogeny 33, 35–36, 45, 54–
55, 84, 89, 112, 118, 123, 143, 154,
157–158, 166, 184, 209, 212, 214,
222, 242
Laramide Uinta Mountain Uplift 211
Last Chance Mine 79, 83
lava 28, 67–70, 77
lava domes 57–58
Lava Falls 93, 95
lava flows 4, 46–48, 64–66, 77, 92–95,
197, 199
Lava Point flows 199
lava tubes 254–257

layercake geology 21–23
Leadville Limestone 21
limestone 18–19, 44, 97, 125, 245
Little Colorado River 78, 87
Little Grand Canyon 154–157
Little Ruin Canyon 128
Lower Calf Creek Falls 174–176
Lower Falls 250

M

Madison Limestone 21
magma 26, 28, 30, 122–123, 232
magnesium 28
Malpais National Monument 16
Manakacha Formation 82
Mancos Shale 20, 227, 235
manganese 25, 100, 196
mantle blowout 234
mantles 31
maps 40–41
marble 29
Marble Canyon 78, 86
Markagunt Plateau 193–196
mechanical weathering 188
members 21
Merriam Crater 57, 69
Mesa Verde 225–228, 240
Mesaverde Group 225, 240
metamorphic rocks 29–30, 32
meteorites 152–153
mica 17, 28–30
microplates 31–32
migmitite 30
minette 236
Mitten Park fault 212
Moccasin Terrace 201
Moenave Formation 185
Moenave Sandstone 201
Moenkopi Formation 96, 104, 111, 138–
139, 152, 154–156, 185
Mogollon Highlands 44, 51, 99, 102
Mogollon Rim 16, 44–56, 69
Monkey Wrench Gang, The 118
monoclines 35, 36–38, 45, 118, 158,
180–182
Monument Canyon 214–216
Monument Uplift 35, 221
Monument Valley 19, 35, 109–112

Moquith Mountains 201
moraines 62
Morgan Formation 212
Mormon Lake 44
Morrison Formation 141–142, 211, 245
Moss Back Member 155–157
Mount Hillers 168–171
Mount St. Helens 61
Mount Whitney 62
Muav Fault 89–91
mud cracks 24
mudstone 19, 97

N
National Geographic Trails Illustrated
    Series 40
Natural Bridges National Monument
    131–136
Navajo Mountain 169
Navajo Sandstone 21–22, 24, 152, 156,
    158–159, 163, 166, 175, 182, 185,
    192, 197, 201, 203–204
Navajo Volcanic Field 234
normal faults 38
North American Plate 58
North Bass Trail 89–90
North Rim 84–92
North Vista Trail 222–224
North Wilson Trail 52–56

O
Oak Creek Canyon 52–56
obsidian 28
O'Leary Peak 58, 66
olivine 17, 28
Organ Rock Shale 109, 154, 222
Owachomo Bridge 134, 136
oxides 25, 196, 203

P
Pacific Plate 35
pahoehoe 66, 256
Painted Desert 96–116
Painted Walls 222–223
Pangea 99, 244
Panorama Trail 177, 179
Paradox Basin 208–209, 221
Paradox Formation 124–125, 127

Paradox Valley 144
Paria Canyon–Vermilion Cliffs
    Wilderness 112–116
Paria River 193
Paunsaugunt Fault 185, 192–193
Paunsaugunt Plateau 186–190, 193
pegmatite 216, 224
Pennsylvanian Naco Group 50–51
Peralta Tuff 250–251, 253
Petrified Forest National Park 21, 96,
    98–101
petrified lightning 177
petrified wood 98, 100, 156, 238
pictographs 131, 134, 154, 157
Pine Creek 205
Pink Member 187
plate tectonics 31–39, 77
plates 31
plutonic igneous rocks. See intrusive
    igneous rocks
plutons 26
Point Lookout Sandstone 227
Point Supreme 195
Powell, John Wesley 88, 168, 185, 191,
    221
Powell Plateau 88–91
Powell Point 191–192
Powell Reservoir (Lake Powell) 118
Prospect Canyon 93, 95
Pueblo Alto Trail 239–242
Pueblo Bonito 241
pumice 247
pyroclastics 73
pyroxene 63

Q
quartz 17, 19–20, 25, 29, 88, 100, 203,
    216
quartz monzonite 28
quartzite 29, 205

R
red chert (jasper) 125
Red Mountain 71–73
Red Rock Country 25, 242–245
Redlands Monocline 214
Redwall Limestone 21, 51, 75, 79, 82–83
reverse faults 38

rhyolite 28, 57
rifting 31
rim gravels 46
Rim Overlook 162–165
Rio Grande Rift 33, 232–233, 243
ripple marks 24, 203, 227
rocks 16–30
Rocky Mountains 3, 16, 36, 208–209
Roosevelt, Theodore 90–91
Ruth Hall Museum of Paleontology 243

S

safety 42
salt 127
salt anticlines 143–144
salt tectonics 143–144
Salt Valley 144
San Andreas Fault 31, 39
San Francisco Mountain 44, 58, 63–64
San Francisco Volcanic Field 16, 57–73
San Juan Basin 237–239
San Juan Mountains 16, 59–60, 222, 225
San Juan River 123–127, 221
San Rafael Group 105
San Rafael Reef 157–160
San Rafael Swell 35, 154–160, 183
Sandia Mountains 232
sandstone 19, 25, 97, 118–119, 140–
    143, 148–149, 162–165, 171–173,
    176–179, 214–216
Sangre de Cristo Range 232
schist 29–30, 33
Schnebly Hill Formation 44, 47, 50–51,
    54
scoria (cinders) 66
sediment 17
sedimentary rocks 17–26, 44–45, 47,
    122–124, 148
sedimentary structures 24
Sedona 47–48
Sevier Fault 185, 192–193, 201
Sevier Highlands 130
shale 19–20, 97, 148
Shinarump Conglomerate 20, 102, 104,
    111–112
Ship Rock 232–237
Silent City 187
siltstone 19

Sinking Ship 189
Sipapu Bridge 133–135
slate 29
Slick Rock Member 148
slickenside 82
slickrock 104
slickrock country 18–182
soft sediment deformation 116
Sonsela Sandstone Bed 98–99
South Rim 34
Southeastern Plateau 230–257
spatter cones 66
Spectra Point 194–195
spheroidal weathering 161
Split Mountain 221
Spooky Gulch 173
star dunes 203
Steamboat Rock 212
Straight Cliffs Formation 185
strata 14, 21
stratigraphy 21–23
stratovolcanoes (composite volcanoes)
    28
stream piracy 78, 217–219, 221
striation 206
strike-slip 232
strike-slip faults 36–39
Strike Valley Overlook 165–167
strikes 166
subduction 32, 35, 232
Sugarloaf Mountain 62
Sunset Crater 16, 58, 65–66
Sunset Point 186–187
Supai Formation. *See* Schnebly Hill
    Formation
Supai Group 75, 85, 93
supergroups 21
Surprise Canyon Formation 75
synclines 33

T

Table Cliffs Plateau 184–185, 187, 189,
    191–193
talus 188
Tapeats Sandstone 21–22, 74, 85
tectonics 31–35
Teddy's Cabin 90–91
tent rocks 247

Tent Rocks National Monument 250–254
Thors Hammer 187
Thousand Lake Mountain 163
Threatening Rock 241
thrust faults 38
Todilto Formation 245
topographic (topo) maps 40–41
Toroweap Formation 44, 54–55, 81, 86, 89, 93, 104
Toroweap Point 92–95
Toroweap Sea 75–76
trace fossils 227
trilobites 75
tuff 28
tuff-breccia 236
Tushar Mountains 204–206
Tushar Mountains Volcanic Field 60, 204
Twin Towers 128–130

U
Uinta Mountains 212
Unaweep Canyon 217–221
Uncompahgre Plateau 30, 33, 208–209, 214, 216–221
Uncompahgre Uplift 35, 104, 124
unconformity 22, 102, 106
Unkar Group 86–87
Upheaval Dome 150–154
uplifts 45
Upper Falls 249
upwarps 35
uranium 156, 160
U.S. Geological Survey (USGS) 40–41

V
Vermilon Cliffs 185, 201
vesicles 28, 66, 70, 197
Virgin River 197
Vishnu Schist 26, 29, 33, 74
volcanic rocks 44, 97
volcanoes 58–60
Vulcans Anvil 93
Vulcan's Throne 77, 92–93

W
Wall Arch 147–148
Wall Street 189
Watahomigi Formation 82

water 188–189
Waterpocket Fold 162–167
Wave, The 115–116
weather conditions 39
weathering 38, 47, 97, 142–143, 149, 161, 188–189
Weber Sandstone 212
Wescogame Sandstone 82
West Elk Mountains 222
Western Slope 208–228
White Canyon 131–136
White Cliffs 185
White House Trail 102–104
White Member 187
White Mountains 16, 58, 69
White Mountains Volcanic Fields 44
White Rim Sandstone 154
Wilson Bench 52, 56
Wingate Sandstone 118, 142, 151–152, 154, 156, 166, 214–216, 219–220

Y
Yampa River 211–212

Z
Zion Canyon 21–22, 196–200
Zoroaster Granite 26, 74
Zuni Mountains 255
Zuni Uplift 35

About the Author

Ralph Lee Hopkins has a passion for hiking and interpreting the landscape. Ralph's interests in geology and photography led him to do his master's thesis in geology at Northern Arizona University where he studied rocks along the rim of the Grand Canyon. He authored a chapter on his research in *Grand Canyon Geology* (Oxford University Press, 1990). In 1990, Ralph was photographer on a Colorado River expedition sponsored by the U.S. Geological Survey matching historical photos from the 1890 Stanton River Expedition. A selection of his photos from this trip appeared in the book *Grand Canyon, a Century of Change* (The University of Arizona Press, 1996).

Ralph leads natural history voyages and photo expeditions around the world for Lindblad Expeditions. Photos from his travels appear regularly in books, calendars, and magazines including *Arizona Highways, National Geographic, New Mexico,* and *Outside.* He is co-author/photographer of the book *Baja—A Special Expedition to Baja and the Sea of Cortez* (Lindblad Expeditions, 1995) and he also co-authored and photographed the book *Hiking Colorado's Geology* with his wife, Lindy (The Mountaineers Books, 2000). To view Ralph's online photographic portfolio visit *www.wilderland images.com.*

Between adventures Ralph lives with his wife and their faithful "rock hound," Coconino, in the foothills north of Santa Fe, New Mexico.

THE MOUNTAINEERS, founded in 1906, is a nonprofit outdoor activity and conservation club, whose mission is "to explore, study, preserve, and enjoy the natural beauty of the outdoors. . . . " Based in Seattle, Washington, the club is now the third-largest such organization in the United States, with 15,000 members and five branches throughout Washington state.

The Mountaineers sponsors both classes and year-round outdoor activities in the Pacific Northwest, which include hiking, mountain climbing, ski-touring, snowshoeing, bicycling, camping, kayaking and canoeing, nature study, sailing, and adventure travel. The club's conservation division supports environmental causes through educational activities, sponsoring legislation, and presenting informational programs. All club activities are led by skilled, experienced volunteers, who are dedicated to promoting safe and responsible enjoyment and preservation of the outdoors.

If you would like to participate in these organized outdoor activities or the club's programs, consider a membership in The Mountaineers. For information and an application, write or call The Mountaineers, Club Headquarters, 300 Third Avenue West, Seattle, WA 98119; 206-284-6310.

The Mountaineers Books, an active, nonprofit publishing program of the club, produces guidebooks, instructional texts, historical works, natural history guides, and works on environmental conservation. All books produced by The Mountaineers fulfill the club's mission.

Send or call for our catalog of more than 450 outdoor titles:

The Mountaineers Books
1001 SW Klickitat Way, Suite 201
Seattle, WA 98134
800-553-4453
mbooks@mountaineers.org
www.mountaineersbooks.org

The Mountaineers Books is proud to be a corporate sponsor of Leave No Trace, whose mission is to promote and inspire responsible outdoor recreation through education, research, and partnerships. The Leave No Trace program is focused specifically on human-powered (nonmotorized) recreation.

Leave No Trace strives to educate visitors about the nature of their recreational impacts, as well as offer techniques to prevent and minimize such impacts. Leave No Trace is best understood as an educational and ethical program, not as a set of rules and regulations.

For more information, visit *www.lnt.org,* or call 800-332-4100.